Missing, Murder Suspected

(A TRUE CRIME TRILOGY)

AUSTIN STONE

EDITED BY EDMUND (ED) J.A.STONE

 FriesenPress

Suite 300 - 990 Fort St
Victoria, BC, V8V 3K2
Canada

www.friesenpress.com

Copyright © 2017 by Edmund J.A. Stone
Editied by Edmund (Ed) J.A.Stone
First Edition — 2017

ISBN
978-1-4602-9883-1 (Hardcover)
978-1-4602-9884-8 (Paperback)
978-1-4602-9885-5 (eBook)

1. TRUE CRIME

Distributed to the trade by The Ingram Book Company

Contents

By the Same Author

Novels

1936 *Murders in the Mortuary* (Eldon Press & Putnam, NY)

1936 *The Headsman* (Eldon Press)

1948 *Hangman's Harvest* (John Gifford)

1949 *Blood Stays Red* (John Gifford)

1949 *Death Throws a Party* (John Gifford)

1950 *Deadly Night-Blade* (John Gifford)

1953 *In The Shadow* (John Gifford)

BBC Radio Plays

Crime on the Sands

Malice an Afterthought

The Mind of Murder

Mystery in Pimlico

An Affair of Honour

Two Clues To A Murder

Melody of Death

Beautiful For Ever

A Pearl in the Hand

Etc.

Stage Play

1953 *Burgundy and Mrs Cox* (Great Malvern Winter Garden's)

Editor's Foreword

My father Austin Stone was a well known English author and playwright, whose first book *Murders in the Mortuary* was written in 1936, followed by *The Headsman* also in 1936. During the second World War he joined the British Army and became a 2nd. Lieutenant in the RASC. It was not until a few years after the war, that he moved with the family to a quiet location in Wales, where he continued his writing career and in 1948 published his 3rd book *Hangman's Harvest*. After moving to Malvern in 1949 he wrote 2 more books, *Blood Stays Red* and *Death Throws a Party*, then in 1950 he wrote *Deadly Night Blade*. In 1953 (Queen's Coronation Year) he became chairman of the Malvern Writer's Circle, a position he held for several years. This association meant that he was acquainted with many well known literary author's of the time, including for example Barbara Cartland and Daphne du Maurier. Also in 1953 he wrote his last published book *In the Shadow* . As you can probably tell from the book titles, these were all crime novels, most of which were based on and written around "true crime" events.

In the mid 1950s, Dad decided to progress to radio plays and his first play "Crime on the Sands" was aired on BBC Radio's, Thursday night play, broadcast live @ 7.00pm on October 28,1954. This was to be followed up with as many as 8 more plays, which were broadcast live by the BBC Radio. Once again these were based on 'true crime' events. Many of the people who played character roles in these plays, went on to become famous actors - such as Donald Pleasance (OBE), Billy Whitelaw (CBE) and John Laurie (of "Dad's Army" fame).

After my mother died in 1959, Dad stopped writing - other than occasional newspaper articles - (see note 2 below) and went to work for an engineering company, until his own death in 1979. As I had emigrated to Canada in 1974, my older brother took care of Dad's documents and paperwork, which included manuscript copies of his many books and radio plays etc. In 2006, many years after my brother had died, I was given most of these documents/manuscripts and found there were two books he had written which were never published! As a young boy I remember clearly going to bed at night and hearing dad's typewriter "tap-tapping" away for hours as he worked his way through another book or play (how he would have loved to have had a computer, making typo, spelling and word errors that much easier). Because so much time and effort had gone into writing these books, I decided that it would be the right thing to do to publish and edit at least one of these books *posthumously* in his memory. *"Missing, Murder Suspected"* was originally written just a few years before Dad's death. Since then, there have been a number of articles written about these specific murders. However,

my fathers comments (see authors notes attached), explain well the essence of this particular book, written about three famous "true crime" events. I hope you will enjoy reading this book as much as I have enjoyed transcribing and editing his original manuscript, in order to complete it for publication.

Dad's Typwriter

Notes:

(1) For authenticity, I have kept the original English spelling.

(2) I had assumed Dad had stopped writing books c1955. However, when editing the last story of *"Missing, Murder Suspected"* there was reference to Britain having abolished the death penalty in 1965 and also on pg.247 the sentence "Barely thirty years have passed since then" (Crime was committed in 1944), he must have written this book somewhere around 1973!

Edmund J.A.(Ed) Stone

Author's Notes

"The library shelves offer many volumes dealing with the true cases of murder, the details of which, however, are mostly contained in biographies describing the brilliant part played by some famous Defense Council, Detective, Pathologist or other forensic expert, the story of the crime itself being dismissed objectively in a page or so--often a couple of paragraphs. The result is that the reader is introduced to an accused person virtually for the first time when he or she is a prisoner in the dock and to the victim as a corpse on the mortuary slab. Yet, behind every domestic murder (as apposed to gang killings and murder in the furtherance of robbery or theft) there lies a deeply human story. The characters involved are human beings with their own thoughts, problems and emotions, rather than mere puppets brought on to set the stage for the brilliance of the expert.

In this volume I have taken three cases where the victims were missing for some time before discovery of the crime and have endeavoured to present them in such a way that the reader is not only given an early glimpse into the lives of both victim and accused, but is able, thereafter, virtually to live and breathe with them over the vital period, so that when eventually the crime is revealed , every detail, both factual and psychological, is already known. The brilliance of the expert comes afterwards.

Although at times this may read as fiction, only a minimum of 'author's license' is involved, every fact being authentic, every conversation based on the evidence of witnesses. In this way it is hoped that the reader will be able to appreciate fully the tension and drama, as well as the workings of providence, which often conspire to bring tragedy into the lives of ordinary people."

My own darling Elsie -- Thank you for your letter received this morning. What I haven't told you is that on certain occasions a girl has been here late at night, I am not going to mention the name, nobody knows. When you gave in to your nerves, I gave up hope in you and let myself go; this is the result......I must have time to think. She thinks I am going to marry her, of course, and I have a strong feeling for her or I shouldn't have done what I have. Don't tell anyone yet, but I am in a proper fix now..........

Poor Elsie ... had an immediate nervous collapse. ... Instead, her reply was charged with pathetic recriminations ... a stubborn tenacity.

You ... thought you capable of such deception....... gone off my head... would have been no excuse for you carrying on with another girl! You are engaged to me ... have first claim on you.....Whatever this other girl expects of you, your duty is to marry me. Oh Norman, you have broken my heart ... betrayed your ... never have betrayed your ... Norman, I expect you to marry me [and finish with the other girl] as soon as possible. My baby must have a name; and another thing, I love you in spite of all!.........with all my fondest love and kisses for ever and always, your own loving Elsie.

Love And Hate Among The Chickens

(Rex V. Norman Thorne)

"In my opinion, you can't beat White Leghorns when it comes to a matter of egg-yield."

(Norman Thorne to his solicitor whilst awaiting the jury's verdict at Lewis Assizes.)

The recrimin... he justly deserved; but ... took him completely by ... ic, least of all any trout... slandered despicably to me ... next day, Sunday 30th., ... an unexpected visit in person, ... , humouring her in every way. She cried copiously, at times coming near to hysteria; but he managed to pacify her by reaffirming his promise of marriage should her pregnancy become fully established.

"I shall see my father next week," he told her. "You know I

1

Thorne, Wesley Poultry Farm, Blackness, Crowborough:

ELSIE LEFT FRIDAY. HAVE HEARD NO NEWS. HAS SHE ARRIVED? REPLY. CAMERON.

The chances were that Norman Thorne's hand was just a little unsteady as he held and read the telegram. All at once, what had been a living nightmare for several days was now plunged into stark reality by the tele-typed words, pasted in strips on the buff official form. The wire had been handed in by Mr. Cameron, Elsie's father, at a North London post office half an hour earlier on that morning of December 10, 1924 and Thorne now stood reading it at the door of his hut, forty miles away on a Sussex poultry farm.

The hut itself was little more than a converted brooder, squalid in muddy surroundings and made almost pitiful by the many attempts at improvisation; for the scanty furniture was knocked together from odd pieces of raw timber, while the iron bedstead could boast of no better mattress than a few linen bags stuffed with spare clothing.

Yet, by contrast, the occupant himself was tidy, well-groomed--a young man of twenty-four, on the short side but sturdily built, with sleek dark hair brushed back from a narrow forehead. Indeed, he possessed a certain naive charm which caused visitors to the hut-- women in particular--to ignore the squalor and to experience only a sense of pity and admiration.

The telegraph boy, in blissful ignorance of the dramatic message he had just delivered, stood by the door of the hut, whistling and watching the antics of two Leghorn cockerels as they jumped crazily to peck at one another's heads. Vaguely he was aware that Thorne had moved over to a table and was busy writing.

Nearby, in the hamlet of Blackness, a clock chimed the three--quarters--9.45 a.m. **Blackness**! The very name was sombre, suggesting dark deeds. Yet, in the dialect of East Sussex, accent falls on the last syllable of all place names; in this instance affording the more attractive pronunciation of *Blackness....*

"Thank you," said Thorne, appearing in the doorway again with a gracious smile. "The reply is pre-paid up to twelve words. I think you'll find that just about covers it."

The telegraph boy dragged his gaze reluctantly from the feathered combatants to study the wording of the reply:

NOT HERE. OPEN LETTERS. CANNOT UNDER-
STAND. <u>THORNE</u>.

The telegraph boy took the sixpence that Thorne held out, touched his cap, jumped on his bicycle and skidded away down the muddy path. Norman Thorne watched as the rider disappeared among the high hedges of the lane. He watched for a few minutes longer, his eyes darting frequently to a spot where the White Leghorns scratched and scavenged. Then he braced his shoulders, almost with an air of defiance, and closed the door of the hut.....

‡

When John Norman Thorne first saw the light of day, at Portsmouth in the opening year of this century, eighty odd miles away at Kensal Rise in London, Elsie Cameron was trotting about the nursery, a light if somewhat pensive two-year-old. Some believe in affinities; others in pure chance. Whichever the right school of thought, twenty years later the tangents of those two lives were to cross.

They did so at Evensong in a Wesleyan church...a strange place of encounter in view of the events which followed. Yet, if the morals of youth are diligently wrapped in cotton-wool one of two things is likely to result: either the morals remain thus wrapped throughout life, or else there comes a time when repression bursts its shackles and the original object is defeated in a welter of promiscuity. Norman Thorne, however, was an exception to both contingencies, steering a middle course, never quite flinging aside the cotton-wool, merely flirting with immorality in a degrading manner, aided by a willing partner. Taken individually, it would be hard to find two characters less inspiring than those of Norman Thorne and Elsie Cameron; but thrown together, their joint actions and behaviour at once become an object lesson to all students of human nature, psychology and criminology.

What had happened to Norman Thorne during those first twenty years of his life, before he met Elsie Cameron?

Mr. Thorne senior was an engineer employed in the Admiralty dockyards at Portsmouth, He was also a staunch member of the Wesleyan Church and drilled his only son in the same teachings from the start. In this he met with no difficulty, for Norman proved an apt pupil, willingly entering into the spirit of the many religious activities as well of those of numerous societies pertaining to moral welfare. Nevertheless, tragedy struck early at this model family with the death of his mother when Norman was barely seven years old. In little more than a year, however, Mr. Thorne had married again, and whilst many shortcomings in adult life can be traced indirectly or otherwise to a step-parent, there is nothing to suggest that the new Mrs. Thorne treated Norman other than as a child of her own bosom; even more so, as the years went by and no new offspring blessed this second union.

In 1911, Mr. Thorne's promotion to overseer caused them to move from Portsmouth to London, where they took a house in Willesden; and a few years later Norman went to Kilburn Grammar School. World War 1 had been raging for just over twelve months when he left and became apprenticed to the Aster Engineering Company. At fifteen, he was a youth of pleasing appearance, intelligent, affable and adhering strictly to the high moral code of his upbringing. In fact, during the three years that followed he became, among other things, a Sunday-school teacher, a speaker at open-air meetings of the Band of Hope and a keen organizer of the local Boy Scouts. In due course, he also joined a society calling itself the Alliance of Honour and having as its aim the prevention of sexual intercourse between young people before marriage--a membership which, a few years later, was to have sinister repercussions. Thus, when in the early part of 1918 Norman Thorne enlisted in the R.A.F., his absence was keenly felt by certain sections of the community and in particular at the nearby Wesleyan chapel in Kensal Rise.

To many a youth of eighteen, the sudden cutting adrift from so rigid a moral discipline in favour of life in the services--particularly in war time--might have had disastrous effects. But with Thorne the tenets were too deeply ingrained to be uprooted during a mere twenty months in the Royal Naval Air Arm, even though half of them were spent on active service in France. There were temptations, of course, as well as the bad example of many comrades; but Thorne remained above it all. For his leisure hours, instead of women and wine there were always the Y.M.C.A. and various forms of harmless recreation. In other words, the cotton-wool wrapping remained undisturbed; and when in November 1919 he returned to Willesden to take up the threads of his former life it was with an exemplary character, not only in the records of the Admiralty but sufficient to satisfy the most exacting moralist.

The tangent of Norman Thorne's life, however, was fast approaching that of Elsie Cameron.

2

He had seen her before and knew her name; but he had never spoken to her until that Sunday evening towards the end of 1920. The chapel at Kensal Rise was more crowded than usual and Thorne was a few minutes late--squeezing into a vacant seat in one of the back pews. Some minutes elapsed before he became aware of the figure next to him who had moved up a few inches to make more room. She was about the same height as himself, though somewhat frail and slender. She wore a fawn topcoat and a large hat to match, which, in the ugly style of the period, swept downwards almost concealing her face. Nowadays, many women can derive added allure from the wearing of glasses; but in 1920 plastics were less than a far off dream and Elsie Cameron's spectacles were framed in plain steel, plunging behind the ears to stop just short of the neat bun of auburn hair at the back of her head. Thorne was vaguely aware that she only whispered the responses and remained altogether silent during the singing. He was aware of that much and no more--until the congregation finally rose and began to file out. It was then that he saw Elsie Cameron groping on the floor among the hassocks and he stooped quickly to pick up her glove. She took it, throwing him a grateful smile; and he noticed that the eyes behind the spectacles were large, grey and strangely expressive. He stood aside, allowing her to pass up the aisle ahead of him. Outside, the pavement glistened under a thin blanket of sleet and Thorne worked at the swivel of his umbrella.

"Allow me, Miss Cameron," he said. "You'll get soaked in that thin coat!" It was a genuine act of chivalry with no other motive behind it; the boy scout doing his good deed for the day. Moreover, they needed no introduction, for Thorne knew that his father and Mr. Cameron worked together on several church committees.

He escorted her, holding the umbrella aloft, throughout the half mile to Clifford Gardens where the Cameron's lived. She told him about her elder sister Margaret who was engaged to be married, and her brother just out of the army. She also told him of her job as shorthand typist with the Triplex Glass Company and Thorne seemed genuinely interested.

"The trouble is," he said laughing, "now that the war is over, all the women who did jobs want to keep them and there isn't enough work for the men!"

"Haven't you got a job?" she asked.

"Oh, yes. I managed to get taken on by the Fiat Motor Company in Wembley. I'm an engineer, you know."

There was a street lamp immediately outside the gate of 86, Clifford Gardens, and as they paused there she looked at him with lips slightly parted. She had removed her glasses and there was something undeniably attractive, if a trifle sensual, in the face thus revealed.

"Well, it was ever so kind of you to see me home, Mr.Thorne. I'd have got drenched!"

"Not at all," he said. "Perhaps we'll meet again sometime."

"I hope so."

"D'you go--every Sunday evening?"

She nodded: "I prefer it to the morning service."

"Me too," said Thorne.

It became a weekly habit . Every Sunday evening they would meet in church and afterwards he accompanied her home. There was nothing in it, except that each week the lingering at the gate in Clifford Gardens grew longer. Thorne made no attempt to analyze his own feelings at this stage; and how much his thoughts dwelt upon Elsie Cameron during the week, amid the roar of machinery in the Fiat motor works, was anybody's guess.

But what of Elsie Cameron? Outwardly, she was no different from any other girl of twenty-two, although a little nervous and shy perhaps in public and conscious of the spectacles. Her tastes were simple; and the thoughts of everyday life ran in normal healthy channels, held there--as with Thorne--by a strict Wesleyan upbringing. Her sub-conscious mind, however, presented a very different picture, being filled almost exclusively of sex and marriage. On her own admittance to two different doctors, she enjoyed erotic dreams at night and was even in the habit of stimulating these. Yet, it was all in a world and on a plane essentially far removed from that of her family and her place of work. Moreover, left to her own devices, Elsie Cameron would never have become a nymphoma-niac, for somewhere in the background there always hovered an ideal; nor had she ever been known to assess or even to smile at any strange man.

Such, however, was the girl whom cynical providence had chosen to throw in the path of a young man two years her junior, utterly inexperienced, and in the unfortunate all-round circumstances of Norman Thorne.

Soon the meetings became more frequent; and they began "walk-ing out" together. There was kissing, of course, in which it was Elsie who was apt to cling just that much longer. Thorne had never kissed a girl in his life before, except under the mistletoe in public, and what he began to experience in the shadows of Clifford Gar-dens alarmed--even shocked him a little at first--as the cotton-wool wrapping became disturbed. This state of affairs continued for the better part of a year, by the end of which time Thorne was generally excepted by Mr. and Mrs. Cameron as a future son-in-law. There had been talk of marriage between them particularly on Elsie's part, although for Thorne the prospect was remote. he was still living with his father and step-mother in Willesden, but for which his wages would barely have kept him. Worse still, the country was on the verge of its worst ever trade slump, with redundancy and unemployment already raising an ugly head; and in the early part of 1922 Thorne, along with many others from the Fiat works, found himself on the dole.

During the months which followed, while he tramped the streets in search of work, Elsie was sympathetic, loyal, and helpful; for the ideal of her sub-conscious imaginings had long since materialized in the shape of Norman Holmes Thorne, and the fact of his continued unemployment made no difference to her except as an obstacle to their marriage.

Then, as they met one evening in the Summer of that year, Thorne's air of despondency seemed to have lifted.

"It's been at the back of my mind for some time," he told her. "What's the use of trudging around looking for jobs when there aren't any to be had? I've decided to start a business of my own-- not engineering, of course--but a poultry farm!"

"A poultry farm?" Her eyes widened behind the lenses.

"There's money in chickens if you go about things the right way. I've been reading it up in books. What's more, my father has promised to finance me. Everything's settled!"

"Oh, Norman, how wonderful! But--where? When?"

"I'm going to Sussex tomorrow to inspect a plot of land that's advertised for sale. It sounds just the thing. Near Crowborough."

"Crowborough!" She frowned. "But that's an awful long way away!"

"Only forty miles. But don't worry, Elsie--you'll be able to come there at week-ends. Of course, I shall be pretty busy to begin with--building the huts and all the rest of it, but--you never know--if the farm's a success, maybe we can get married sooner than we thought."

The frown disappeared immediately. They were the only words she ever wanted to hear these days....

3

It was a two-and-a-half acre field in open country, just above the village of Blackness and a mile or two out of Crowborough. At first sight the immediate vicinity appeared desolate and lonely, yet there were cottages nearby and from one corner of the field a footpath led to a small farmhouse less than two hundred yards away, hidden behind trees. The soil was a heavy clay, cumbersome in Winter; but on the whole the place suited Thorne's requirements admirably, and in the following month of August he moved there with all his belongings, securing temporary accommodation in a cottage half a mile from the site with a Mr. and Mrs.Piper. His father had generously provided an additional sum of money for timber and the stocking of the poultry farm; and Thorne at once set about the task of building the runs.

In those early days he cycled the forty miles back to London most week-ends, but later, when the first batch of roosters arrived they kept him tied there and it was Elsie who visited Blackness as often as possible, also lodging with the Pipers. Ostensibly, she did her best to help, but in fact her presence was only a hindrance, for the building of the hen-coops was taking longer than he thought; Winter was approaching; the cost of furnished rooms a big drain on his scanty resources. Midway through December he decided to economize by converting the biggest of the brooders into living-quarters. When complete, this consisted of a hut crudely assembled and measuring six feet long by seven feet five inches wide. The furniture comprised of an iron bedstead, a home-made table, a wickerwork armchair and two upright wooden ones. At the far end of the hut he installed an ancient coal cooking-stove, its patched-up sheet-metal chimney piercing a hole in the roof.

In this primitive dwelling Norman Thorne took up his permanent abode shortly before Christmas 1922, significantly dubbing it "Wesley Poultry Farm". It was here also that from now on Elsie Cameron was to spend her entire time whenever she visited Crowborough, returning only to the Piper's cottage late at night, often long after the elderly couple had retired to bed....

What went on in the privacy of that lonely hut with only the nearby roosters for company--not only on dark Winter nights but in the daytime as well? For none of the neighboring buildings over-looked it.

The sexual relationship which developed between Norman Thorne and Elsie Cameron formed a vital link in the change of events. Afterwards, Thorne was to give the details freely, unspar-ingly, in a long statement to the police, little realizing that this would later be read aloud to an Assize Court filled to overflowing with more women than men.

"We were intimate," he said, *"but in such a way that. in my opinion, conception could not take place...."*

What in fact he went on to describe was, virtually, a leading right up the very threshold of the sex act and there stopping. Not once did the situation get out of hand so far as he was concerned; not once did matters go beyond that point....

In the seclusion and confinement of that tiny dwelling, with scarce room for two people to move without falling across the bed, Thorne's self- control, if true, was an object of marvel. Yet it was clearly prompted by two motives. Firstly, the fear of creating preg-nancy; secondly, and perhaps the stronger of the two, a smug adher-ence to the "cotton-wool wrappings" of childhood and early youth. If occasion demanded, could he ever again face a Sunday-school class, address a meeting of the Band of Hope, least of all mingle with fellow members of the Alliance of Honour, whilst as an unmarried man he was secretly enjoying full carnal relations? By his exercise of caution and reserve, on the other hand, he managed to persuade himself there was some mitigation, if only partially allaying the burning conscience.

"This practice continued on almost all the occasions when Miss Cameron visited the hut...."

For a man, "this practice" may offer a certain amount of crude satisfaction--even satiety. For a women, it is the shortest route to a mental home; and Elsie Cameron's nerves had been none too stable in the first place. According to Thorne, no such incident occurred between them until she started to visit the hut. Yet Mr. Cameron could date a decline in his daughter's health to the time when the couple first started walking-out together. Whatever the truth of the matter, by the Spring of 1923 Elsie Cameron was obliged to receive treatment from the family doctor for neurasthenia and mental depression. On these grounds also she had lost her job of eight years standing with the Triplex Glass Company; and thenceforth was to be incapable of remaining in any one place of employment for more than a few weeks at a time. Yet, despite Thorne's selfish behaviour to which she more than willingly submitted, in his company she was normal and passably happy; although the harpings on marriage grew daily more insistent. It was only when they were separated that the nervous depression took a hold, alarming her parents who, at this stage, were quite ignorant of what was going on. She wrote to him several times a week--the passionate outpourings of frustration in which the main theme never varied:

"Oh, Norman, my love, why can't we be married right away?...."

In the Summer of that year, 1923, being out of a job yet again, she was only too glad of the excuse to visit Crowborough. As usual, she took a room at the Piper's if only for the sake of convention, and this time she would have stayed on for ever, but for the question of money. Her own savings were scanty and she had earned very little during the past few months owing to ill-health. As for Thorne, the poultry farm was far from showing a profit, the pound a week allowance from his father being his only stable income. The possibility of marriage, therefore, was as remote as ever and her constant outbursts and pleadings on the subject had already begun to cause him deep concern. Thus, when they learned that a Mr. and Mrs. Smethwick in the neighbourhood were requiring a nursemaid for their two children, it was Thorne who suggested that Elsie should apply for the post. Somewhat reluctantly she did so, leaving Crowborough a few days later with the Smethwick family for Pevensey where they were to spend the Summer holidays.

The sea air, however, did little to restore Elsie Cameron's health. Within three weeks she was back again in Crowborough, her state of nervous depression having proved too much for Mr. and Mrs. Smethwick.

Back to the hut. Back to the Piper's. They were an understanding couple, the Piper's--even broadminded in face of the local gossip to which Elsie Cameron's visits had, not unnaturally, given rise. Yet there were limits to all things; and so far as Mr. and Mrs. Piper were concerned the climax was reached two nights after her return from Pevensey. They were about to retire to bed when Elsie Cameron came in, somewhat earlier than usual. She had of course, spent the entire day with Thorne, yet she now appeared sullen, morose, and the candlestick shook in her hand as she mounted the short flight of rickety stairs to the bedroom.

"Had a row with him, I'll be bound!" whispered Mrs. Piper, as the door on the landing above them closed.

They were in the kitchen parlour and Mr. Piper nodded, reaching up to extinguish an oil lamp that hung on the wall.

"He be a nice young fellow--but why don't he marry her and have done with it?"

"Money, I suppose," said Mrs.Piper. "Anyway, it's none of our concern. We've our own troubles to look to. Just the same...."

She broke off suddenly, as the landing door opened again and footsteps sounded on the staircase. A moment later Elsie Cameron appeared in the doorway. Her face was pale, her lips trembling, the hands clasping and unclasping themselves; nor had she even removed her hat and coat.

"What's the matter, dear?" said Mrs.Piper kindly. "Aren't you feeling well?"

"I'm all right," Elsie said, but she was on the verge of tears.

"There!" Mrs.Piper took a step towards her. "Just you go to bed and have a good sleep. Things always look brighter in the morning!"

"No!" Elsie glanced up quickly, almost shouting. "I don't want to go to bed! I want to go back to Norman!"

"What, at this time o'night? Come, now...."

But Elsie avoided Mrs.Piper and, launching herself at Mr.Piper, threw her arms about his neck and clung there like a frightened child.

"Take me back to him!" she wailed. "*Please* take me back to Norman!"

Mr.Piper, thoroughly embarrassed, disengaged himself gently, and she fell sobbing in a chair. In vain they pleaded with her but she remained adamant, stubborn in her demands, until finally Mrs. Piper stood back with lips compressed.

"Piper," she said curtly, "you'd best go and fetch Mr.Thorne. Maybe he'll make her see reason--and tomorrow she must leave. I've had enough of this!"

Elsie Cameron rose quickly from the chair. She had removed the misted spectacles and her eyes were red and swollen.

"I'll go with you!" she said. "Take me back to the hut!"

Without a word, Mr.Piper reached for his cap, unbolting the kitchen door; and a moment later Elsie followed him out into the warm night air. In a silence broken only by her occasional whimpers the two of them trudged the half mile to Wesley Poultry Farm. The entrance gate in the lane was padlocked and, being anxious not to arouse the neighbourhood, Mr.Piper called out softly and whistled for some time before a light showed in the hut; and presently Thorne appeared in the doorway in his pyjamas. He had been sound asleep.

"The missus and me, we can't do nothing with her," said Mr.Piper when Thorne eventually arrived to unlock the gate. But explanations were scarcely necessary, for Elsie had already thrown herself at Thorne and was begging him to let her stay the night in the hut.

"Don't be silly, Elsie," he said, in a tone that suggested shocked bewilderment. "You can't possibly do that!"

"Why not?" she moaned. "Why ever not Norman? We're going to married soon, aren't we?"

"You'd best come back with us, Mr.Thorne, and help get her to bed," said Piper. "She won't listen to the missus nor me!"

"I don't want to go back there!" She was on the verge of scream-ing. "I want to stay with you, Norman!"

"Come on, Elsie," he said, taking her arm. "I'll go with you. You're not well. You'll have to see the doctor again!"

They each took one of her arms and started off down the lane.

It was a pitiful sight as they half dragged her along screaming and protesting. They had not gone far when Mr.Piper called a halt.

"It's no use, Mr. Thorne…we can't go on like this. You'll have to take her back after all!"

"But--Thorne hesitated. "Whatever will people say? I mean--they wouldn't understand!"

"Just for the one night--" said Piper, "there's no reason for any-one to know of it. Anyway, you can count on me and Mrs.Piper!"

Thorne took her back to the hut. She was quiet and docile now that she had her own way. If he was angry with her he managed to conceal it; although, once inside the hut he ignored her amorous advances, laying her on the bed and throwing a blanket over the trembling body. Mental exhaustion soon took charge and she fell fast asleep. He pulled another blanket from the foot of the bed and sat in the wickerwork chair. Long afterwards he was to be asked in public:

"Had intimacy taken place between you earlier that evening?"

"Oh, yes," was the glib reply.

To give him his due, it never occurred to Thorne that he might be the primary cause of Elsie Cameron's nervous condition; and that night , for the very first time, he found himself regretting the association. He was beginning to enjoy life at Crowborough. The neighbours were friendly and had already accepted him. There were whist drives and dances at the Village Institute Hall, as well as other social activities. Now Elsie Cameron's alarming behaviour threat-ened all this. She was in fact becoming a nuisance. Yet, once again the ethical teachings of youth came to the rescue and all his better instincts rebelled at the thought of letting her down….

In the morning she was at it again, begging him to allow her to stay--to marry her--although in the cold light of day there was no hysteria behind it.

"You know it's impossible right now," he told her for the hundredth time. "You'll have to be patient!"

During the wakeful hours of the night he had made up his mind to take her back to London that day, not trusting her to make the journey on her own. He fed the chickens early and soon after breakfast they set out to walk the mile and a half to the station, she under sullen protest. On the way they called at the Pipers' to collect her belongings; and at the post office he sent off a telegram to Elsie's sister Margaret who was now married, asking her to meet their train at Victoria, Mr. and Mrs. Cameron being away until the end of the week.

At Crowborough they secured a compartment to themselves, and just as the train began to move out Elsie jumped up, grabbing at the handle of the carriage door.

"I don't want to go back to London!" she cried. "I want to stay here with you! Please Norman--*please*!"

Somehow he managed to quieten her; and at the next station the compartment mercifully began to fill up. It was a journey he was not likely to forget in a hurry.

Margaret was waiting at the barrier when they arrived and Thorne took her aside, whispering: "Elsie's in bad shape! Better take her to see Dr. Walker again. D'you know--she threatened to throw herself out of the carriage on the way here!" If this was an exaggeration at least it helped to explain his motive in bringing her home.

He caught the next train back to Crowborough, arriving in good time to complete his daily chores among the birds. That evening he went to a whist drive; but it was not until the following Whitsun that he made the acquaintance of Elizabeth C....*

---

* In order to avoid any possible embarrassment or distress the name of this girl is not given in full.

4

Dr. Walker's treatment, consisting of bromides, strychnine and iron tonics took partial effect. At any rate during the next few months Elsie showed a marked improvement. She continued to visit Thorne whenever possible and although there were no repetitions of the Piper incident she never ceased to talk of marriage; whilst the intimate relationship between them continued unabated. She could no longer lodge with the Pipers, of course, but Thorne had by now formed a close friendship with Mr. and Mrs.Cosham who lived at the farmstead adjoining his property and where he called daily for his milk. They were a much younger couple than the Pipers, mixing freely in the social activities of the village. Sometimes they held parties at their house and on these occasions Thorne was always invited. Moreover, whenever Elsie Cameron visited Crowborough they generously gave her a room free of charge.

Such was the general state of affairs just before Whitsun, 1924, when Thorne first met Elizabeth C-----. He met her at a village dance; and although he had seen her there before at these functions, he had never spoken to her until that evening when the music stopped abruptly in the middle of a Paul Jones and they found themselves face to face. She was slim, attractive and vivacious; the very opposite in type to Elsie Cameron. Dancing was not among Thorne's better accomplishments and she teased him about this good-naturedly. He learned that she lived with her parents in a cottage half way between Crowborough and Blackness; that to help the family coffers she took in needlework. They had several dances together that evening, arranging vaguely to repeat things the following week.

"What about your fiancé?" she asked, a trifle mischievously, for there were few in the neighbourhood who did not know that the young owner of Wesley Poultry Farm was engaged to a girl who paid frequent visits from London.

"She's none too keen on dancing," Thorne said. "So I may as well make the most of it before we're married!"

Elsie came for the Whitsun holiday; and on Saturday night he took her down to the dance in the village hall, introducing her to Miss C....He persuaded Elsie to take the floor now and again, but for the most part she was content to sit out--somewhat awkwardly on a hard upright chair, clasping and unclasping her hands and smiling faintly whenever Thorne and his new-found friend glided past. Her simple faith in him was proof against the pangs of jealousy that most girls would have felt at the sight of the couple dancing almost cheek to cheek one moment, gay and abandoned the next. As for Thorne, he must have been acutely aware of the steep contrast between the two girls. There was something wholesome and refreshing about Elizabeth C....He could not imagine her as a victim of nervous depression or hysterical outbursts. She was meticulously neat and tidy too, the floral pattern of her frocks somehow matching the freshness of her skin. Thorne did not know it yet, but he had already begun to fall head over heels in love with Bessie C....

Elsie Cameron caught an early train home on the Monday evening, having managed for the few weeks to hold down a job with the Dorco Engineering Company where she was due back at work the following day. Thorne saw her off amid many terms of endearment and the usual promises of marriage as soon as this was possible. Yet, as he walked back to the lonely hut his mind was filled with conflicting thoughts and emotions.

The friendship between Thorne and Elizabeth C...ripened slowly and inevitably as the Summer months went by in a round of whist drives and dances, interrupted at intervals by the visits of Elsie Cameron. It was not until the early Autumn, however, that Miss C... paid her own first visit to the hut; and whatever Thorne's conscious feelings in the matter he was bold enough to mention this possibility in a letter to Elsie the previous day:

Went to a partner whist drive last night, and had Miss C. She may come to tea tomorrow, but it's doubtful....

"Miss C.", however, did not disappoint; although her visit was partly the result of a mild joke between them. She had been teasing him about doing his own cooking and other domestic chores --- even hinting that it might not in fact be true.

"All right," Thorne had said. "Why not come and see for yourself? Why not come to tea with me tomorrow afternoon?"

"I couldn't come tomorrow!" She had coloured perceptibly.

"Then the day after! Your mother said she wanted some eggs. You could collect them."

"Well, I--don't know that I ought to really! I'll - I'll have to think about it."

"I hope you'll think very hard," he said.

She came. He made tea, setting it down on the rickety home-made table. They chatted and laughed, if in a somewhat strained atmosphere, for they had never been alone together before and each was acutely aware of the intimacy of the tiny hut. She expressed genuine amusement, as well as concern, at the short length of cord suspended above the stove and from which dangled several pairs of socks badly in need of darning.....and presently her critical eye caught sight of two large wooden objects standing upright in a corner.

"Whatever are those things?" she asked.

"They're Indian Clubs," he told her. "For exercise. I do my daily dozen every morning without fail!"

She stayed less than an hour, half promising to come again one day. Three weeks elapsed before she did so; and by that time Thorne had thrown discretion to the winds, declaring himself deeply in love with her.

It was an invidious position for Elizabeth C-----, who was no longer able to hide her own reciprocal feelings in the matter. A highly respectable girl, she was the very last to have enticed a man wittingly from his obligations to another. They were both young, and what for her had begun as a mild, innocuous flirtation had somehow got out of control, entangling the pair of them. As for Thorne, his conscience was on the rack. Even now he still shied at the cruel and infamous step of wrecking Elsie Cameron's entire world at a single stroke. Instead, he sought the least line of resistance, in compromise -- by telling Bessie C----- that if he could manage to obtain his freedom they would be married. Meanwhile, his very circumstances afforded breathing space, for right now he was in no position to offer marriage to any women. The poultry farm was running at a dead loss and he owed money to local tradesmen. In fact, for some months past he had seriously contemplated selling out and offering the land in building plots. Nothing could be done in the matter, however, without consulting his father; and in October Thorne paid one of his rare visits to London, leaving the obliging Mr. and Mrs.Cosham to tend the chickens in his absence.

Needless to say,Elsie Cameron was overjoyed at the sight of him. During the preceding weeks she had suffered a relapse and had again been under Dr. Walker's care for neurasthenia. She found herself incapable of concentrating on any job of work and had been brought home early one day by two girl colleagues from her last place of employment. On the way, she had been afraid to cross the road even in their company and had the fixed idea that everyone was laughing at her. But now, with Thorne at her side once again, she was almost back to normal, acclaiming her love for him aloud to the passing traffic, praying only for the day when they could be married. Perhaps Thorne had come to London with every intention of telling her the truth. If so, he was unable to muster sufficient courage. Instead, he took her to the great Wembley Exhibition of that year, where for a few hours at any rate the uppermost thoughts of both were diverted by the hectic, swirling cosmopolitan crowds; the largest swings and roundabouts the world had ever seen and, in particular, the Giant Racer -- a mountain switchback that hurtled carloads of screaming people down almost perpendicular slopes at eighty miles an hour.....

They had just left the Amusement Park and found themselves in a section flanked on either side by stalls and booths. Quite apart from Industry, almost every league, movement or mission of any importance had secured a pitch within the perimeter of that vast exhibition; and suddenly Thorne jerked to a standstill, the blood beginning to pound at his temples as he found himself staring up at the large words splashed across the facade of a nearby stall:

THE ALLIANCE OF HONOUR. YOUNG PEOPLE JOIN NOW, AND BE SAVED FROM THE SINS OF THE FLESH.

An elderly man in sombre attire was handing out literature and doing his best to attract an audience, but only a few paused to stare up at him in vacant curiosity. To Thorne, it was as though providence had guided his footsteps to this very spot and his immediate reactions were twofold. Firstly, a reminder that he had not paid his subscription to the society for two years. Secondly, that as a prelude to more drastic steps here was a plausible excuse for discontinuing the physical relationship which had existed for so long between himself and Elsie Cameron and which, since the advent of Elizabeth C...upon the scene, had become increasingly distasteful to him.

"What is it, Norman?" Elsie was tugging at his sleeve. "What's that man shouting about?"

In lowered tones he explained the object and principles of the Alliance of Honour, even expressing remorse at his own short-comings as a member. In fact--he told her--it would be proof of her love for him if she too were to join the society.

"After all," he forced himself to utter the final words of deception, "it's only until we're married!"

She was in a mood to obey his slightest whim and proceeded at once to enrol as a member. Thorne paid his own outstanding subscriptions and together they walked away arm in arm....

It was not until Thorne had returned to Crowborough--having come to no definite arrangements with his father regarding the poultry farm--that in the loneliness of her thoughts a nagging fear began to assail Elsie Cameron. Could it be that Norman was tiring of her? Why was he so anxious to discontinue the intimacy which had been an essential part of their lives for more than two years? A moment's self-analysis told her that such a suggestion would never have come from her side of the fence; yet her simple faith still precluded the possibility of a rival. For a day or so she brooded, until finally a fierce tenacity, a possessive determination, gripped her and she wrote him a long letter telling him she was pregnant; that it was now essential that they should get married as soon as possible. Perhaps, in her state of nervous debility, she even persuaded herself it was true.

Back at Crowborough, Thorne had begun to "walk-out" openly with Elizabeth C..., both of them apparently heedless of the gossip this was causing in the village. She also began to visit the hut several times a week, arriving about 8.30 p.m. and staying until half-past ten. Later, Miss C...was to be asked:

"What did you do on these occasions?"

To which she made the somewhat surprising but no less honest reply in it's bland innocence:

"Mostly I sat on his knee in the armchair. We were love-making and talking about Miss Cameron."

Into this idyllic setting came Elsie's jarring letter announcing her pregnancy. Yet Thorne made no mention of it to Miss C....In fact, he was not unduly perturbed at this stage, for once before Elsie Cameron had made a similar claim, later to find herself mistaken. Also, he was convinced in his own mind that such a state of affairs was impossible. Nevertheless, in order to pacify her he now wrote, saying that if it turned out to be true he would, of course, marry her as soon as matters could be arranged.

Perhaps he underestimated Elsie Cameron -- women in general -- for the tangled web of subterfuge had already begun to catch up with him and he now had a secret from Elizabeth C----- as well.

Was Elsie Cameron really pregnant? She intimated as much to her parents which in itself entailed a confession of her behaviour with Thorne and, shocked beyond measure, they sent her at once to Dr.Walker. Like everyone else, the family physician had only her word for it when she told him she had missed two periods.

"There are signs of pregnancy," was as much as he could say after an examination. "Come back again in a month's time and we shall know for certain." Meanwhile--he looked at her as though taking her whole case history into account, "the best thing you can do is get married!"

That was on November 18, and the following Friday she caught an early train to Sussex. In the circumstances, Mr.Cameron had, not unnaturally, forbidden her to stay overnight and Thorne met her at Groombridge, a branch-line station, from which they went on to Tunbridge Wells to spend the day there. It was a gruelling day for Thorne, her sole topic of conversation centering around her pregnancy and the urgent need for a speedy wedding.

"Dr.Walker says there's absolutely no question," she exaggerated. "Really, Norman, you've got to do something about it!"

"I still find things very hard to believe, " Thorne said. "in any case, how can Dr. Walker tell for certain so soon?" He had no wish to continue the argument, however, for her voice had already reached a high, whining pitch and he feared another Piper incident in the main shopping centre of Tunbridge Wells. By now, also, he had become adept in the art of procrastination and when the time came to wave good-bye to her on the station platform she was moderately happy, moderately assured of his good intentions. Afterwards he returned to Crowborough to spend the rest of the evening in the far more congenial company of Bessie C....

Nevertheless, even Thorne knew that he had merely gained a further respite --- that sooner or later a move would have to be made either one way or the other; and a few days later he plucked up sufficient courage to throw out a first, ambiguous hint of the truth in a letter to Elsie Cameron:

> There are one or two things I have not told you for more
> reasons than one, he wrote. It concerns someone else -- who,
> you do not know. I'm afraid I am between two fires, but
> don't go and tell anyone else. And please return this letter
> to me as soon as you've read it....

Elsie's reply came back swiftly; but not before she had been astute enough to make a copy of his letter;

My own darling Norman--Your letter received last night and I am returning it, although I don't see why you wanted it back....After what you said on Friday I shall expect you to go and arrange our marriage as soon as possible. Why aren't you going this week? Every day is making a difference to me!....Really, Norman, your letter puzzles me. I can't make it out. Why are there one or two things you haven't told me, and in what way does it concern someone else? I have never kept a single thing from you and I don't think it fair of you to keep things from me. What d'you mean by "You are afraid you're between two fires?" Oh, I don't understand things at all ! Well, Norman, please arrange about getting married as soon as possible. I feel sick every day and soon things will be noticeable to everybody, and I want to be married before Christmas, which is only a month tomorrow....

Thorne received this letter on November 27. Having broken the ice to some extent he was emboldened to take matters one stage further. This he did in a second letter by return of post:

My own darling Elsie--thank you for your letter received this morning. What I haven't told you is that on certain occasions a girl has been here late at night, I am not going to mention the name, nobody knows. When you gave into your nerves, I gave up hope in you and let myself go; this is the result...I must have time to think. She thinks I am going to marry her, of course, and I have a strong feeling for her or I shouldn't have done what I have. Don't tell anyone yet, but I am in a proper fix now....

Poor Elsie Cameron! Yet this mortal blow evoked no immediate nervous collapse. Instead, her reply was charged with pathetic recriminations and a stubborn tenacity:

You have absolutely broken my heart. I never thought you capable of such deception....Had I gone off my head, it would have been no excuse for you carrying on with

*another girl! You are engaged to me and I have first claim
on you....Whatever this other girl expects of you, your duty
is to marry me. Oh, Norman, you have broken my heart!
Had you been a raving lunatic I could never have betrayed
your trust and gone with another man....Well, Norman, I
expect you to marry me (and finish with the other girl) as
soon as possible. My baby must have a name; and another
thing, I love you in spite of all!....With all my fondest love
and kisses for ever and always, your own darling Elsie.*

The recriminations he had expected and knew he justly deserved;
but the possessive fire and tenacious resolve took him completely by
surprise. He wanted no wrangling in public, least of all any trouble
involving Elizabeth C...whom he had slandered despicably to suit
his purpose. Thus, when the very next day, Sunday 30th, Elsie
Cameron followed up her letter by an unexpected visit in person,
he put himself out to be nice to her, humouring her in every way.
She cried copiously, at times coming near to hysteria; but he managed to pacify her by reaffirming his promise of marriage should
her pregnancy become fully established.

"I shall see my father next week," he told her. "You know I can
do nothing until I've talked it over with him. But don't worry, Elsie-
-everything'll work out all right."

It cost him nothing to say this, for he was still convinced that the
pregnancy was a myth. Nevertheless, her faith in him was to a large
extent restored and by the time she left him to return to London
that evening it was in a far happier frame of mind. In other words,
they were right back where they had started....

He had not lied to her, however, regarding his father. A meeting between them had become of paramount importance, for Mr.
Cameron had lost no time in approaching Mr.Thorne concerning
Elsie's supposed condition, the whole business coming as a smack
between the eyes for both Wesleyan parents. Thus, on Wednesday,
December 3, Mr.Thorne visited Crowborough and a long discussion took place between father and son. Mr. Thorne, admittedly,
had never regarded Elsie Cameron any too favourably as a future

daughter-in-law on account of her nervous disposition. At the same time, he was a man of strict principles and if his son had indeed got a girl into trouble, then there was only one proper course open. The outcome of this meeting, therefore, was that they should wait a few weeks in order to make quite sure, before going ahead with any definite arrangements; a policy of deferment which suited Thorne down to the ground, and that evening he wrote to Elsie telling her of the decision, buoying her up with hope. His letter was chatty and light-hearted:

> *The Cosham's are having a party on Saturday evening and I have been invited. They have some friends coming for the week-end...so I shall have a night out. Don't think there is any more to say now. Cheerio. With fondest love and kisses, your own loving Norman.*

Later that same evening his *"fondest love and kisses"* were in fact bestowed upon Bessie C....

But how long could Thorne keep this up? Alternatively, if she was not really pregnant how long could Elsie Cameron keep it up?

Sooner or later there must be a showdown, on one side or the other.

5

The morning of December 5 dawned bright and clear over Kensal Rise, as over most parts of the country; the more welcome after an Autumn of intermittent rain and gales. It was to be a fateful date in a calendar of grim happenings; a date which marked the beginning of a series of events, apparently isolated and disjointed, yet all falling, weeks later, into a co-ordinated pattern.

Mrs.Mottier and her husband, an elderly couple, occupied rooms on the first floor at 86, Clifford Gardens, Kensal Rise, sharing the house with the Cameron's. At nine o'clock that morning Mrs.Mottier was going about her daily chores when Elsie Cameron knocked on the door and came in for a chat, as she frequently did. She wore a green knitted woollen dress and over one arm was proudly displaying a new jumper, purchased the day before. She also held out a new pair of shoes for the older women's approval. In all, she seemed in the best of spirits that morning and not even Mrs.Mottier was let into the secret of a resolution formed overnight, deep at the back of her mind: these pathetic garments were to be in the nature of a trousseau.

"Oh, Mrs.Mottier," Elsie said presently, "I wonder if you'd do me a big favour!"

"What is it, dear?" asked Mrs.Mottier, who had always been very fond of Elsie.

"I've bought rubber soles for these new shoes but I don't know how to stick them on. Will you do it for me?"

"I'll see what I can do," the older women replied. "How soon d'you want them?"

"I have an appointment with the hairdresser this morning," Elsie said, "But if possible I want to wear them this afternoon--early."

"Leave it to me, dear," said Mrs.Mottier.

Shortly afterwards Elsie went out, returning at mid-day, by which time the obliging Mrs.Mottier had fixed the rubber soles.

"How d'you like my hair?" Elsie asked, removing her hat. "It's a new style!" She was flushed and a little excited.

"It suits you fine," said Mrs.Mottier.

They were alone in the house, Mrs.Cameron being away for the day and the two men at work. Elsie remained talking for a few minutes before going to her own room; and although Mrs.Mottier heard her leave the house at two o'clock, she never again saw Elsie Cameron alive....

At ten o'clock that night Thorne was at Crowborough station waiting for the Brighton train to come in. When it arrived Miss C...and her mother alighted. They had spent the day in Brighton doing the Christmas shopping well in advance; and Thorne carried the heavy suitcases containing their purchases one and a half miles uphill from the station. On the way, all three chatted gaily until they reached the cottage where Miss.C...went inside, leaving the other two to linger by the gate. They remained there for nearly half an hour in the shadowy darkness, and Elizabeth's watch said just after eleven-fifteen by the time Thorne left her. From there it was ten minutes walk back to the hut....

In a chill, misty dawn the following morning, Saturday, December 6, he was moving about in the hen-runs. By the time the mist cleared he had completed all the work he intended doing that day, but for some reason he had little appetite for breakfast. He waited until the postman had gone past the gate without stopping to deliver anything, then he took his bicycle out of the shed and rode down to Crowborough station, catching the 10.10 a.m. train for Tunbridge Wells. At Groombridge he jumped out and stood for a few seconds by the open door of the carriage, glancing up and down the platform. It was only a brief halt and a minute later he continued his journey. He spent an hour or so in Tunbridge Wells, idly gazing into shop windows--and was back again at the poultry farm by two o'clock. He took his milk can and strolled over to the Cosham's. As a rule it was Mrs. Cosham who served him with the milk, but being a Saturday afternoon she was out shopping and the farmer himself greeted Thorne in the dairy.

"The very man I want to see," said Mr. Cosham. "Just been over to your place!"

"Oh?" There was a sharp edge to Thorne's voice, but he added quickly in a milder tone: "Sorry I was out. I've been to Tunbridge Wells. Was it--anything important?"

"Only to tell you the party's off for tonight. Sorry to disappoint you, Norman, but the folks we were expecting for the week-end can't come after all. So we decided to postpone it for a week or two."

"That's quite alright," Thorne said. "Although naturally I was looking forward to it."

He remained for some time, discussing the situation in the poultry business and local village affairs, before returning to the hut for tea. Later, by way of compensation for the cancelled party, he took Elizabeth C...to the pictures.

The following morning he wrote and posted a letter to Elsie Cameron:

Sunday, December 7th.

My own darling Elsie--Well, and where did you get to yesterday? I went to Groombridge and you didn't turn up. I suppose you were detained unexpectedly for some reason or other...I came back again and looked for a letter at midday, but was unlucky, so I shall have to wait until tomorrow. I didn't go to the Cosham's last night after all....Well, lovely, you must let me know when you think of coming again. Cheerio, darling, with my fondest love. Your own loving Norman.

The very next day he followed this up with another:

Monday, December 8th.

My own darling Elsie--I was expecting a letter today, especially after not seeing you on Saturday and not hearing from you. I do hope everything is all right and that your nerves are not bad again. If they are, try to fight against it for everybody's sake. Write as soon as you can or I shall be

*worrying….Cheerio, sweetheart. With all my fondest love
and kisses, Ever and Always your own loving Norman.*

Even a casual observer could scarcely fail to note the marked
change of tone in these letters--the avowals of love, the deep concern
over her health and the worry at her continued silence--compared
with the callous, almost cruel indifference which had flavoured
those of the past few weeks....

The two letters remained unopened on the hall table at 86, Clifford Gardens until the Wednesday; for it was on that morning that
Mr. Cameron had dispatched his urgent telegram:

ELSIE LEFT FRIDAY. HAVE HEARD NO NEWS. HAS SHE
ARRIVED/. REPLY.

And Thorne's answer:

NOT HERE. OPEN LETTERS. CANNOT UNDERSTAND.

6

Soon after the telegraph boy had pedalled away that morning, carrying the reply to Mr.Cameron, Thorne took his milk can and strolled over to the Cosham's. He appeared mildly worried and perplexed as he showed the telegram to Mrs.Cosham.

"I can't understand it," he said. "She certainly never came here on Friday."

"Were you expecting her?" Mrs.Cosham asked.

"That's just it," he said. "There was never any question of her coming on Friday, but I <u>had</u> arranged to meet her at Groombridge on Saturday. I went there, but she never turned up!"

"Saturday?" Mrs.Cosham's eyebrows rose sharply. "That was the day of our party. You never told us Elsie was coming!"

"Didn't I!" Thorne's tone was casual, but a slight flush had appeared in his sallow cheeks and he passed a hand over the sleek black hair. "I must have forgotten. Anyhow, she was only coming for the day."

"But according to this"--Mrs.Cosham was still holding the telegram--"she left home on Friday. What d'you think can have happened to her?"

Thorne shrugged. "Almost anything--particularly in her state of nerves. She might even have thrown herself in the Thames!"

Florence Cosham looked worried. Like the Piper's, she too had good experience of Elsie Cameron's neurotic disposition. Moreover, there was very little she did not know about Thorne's private affairs, not as a result of any inquisitiveness on her part, but because for more than a year he had confided everything to this couple, she taking almost a motherly interest in him. Although he had not mentioned Elsie's claim of pregnancy, they knew all about Elizabeth C...and more than once, in comparing the two girls, Mrs.Cosham had expressed disapproval of Elsie Cameron as a future wife for

him. Now, however, Thorne's glib suggestion that she might have
thrown herself in the river caused her deep concern.

"Poor creature," she said. "Let's hope nothing like that has happened! All the same, when she was staying here this Summer she
did seem worried. Over money, I thought it was--being out of work
for so long."

Thorne nodded: "Anyway, best not to say anything about it
at present--locally!"

Several days went by, during which time Thorne wrote to Mr. and
Mrs.Cameron expressing his utter bewilderment, as well as his grief,
at the continued absence of news. Otherwise, life at Wesley Poultry
Farm resumed it's normal routine; his leisure hours being spent in
the company of Elizabeth C...who, as yet, was quite unaware that
Elsie Cameron had apparently vanished.

It was a few mornings later that Police Constable Beck, of the
Crowborough Constabulary, pedalled slowly up the lane, alighting
to rest his bicycle with meticulous care against the hedge. Thorne,
who had fully expected some such visitation sooner or later, met
him at the gate.

"Morning, Mr.Thorne," said Beck, a stalwart native of Sussex.
"I'm making enquiries into the whereabouts of Miss Elsie Emily
Cameron. Possibly you can help." He fumbled at a breast pocket,
producing several documents. It was the first cog in a vast piece
of machinery, set in motion by Mr.Cameron in far off Kensal Rise.
Thorne met it with the utmost calm.

"I'm glad they're doing something about it," he said. "I've
been very worried--especially as I can't be of very much help in
the matter."

"She is known to have left home--86, Clifford Gardens, Kensal
Rise--at approximately 2 p.m. on Friday, December the fifth," said
Constable Beck, consulting one of the documents. "Thought to have
been carrying a small suitcase and to have been on her way to visit
you here."

"If so, she never arrived," said Thorne. "In any case, I wasn't expecting Miss Cameron that day, and it's most unlike her to come without letting me know beforehand."

Beck nodded and made an entry in his notebook.

"When would be the last time you actually saw her, Mr. Thorne?"

"On Sunday, November thirtieth, she came here just for the day, returning on the 8.15 p.m. train. I haven't seen her since." He went on about her failure to meet him at Groombridge on the Saturday, as he claimed they had arranged. With the formality of his calling, Constable Beck put a number of routine questions all of which Thorne answered with complete self-assurance.

"What'll be the next step?" he asked, as Beck stuffed the documents back in his pocket.

"There'll be a description circulated--both here and in London. I expect it'll go out tonight. Oh, we'll find her all right, but these things take time, you know!" He paused suddenly, looking at Thorne. "You don't happen to have a photograph of Miss Cameron, I suppose?"

"Why, yes," said Thorne, almost with enthusiasm. "Wait here, I'll fetch it!"

He ran back to the hut, returning a moment later with a leather frame, postcard size. He slid the picture out, handing it to Beck.

"It's quite a good likeness," he said. "But, of course, she wears glasses, normally."

Beck nodded, pocketing the photograph. "Well, thanks very much, Mr.Thorne;...."

With enquiries by the police, however, Elsie Cameron's sudden disappearance could no longer be kept a secret in the locality; and within twenty-four hours Crowborough and the hamlet of Blackness were inevitably buzzing with rumours and speculation. It was late the following afternoon, while Thorne was feeding his birds, that he looked up to see Mr.Cosham approaching along the footpath that separated the two properties. The farmer halted by the hen-runs and his face bore a look of puzzled concern as he spoke to Thorne through the wire netting.

"Norman," he said, "I don't rightly understand it, but you'd best go and have a word with George Adams. He's got some news for you!"

"George Adams? What kind of news?" Thorne frowned.

"It's best he tells you himself--I might get it wrong. Anyway, it's what he told me at dinner-time today--and you know the stories that are going around--about Elsie! My advice is to pop over and see him right away. He'll just about be home from work."

It was only a short distance to Grovehurst Villas, where the Adams lived. They were a London couple, having left their native Tottenham some years before to settle in the wilds of Sussex, Mr. Adams being employed as a fruit grower at the nearby nurseries. As neighbours, Thorne knew them quite well and often met them at whist drives. Mrs.Adams now answered his knock and invited him over the threshold.

"I understand you have some news for me," Thorne said, as George Adams appeared in the hall.

"Well--yes, in a way," said the fruit grower, with just a hint of embarrassment. "It's about Miss Cameron. Fact is, me and my mate Albert Sands--seen her late that Friday afternoon on the way back from work. Carry'n a suitcase and all, she was--and making for your place!"

Thorne licked his lips and appeared to swallow something, but his voice remained perfectly calm.

"You must have been mistaken," he said.

"No mistake--as Albert Sands'll vouch. It was dark, of course, but we seen her plain enough. We stood aside to make way for her on account of the mud, and she passed as close as I am to you now! Be about ten-past-five."

"In that case," said Thorne, "I take your word for it, although I still think you might have been mistaken in the darkness. All I can say is that I was at home at that time and she never came near the hut, to my knowledge. The trouble is, I can't remember whether the gate was locked or not. If it was, she might have strolled on up the lane, thinking I was out." He searched his brain for more, finally adding: "The gypsies might even have got hold of her!"

"It's a possibility, I suppose," said George Adams dubiously. "Anyway, me and Albert Sands reckon we ought to tell the police."

"Yes, of course," said Thorne. "And thanks for letting me know."

If the fruit grower's statement disconcerted him in any way he never showed it. To those who offered their sympathy, or even alluded to Elsie Cameron during the next few days, he expressed the opinion that she had either met with an accident or was suffering from loss of memory. Nevertheless, the tongues continued to wag; and whilst many a girl in Elizabeth C...'s position would have fought shy of him even at this early stage, she continued to visit the hut and to be seen about with him, never once doubting his word on any point, fully confident that the whole unfortunate business would be cleared up to the satisfaction of everyone.

Meanwhile, the machinery of the law continued to turn with its slow but inexorable revolutions; and soon Detective Inspector Edwards, of the East Sussex Constabulary, appeared in Crowborough to carry investigations one stage further. He was joined a few days later by Superintendent Budgen of the same Division; and to both officers Thorne repeated his story, never adding a discrepancy, never for a moment losing his calm self-assurance. In fact, his attitude expressed itself clearly in the very first words to Superintendent Budgen when that officer, accompanied by Inspector Edwards, called and asked permission to look over the hut and poultry farm.

"Of course!" said Thorne. "I can't tell you how glad I am that someone responsible has arrived at last to clear matters up!"

With his willing co-operation they carried out a thorough search of the hut, the outhouses and the chicken-runs. It was, as the Superintendent politely pointed out, a mere matter of routine; and by the time they were through both officers appeared satisfied, if none the wiser.

"You know," Thorne said, as they were about to leave, "that Mr.Adams and Mr.Sands say they saw Miss Cameron in the lane there, on the afternoon of Friday, December the fifth.---Well, it's my firm belief they mistook her for someone else in the dark. Also, I was here in the hut at that time and even if the gate was locked she would have seen the light and called out to me."

Superintendent Budgen nodded thoughtfully. Even as a country police officer, experience had taught him the fallibility of witnesses to identification-- especially in the dark; and he left Wesley Poultry Farm that morning, prepared to strike out on entirely new lines of investigation....

Yet, Christmas came and went, without any fresh development. For the inhabitants of Crowborough and Blackness, every day that passed in this manner added to the tension as well as to the mounting suspicion. Even Elizabeth C...began to feel the strain and ceased to visit Thorne at the hut. Instead, they met at her house or went for lonely walks. Routine enquiries had also been stepped up in London, and news of Elsie Cameron's mysterious disappearance had crept into the national press; although commanding, as yet, only small, insignificant paragraphs. Thorne had interviewed several local reporters, freely supplying them with copy, but he was quite unprepared for the host of London pressmen and photographers that descended on Wesley Poultry Farm one morning in the second week of January, for he did not know what they knew: that the Sussex police, finding themselves at a deadlock, had called in the help of Scotland Yard. Although taken by surprise, Thorne maintained an air of cool defiance--even of aplomb--as he faced the battery of cameras, answering questions without hesitation. They photographed the hut and its owner from every angle, until Thorne became a trifle conscious of his own importance.

"Listen gentlemen," he suddenly exclaimed above the clamour of voices. "I'm a poultry farmer and if you want a really good picture, why not take one of me out there, among the chickens!"

They agreed unanimously, and followed as he led the way into the White Leghorn run, between the hut and the gate. The birds took fright at this mass intrusion but returned quickly enough to cluster at Thorne's heels as he threw them a handful of corn. He stooped and grabbed one of them, stilling it's fluttering wings. Then, with the bird tucked under one arm he adopted a pose. It was a defiant, arrogant pose and his lips curled back in a smile as the cameras clicked. For a few fleeting seconds the quiet young Wesleyan had darted forth from his shell of reserve to reveal something of the man it concealed....

At almost that identical moment an elderly women was climbing the front steps of Crowborough police station. Doubtless, she had hoped to be greeted by the familiar smile of Constable Beck or the local sergeant; but as soon as she had stated her business she found herself in the presence of two strangers--big men in belted raincoats and Trilby hats. They were Chief Inspector John Gillan and Detective Sergeant Askew, both of New Scotland Yard, who had in fact arrived that morning to take over investigations into the whereabouts of Elsie Cameron.

"My name is Mrs.Annie Price," she began. "I live with my husband at No.2, Blackness Cottages--"

Mrs. Price, like everyone else in the neighbourhood, knew Elsie Cameron by sight. She had also heard various rumours concerning the girl--particularly since Christmas. But because neither she nor her husband went out very much and seldom mingled with the village gossips, she was quite unaware of the true facts--until that very morning, when she had read them in the papers.

"I remember Friday, December the fifth, very well." She now told Inspector Gillan. "That afternoon I went to visit a friend who lives up by the nurseries. I also know it was just five o'clock when I left there, because I had to get home to attend to my husband's tea. Therefore, it must have been about five-fifteen as I passed the gate of Wesley Poultry Farm--and I saw Miss Cameron."

Gillan said: "Exactly where was she when you saw her, Mrs.Price?"

"She had entered by the gate and was just approaching the door of the hut. I remember she was carrying either a small suitcase or a bag--I couldn't quite see which in the darkness. As I say, I only remembered about it this morning when I read the newspapers."

"You've no doubt in your own mind that it was Miss Cameron, I suppose?"

"Oh, it was her all right! I know Miss Cameron well by sight."

Inspector Gillan flicked through the file of statements on the table in front of him.

"Did you see anyone else in the lane about that time?" he asked.

"There were two men walking in the lane ahead of me," said Mrs. Price. "I think it was Mr.Adams and Mr.Sands from the nurseries, but it was dark and I couldn't be sure."

Gillan nodded: "And you're quite certain of the date?"

"I'm positive. December the fifth was my friends birthday. That's why I went to visit her. I don't go out very much as a rule."

Gillan said: "Thanks very much, Mrs.Price!"

On the evening of January 14, Thorne sat at the home-made table penning a letter to Elizabeth C....Words did not come easily, for the letter followed a painful decision arrived at mutually the night before. It was dark outside and he could hear the occasional fussing and fluttering of hens in the roosting-cots. They were his only companions right now; yet somehow the hut no longer retained its atmosphere of intimate seclusion, for Thorne was aware that the eyes and thoughts of the neighbourhood--indeed of most of the country --were focussed upon Wesley Poultry Farm at this very minute. He was aware also that two officers from Scotland Yard had been in the vicinity for three days but--significantly or otherwise--had not seen fit to come near him as yet.

He read through what he had written:

> Dear Bessie--It was a hard struggle last night, but since it is for the best I must be brave and wait till you send for me again. The sooner the papers find something fresh to boom about the better, for then the police can get to work without so many rumours to put them off....Never mind about me. It's my affair until it's cleared up. I am very sorry for you indeed, but you know I did not know at the time of making your acquaintance all this anxiety was coming, or that we should begin to fall in love....Don't worry, I have a clear conscience, however things may look. Yours, as ever, Norman.

He was about to enclose it in an envelope together with a photograph of himself when he heard a car pull up in the lane…voices, and footsteps approaching; and he remembered that the gate was still unlocked. He rose quickly, just as there came an authoritative knock on the door; and a moment later Chief Inspector Gillan and Sergeant Askew entered. Two other officers from the local branch stood outside, for there was scarcely room for any more in the tiny hut.

"Mr.Norman Thorne?" said Gillan; and introduced himself. "I'm making enquiries into the whereabouts of Elsie Emily Cameron and I have a warrant to search this place." He was an enormous man, the rim of his Trilby almost touching the lower slopes of the little wooden roof.

Thorne said: "By all means--but the police have already done so once."

Gillan nodded: "This search will be a bit more thorough! I also propose taking a full statement from you."

"Certainly, " said Thorne. "I have nothing to fear."

Gillan's eyes roamed the hut, finally coming to rest on the letter which still lay open on the table. He picked it up and began reading it. Thorne took a step forward in protest; then quickly changed his mind, shrugging with an air of indifference.

"I'll take possession of these for the time being," said Gillan, picking up the photograph as well.

It was perhaps unfortunate for Thorne that a certain astute Eastbourne solicitor, Mr. E.A.R.Llewellyn, was not on hand at this early stage to safeguard his interests. For instance, Gillan's authority for pocketing this letter is debatable. It was a purely private communication, about to be posted; and there was nothing against Thorne as yet bar suspicion. As material evidence, the letter might establish an association with Miss C…, which Thorne would never have bothered to deny. Otherwise, if anything the letter reaffirmed his innocence. Had it been a blood stained poker or Elsie Cameron's hat there would have been justification for Gillan's action. As it was, he might equally well have impounded Thorne's watch and chain.

"I think it would be better," Gillan was saying, "if you made your statement at the police station. It may take some time."

"Very well," said Thorne. "I'm only too anxious to help in any way I can."

On the way out of the hut he noticed that the two local officers had spades with them; and Gillan paused to give instructions before joining Thorne and Sergeant Askew in the waiting police car.

Down at Crowborough police station Thorne sat facing Gillan across a table. A fire burned merrily in the grate, flicking shadows about the otherwise bleak and cheerless walls. Sergeant Askew sat nearby with pencil and shorthand notebook. To Thorne, it seemed that Inspector Gillan wanted a detailed account of every hour of his life, starting almost from the day he was born. Thorne gave his autobiography willingly so far as memory served him; and when eventually it came to that part of his life involving Elsie Cameron he spared the officer no details, giving a full and frank account of what had taken place between them.

"I didn't believe she was pregnant," he added, "but I promised to marry her if it was true."

From the file in front of him Gillan produced two letters found among Elsie Cameron's belongings at Clifford Gardens. One was in her own handwriting--the copy which she had in fact made of the letter which Thorne had asked her to be returned:

> There are one or two things you do not know...I'm afraid
> I am between two fires....

The other was the original of his second, more explanatory letter:

> What I haven't told you is that on certain occasions a girl
> has been here late at night....Don't tell anyone as yet, but
> I am in a proper fix....

"In this second letter," Gillan was saying, "you infer that Miss C...is also pregnant and expecting you to marry her!"

Much as he had hoped to protect Elizabeth C...'s name from the official records , the cat was now hopelessly out of the bag; and for the very first time Thorne looked uneasy, passing a hand over his smooth black hair.

"That isn't true," he said. "I only put it in the letter, hoping that Miss Cameron would stop pressing me for marriage. I have never been intimate with Miss C...."

Gillan pursued his questioning relentlessly, coming finally to the date of December 5.

"You realize," he said, "that three people have stated they saw Miss Cameron in the vicinity of Wesley Poultry Farm between five and five-fifteen on the evening of that day?"

"Three people?" Thorne looked puzzled. "I know about Mr.Adams and Mr.Sands...."

"Mrs.Annie Price," the Inspector broke in, "saw her actually approaching your hut, just after the other two had passed her in the lane!"

Thorne moistened his lips but otherwise betrayed no sign of emotion.

"They must have been mistaken--all three of them. I tell you, Miss Cameron never came to my hut that evening: I wasn't even expecting her!"

"You say you had arranged to meet her at Groombridge the following day, December the sixth, and she failed to turn up. How was that arrangement made? In writing?"

"Yes," said Thorne, after a moment's deliberation. "I had a letter from her earlier that week, asking me to meet her at Groombridge Station on the Saturday. I went there, but...."

"Have you got that letter, Mr,Thorne?"

Again Thorne hesitated. Then:

"No," he said. "I'm afraid I destroyed it."

Gillan frowned, moving the documents a few inches on the table.

"What were you burning on December the eighth?" he asked quietly.

"Burning?"

"In the stove in your hut. Please think very carefully, Mr.Thorne!"

"I--remember now--I was burning some newspapers and old poultry sacks."

"Nothing else?"

"No--nothing else."

"Do you possess a gun?"

"Good heavens, no!"

"Have you ever had a gun on the premises at Wesley Poultry Farm?"

"Never!"

The interview had lasted for more than seven hours and it was after three in the morning by the time his full statement was read over to him and he signed it. Although weary from the strain of constant questioning, his manner was outwardly as cool and confident as when he had first entered the police station. Even so, it seemed he was not to be allowed to leave again just yet.

"I propose to detain you, Thorne," Gillan said, "pending further investigations."

Thorne knew well enough what was meant by "further investigations"; although once again, had the astute Mr.Llewellyn been there he would doubtless have pointed out that Inspector Gillan had a limited number of hours in which to make up his mind, either to prefer a charge of some sort or else set him free....

With the first light of day digging operations began in earnest at Wesley Poultry Farm; while Thorne passed the seemingly endless time in a police cell. He had slept spasmodically, making only a pretense of eating the breakfast brought in by a uniformed officer. There was even less space here than in the hut, and soon enough the close confinement began to play on his nerves as he paced the narrow floor restlessly, halting now and again to place an ear against the door. Throughout the day there was a great deal of coming and going at Crowborough Police Station, the noises and voices echoing down the corridors to reach him in his cell. It was late afternoon, however, before Thorne became aware all at once that something important had happened--some development--some *find*? He sensed this by the changed tone of the voices--even a subdued undercurrent of excitement. He also recognized the voice of Sergeant Askew who had evidently returned from the scene of operations....

Thorne continued to pace the floor distractedly for a while, until he could stand the suspense no longer. For the very first time the incredible mask of reserve broke down and he began to kick and hammer at the door. When at length Sergeant Askew and another officer appeared, Thorne brushed back the hair which had fallen wildly across his face and said:

"I want to see Inspector Gillan! I've something important to tell him!"

"You'll have to wait," said Askew. "He's up at the poultry farm."

"I know. That's why I want to see him! It's important!"

"I'll pass on the message," Sergeant Askew said curtly....

Thorne had not been mistaken; although a two-and-a half acre field wired off into chicken-runs presented no easy problem to the searchers. Watched by a gaping crowd of village folk and reporters, they adopted a system of elimination, dealing first with those plots of ground unoccupied by the feathered colony. It was early afternoon when one of the officers, probing with a spade in the potato patch, had made contact with some hard object little more than a foot below the surface. When this had been gingerly freed of surrounding soil the relic of a small, cheap suitcase was revealed; and inside it a number of oddments of feminine clothing, including a pair of shoes with rubber soles.

There was no doubt that Elsie Cameron's pitiful luggage had been found!

It was less than an hour later when Inspector Gillan received Thorne's urgent message, yet he seemed in no great hurry to comply with it. Perhaps he was anxious to make the most of the daylight, concentrating digging operations in and around the potato patch. Nevertheless, darkness fell without any fresh developments; and Gillan returned to Crowborough Police Station, leaving the others to carry on by the light of hurricane lanterns. It was a very different Thorne who rose quickly from the cell bed to greet him. In place of the supreme self-assurance of the previous night, his eyes were now hooded and creased with anxiety and the hand that sought constantly to straiten his tie was trembling.

"I understand you want to see me," Gillan said.

Thorne nodded: "I want to tell you the truth about what happened that day--December the fifth!" He sat down on the edge of the bed and spoke with head bowed, as though addressing the floor:

"Between a quarter and half-past five that evening Elsie Cameron arrived at the hut, carrying a suitcase. I was taken completely by surprise and asked her why she had come without letting me know. I also asked her where she intended sleeping, because Mr.and Mrs. Cosham were expecting visitors that week-end. She said she had come to stay until we were married--and that she intended sleeping in the hut. I gave her some tea to calm her down and I also repeated my promise to marry her if she was pregnant. We had no real quarrel or argument, and about half-past seven I left her while I went over to the Cosham's to see if I could arrange about sleeping--but there was nobody at home. I returned to the hut and told her she would have to sleep in my bed, since it was too late to catch the last train back to London. I myself proposed sleeping in the chair. We had some supper, and afterwards I told her I had arranged to meet Miss C...and her mother to help carry their shopping up the hill from the station. She protested at first, but later agreed that I should do this, as I had promised them."

He paused, thrusting the hair back from his face before continuing: "I left the hut soon after half-past nine and met miss C...and her mother at Crowborough Station, just like I told you in my previous statement. I left Miss C...just after a quarter-past eleven and got back to the hut about ten minutes later. The light was still on, but when I opened the door...."

"Well?" Gillan prompted.

"To my horror, I saw Elsie Cameron hanging from a beam! There was a length of cord--clothes line, I think--round her neck, and her feet were just dangling on the ground. She had her frock off and her hair was let down....I cut the rope and laid her on the bed.... She was dead!"

Thorne's face was hidden behind both hands as Inspector Gillan asked quietly: "What did you do then?"

"I was in a daze. I didn't know what to do. I just put out the light and lay across the table for about an hour. After that I was about to go to Dr.Tearle and knock up someone to go for the police--when I suddenly realized the position I was in. People would say I was the cause of her hanging herself--they might even say I'd murdered her!" He looked up suddenly, addressing Gillan directly for the very first time. "I didn't kill her! She committed suicide!" His voice had reached a shrill pitch.

"So what did you do,Thorne?" Gillan appeared unmoved.

"In the end I decided not to go...I fetched my hacksaw from the toolshed...also some sacks....I took off the rest of her clothes and burned some of them in the grate. I put the sacks on the floor by the light of the fire....I took Miss.Cameron--who was then naked--and laid her on the floor by the sacks....Afterwards I intended carrying the sacks away--far away--in a wheelbarrow, but my nerve failed me and I merely took them down to the toolshed and left them there. I went back to the hut and sat in a chair all night. The next morning, just as it got light, I buried the sacks--also a tin box--in one of the chicken-runs." He looked at Gillan as though ridding his mind of an immense burden. "It's the Leghorn run...the first pen from the gate...in the bottom left hand corner!...."

The Leghorn run--bottom left hand corner! The very spot where three days earlier he had posed so jauntily for the press photographers!

Not until half-past ten that night did the spades finally cease their work. By then two bundles of sacking and a large square biscuit tin had been unearthed from a shallow grave among the chickens. With some attempt at reverence these were conveyed to Crowborough Police Station to be opened. The parcels were sodden and swollen in a glistening mould of clay. The first contained the legs, sawn off high up at the thighs and tied together with string, top to tail like sardines. The second bundle revealed the torso with arms attached; even the ring was still on her finger. The contents of the biscuit tin were also wrapped in a thin shroud of sacking, but so tightly wedged that this defied all normal attempts at removal. There followed a macabre tug-of-war in the country police station between Inspector Gillan and Sergeant Askew. The latter gripped the tin, bracing his weight against it, while Gillan took a fistful of sacking in either hand and pulled with all his strength. Inch by inch the tin yielded its secret, until the parcel came clear away. It contained Elsie Cameron's head and neck--severed low down, almost at the point of the collarbone....

At Lewis Assizes later the jury was spared no details of the medical evidence, nor of Thorne's sexual habits. Yet the photographs of Elsie Cameron's remains, as found, were deemed too frightful for the eyes of a layman and were reserved for Judge and Counsel only.

Suicide or otherwise, for six weeks and a day Thorne had lived in that lonely hut with the horror lying buried a few yards away. Did he wake in the night, sweating--even crying aloud--as the fearful truth thundered down at him through the flimsy wooden walls? If so, he never showed it the following day. Nobody--not even Elizabeth C... ever noted the slightest change in him. Not once by so much as the batting of an eyelid had he betrayed the haunting, charnel secret of his mind. The morals may once have been wrapped in cotton-wool, but there is no doubt that Norman Thorne's nerves were cased in tempered steel!

7

Two days later, on January 17, Sir Bernard Spilsbury arrived at Crowborough mortuary to examine the remains of Elsie Cameron. Despite six weeks burial in damp clay, decomposition had not advanced to any great extent; and a preliminary, routine examination revealed to the Home Office Pathologist a young women in her early twenties, well nourished and fairly healthy; who in life had weighed around a hundred and twelve pounds.

Was she pregnant at the time of death? No. In fact, menstruation had already begun internally. In a few hours she would have known of it.

At a hurried police conference beforehand Sir Bernard had been put in the picture regarding Thorne's statement, and he had this uppermost in mind when he looked for the cause of death. Vast experience had taught him that death from hanging--even attempted hanging--leaves its mark in three places internally: the lungs, the brain, and the spinal cord. Yet he could find no trace of asphyxia in Elsie Cameron's lungs; and when he removed the skull-cap the surface of the brain appeared entirely free of contusions or hemorrhage. He probed deeper to reach the centre, but here decomposition had done its work and the whole mass disintegrated at the touch of the instrument. Nevertheless, Sir Bernard had seen sufficient to satisfy him that the brain had sustained no serious injury such as would result from death by strangulation or suffocation. Moreover, the spinal column proved equally intact, without trace of dis-location.

There remained one final check in corroboration of Thorne's story. Had Elsie Cameron been hanging for a matter of seconds only when he found her, the neck would still carry marks of the cord or rope. Sir Bernard could see no such marks externally. True, there were two thin lines or creases running diagonally across the front of the neck, one immediately over the Adam's Apple, the other just above it, but these--he explained to Inspector Gillan who was present at the autopsy--were no more than the natural lines, two of them, to be found on almost every women's neck. Nevertheless, the reputation of the world's greatest pathologist had been founded largely upon a fanatical thoroughness; and not content with a superficial examination Sir Bernard now proceeded to cut into these lines or creases, turning the skin back at fifteen different places, searching for signs of extravasation--the leakage of blood from minute vessels into the surrounding tissues, which is the immediate result of localized pressure. He could find no area that revealed the smallest trace of this and was satisfied that, for some days at least before her death, Elsie Cameron's neck had suffered no undue pressure, either from a rope or any other agent.

Yet, if Sir Bernard Spilsbury ever made a mistake in his life it was in failing to take cuttings from these natural creases, for the purpose of microscopical slides as well as for future reference. On the other hand, why should he? Exhaustive examination by the naked eye both externally and beneath the surface had satisfied him beyond the slightest doubt that no signs of extravasation were present. It was therefore unnecessary to make microscopical slides. Nevertheless, had he done so the trial of Norman Thorne would have been shortened by days....

How then, if not by hanging, had Elsie Cameron died?

Once again it was a matter calling for extreme thoroughness. At a glance, the four sections of human body displayed no evidence of bruising or other injury. Once again it was a question of probing beneath the skin, since a bruise incurred shortly before death is not always visible on the surface. In this way the scalpel revealed no less than eight separate bruises, all beneath the skin and all, in the opinion of the pathologist, sustained shortly before death. Of these, four were on the legs and feet--one in particular extending to a length of fourteen inches between the left knee and ankle; one on the right elbow; the remaining three about the head and face. With one exception, the injuries were comparatively slight and could--Sir Bernard told Gillan--have been received in falling. The one exception, however, a head injury, was of a far more serious nature. Starting at the right temple, this extended down over the right cheek, almost to the level of the mouth, and whilst neither the skin was split nor the bone broken, the tissues between them had been crushed to a pulp. In fact, as opposed to the other injuries this one was clearly the result of a violent blow from some weapon with a hard, smooth surface. It had also been caused last of all--and within a very few seconds of death.

"In my opinion," the pathologist concluded, "death was due to shock, following all the injuries--in particular this last one to the side of the face."

Inspector Gillan said: "We found a pair of Indian Clubs in the hut. Could one of those have done the job,sir?"

Spilsbury thought a moment, then nodded.

"It's possible," he said; and because it was a matter which could not be proved conclusively, his opinion never wavered beyond that point.

But the autopsy had revealed one further sinister fact. Namely, dismemberment had not been carried out until *after the body had passed into a state of rigor mortis*. In other words, a minimum margin of five hours after death. The irresistible inference was, therefore, that Elsie Cameron had been dead before Thorne ever left the hut that night to keep his appointment with Elizabeth C...and her mother!

Armed with all this medical data the police charged Norman Thorne with willful murder.

‡

In due course, Elsie Cameron's remains were conveyed home for more reverent burial in a Harlesdon cemetery. But they were not to be allowed to rest in peace for long. Four weeks later they were dug up yet again for a second post-mortem examination, this time by an eminent Irish pathologist--Dr.Robert Mathew Bront'e, roped in by the defense; for by that time the astute Mr.Llewellyn had come to Thorne's rescue.

In 1925 Sir Bernard Spilsbury was at the height of his fame. Such singular success by one doctor had not unnaturally aroused a certain amount of jealousy within the profession; whilst his apparent infallibility as an expert witness had also given rise to resentment in certain circles of the Bar. Sooner or later, if opportunity occurred, there was bound to be a concerted effort to dislodge the idol from it's pedestal; and for this purpose the case of *Rex v. Norman Thorne*, which must hinge largely upon the medical evidence, seemed a promising field of encounter.

On a bleak, rainy day in the last week of February, both Dr.Bront'e and Sir Bernard Spilsbury were present to witness the raising of Elsie Cameron's coffin; and later, in an adjacent mortuary, to examine the contents. The four weeks which had elapsed since burial, however, had wrought drastic changes, for the coffin was found to be one-third full of a nauseating yellow liquid which had seeped in from the surrounding soil, destroying and washing away in the process most of the vital evidence. Even so, Dr.Bront'e declared that the lines or creases on the neck, described by Spilsbury as natural female lines, were in fact the lines left by a rope. He took minute cuttings, giving half of these to Spilsbury for the purpose of making microscopical slides. The remainder of the body was so decomposed by the action of the fluid as to make further autopsy impossible.

Later, Spilsbury made his own slides of the neck cuttings; Bront'e's were prepared by someone else. Under the microscope Spilsbury could still detect no signs of extravasation. He went further in declaring that the elements were so destroyed that it was not even possible to state with accuracy what in fact the slides portrayed. Bront'e, on the other hand, was convinced that his slides showed definite signs of extravasation; and in this he was supported by the opinions of three other eminent doctors, all of who were either surgeons or pathologists.

The news must have put fresh heart into Norman Thorne as he Languished in a remand cell; still more so when Mr.Llewellyn announced that he had retained the services of Mr.J.D.Cassells,K.C.[*] Everything possible in fact was being done to substantiate his story of suicidal hanging. Yet, if sympathy or pity was due in any quarter

---

[*]   Later Mr.Justice Cassells

it was to the bereaved parents of Elsie Cameron, to Thorne's relatives and trusting friends, not the least of which was Elizabeth C....Guilty or not guilty of murder, Thorne had deceived her shamefully. He had also behaved like a monster; and if she had any feelings left for him they could only have been of horrified disillusionment. However, she was still young with a lifetime before her. Time heals, and the vortex of grim events and distasteful publicity into which her simple country existence had been suddenly swept would not last forever....

‡

The trial opened on March 5th, 1925, at Sussex Winter Assizes, in the County Hall, Lewis. As Mr.Justice Finley took his seat on the Bench amid all the pomp and ceremony he looked very young for a judge, but his record was no less brilliant. Sir Henry Curtis Bennett,K.C. led Mr.R.E.Negus for the Crown; Mr.J.D.Cassells,K.C.,M.P., Mr.Cecil Oakes and Mr.C.T.Abbott appearing for the prisoner. Behind this legal bastion the Defense had in addition subpoenaed no less than eight doctors, as against the Crown's two--Spilsbury and a police surgeon. As Mr.Cassell's was to remark:

"This whole case may well depend upon a microscopical slide!"

As Norman Thorne was brought into the dock, onlookers beheld once again the placid, self-assured young owner of Wesley Poultry Farm, spruce in a well fitting suit, his black hair shining with pomade and brushed strait back from the forehead. Perhaps he derived added encouragement from the impressive array of bewigged counsel, there to champion his cause. Nevertheless, his gaze avoided the many friends whom he had deceived and who now occupied the seats reserved for witnesses, waiting to perform an invidious task; among them Elizabeth C....In a quiet but firm voice he answered "Not Guilty" to the charge of Willful Murder.

‡

Sir Henry Curtis Bennett began to outline the case for the Crown; and this seemed ominously straightforward, backed by circumstantial evidence, Thorne's behaviour before and after, and the findings of the Home Office Pathologist. Thorne had tired of Elsie Cameron and wished to marry Miss C....But the deceased was pressing him for marriage, declaring herself pregnant although this in fact was not true. On the evening of December 5, she had arrived unexpectedly at the hut, but in good spirits and assured that the prisoner was going to marry her if she was pregnant as she undoubtedly believed herself to be. A violent quarrel, however, had followed in which Elsie Cameron was flung to the ground, sustaining severe bruises. In the process, the heavy home-made table had overturned and fallen across her leg, causing a bruise fourteen inches long between the knee and ankle. As she lay on the ground Thorne had struck her a murderous blow across the right side of the head with an Indian Club; and death had followed in a matter of seconds, from the combined shock of all the injuries. Soon afterwards the prisoner had gone out to keep an appointment with Miss C...and her mother, returning later to dismember and bury the body....

Such was the grim story, claimed by Sir Henry as the only logical one to be deduced from the facts he would place before the jury. He began to do so by calling, as first witnesses, all the police officers who had been engaged on the case; and in his cross-examination of these, Mr.Cassells soon made clear the lines to be adopted by the Defense. Thorne's story of suicidal hanging was to be upheld in principle; but in order to bring this into line with the known, indisputable facts, certain modifications were necessary. For instance, none of the Defense doctors were strictly in a position to refute the evidence of Sir Bernard Spilsbury and the police surgeon that all eight bruises on Elsie Cameron's body had been sustained during life--if only a matter of seconds before death. Neither could she have received some of these in the process of hanging. Yet, Thorne in his original statement to Gillan had said: *I cut her down and laid her on the bed. She was dead....* The Defense, therefore, had to keep Elsie Cameron alive just long enough to have sustained the bruises in the process of being cut down and placed on the bed. Thus, Thorne would now change his phrasing to: *"She appeared to be dead...."* No jury could fail to appreciate that a statement given to the police in the stress of panic was open to minor discrepancies, to afterthoughts....In short, the Defense hypothesis was to be: Attempted suicidal hanging--cutting down--followed almost immediately by death from shock; the shock resulting from partial hanging, as opposed to the bruising.

Among a hundred or more exhibits in court was the beam from the hut. Following Thorne's final statement to Inspector Gillan the police had examined this beam for possible marks left by a rope. They had found none, although--as a matter of some significance--whereas all the other beams in the hut bore a coating of dust, this particular one had been wiped clean. From the witness-box Inspector Gillan now went on to describe experiments carried out with the beam, using a length of cord of the same thickness mentioned by Thorne and a weight equivalent to that of Elsie Cameron--first by suddenly releasing the weight and again by gradual suspension. In each case the cord bit into the soft timber, and the marks, including a whisp of hemp fibre, were there on the beam for the jury to see. Against this, Mr.Cassells could do little more than attack a system which had given the police full run of the hut--even to dismantling it--without a representative of the Defense being present.

After the police evidence, during which the Clerk of the Court read aloud Thorne's full and frank statement of his life and relationship with Elsie Cameron, the rest of the picture was gradually built up by all those who had played a part in it: Mr. and Mrs.Cameron and their married daughter Margaret, Mrs.Mottier--even the Cosham's and others living in Crowborough and Blackness who had been in daily contact with the prisoner and the deceased. Quite apart from showing the development of the story-in-chief as unfolded by the evidence, Sir Henry Curtis Bennett sought, through each of these witnesses, to implant one underlying factor firmly in the minds of the jury. Namely, that Elsie Cameron had been deeply in love with Thorne; that he was her whole world, her whole happiness; that only when she was away from him did she resort to moods and depression. In cross-examination Mr.Cassells sought, even more relentlessly, to extract the admission that Elsie Cameron was in fact a neurotic and a likely subject for suicide. In this he made little headway with the Crown witnesses, for whilst none could deny that Elsie had suffered from her nerves, it was a far cry to wishing herself dead. Mr.Cassells, however, was to have his turn later.

All this build-up evidence had occupied more than a day; then it was Sir Bernard Spilsbury's turn to enter the witness-box. In the calm, unruffled manner for which he was renowned, the Home Office Pathologist told of his post-mortem findings. On the ledge of the witness-stand he balanced a human skull, indicating the exact location of the three head injuries, in particular the one which had pulped the tissues and which, in his opinion, had been sustained last of all as the result of a blow. Dealing with his exhaustive examination of the neck at the first post-mortem on January 17, Sir Bernard concluded:

"There was no sign of any sort or kind of damage resulting from attempted hanging or actual hanging. It was therefore not necessary at that time to make any microscopic examination or to make slides."

"Had there been any sign of extravasation as the result of pressure from a rope or cord," Sir Henry asked, "you would have seen this with the naked eye when you turned back the skin?"

"Certainly."

"You were present when Dr.Bront'e conducted a second post-mortem on February the twenty-fourth? What was the condition of the neck by then?"

"The condition of the tissues was then such that no examination, microscopic or otherwise, would help." He added that the slides he had made from Bront'e's cuttings revealed nothing, all the cells and tissues having been destroyed by the action of fluid in the coffin.

Despite a remarkable knowledge of forensic medicine displayed by Mr.Cassells in cross-examination, Sir Bernard remained unshakable; although never failing to cede a point in the prisoner's favour whenever possible.

"Rigor Mortis has been known to set in within an hour of death?"

"Oh yes--less than that in certain cases."

It was when dealing with the main head injury that Mr.Cassells allowed his voice to rise in pitch.

"Do you really tell the jury, Sir Bernard," he exclaimed, gripping the Indian Club and holding it aloft, "that a blow from this weapon, delivered with murderous violence, could produce a bruise such as you describe without breaking the skin or bone?"

"Only on certain parts of the face," came the calm reply. "If it were delivered *here*...." Sir Bernard was again demonstrating with the human skull, "with the smooth, bulbous part of the club, then it would form the exact condition that I found there."

"What is there about this part of the face that would offer such resistance as to give you, upon examination, no broken skin or bone?"

"The question of broken skin," said Sir Bernard quietly, "is one of crushing of skin between the weapon and the bone. If that weapon had been used on the girl's head and a blow struck...say, *there*...it would, of course, almost certainly split the skin. Had it been used on the cheek it would have done the same; but *here*...between the eye and the ear, there is a soft layer of tissue with the bone some distance away. Thus the tissue would have a cushioning effect."

And so it went on, Defence Counsel plugging away remorselessly but never getting anywhere. Every aspect of the medical evidence was turned inside out; death from shock, death from hanging and attempted hanging--resuscitation--. When was a person officially pronounced dead? When the heart stops beating, of course! And here the argument flew to the borders of fantasy, Cassells extracting confirmation from Spilsbury of a known case in which the heart of a guillotine victim had continued to beat for one hour after decapitation. And all to what purpose? Why, to show that whereas Elsie Cameron had assumed every appearance of death her heart might still have been beating faintly; and so long as the heart continues to pump, bruises incurred shortly beforehand will continue to form or spread. The apparent gain by the Defense, however, was to blow back on Thorne later, in a few simple, devastating questions by the Judge....

By the time he stood down after re-examination, the Home Office Pathologist had occupied the witness-box for the better part of one whole day. At this point also the case for the Crown rested. Thorne's life with Elsie Cameron had been laid before the jury, as well as his behaviour during the six weeks immediately following her death. Did Elsie Cameron ever have a rope or cord around her neck? Or had she died by murderous violence? It was Thorne's word now, against the allegations by the Crown; the evidence of the doctors who would support him, against that of Sir Bernard Spilsbury.

8

Mr.Cassells' opening speech was brief, for the jury already knew the line to be taken by the Defense; and after the evidence of a surveyor, the first material witness to be called was the prisoner himself. It was a big moment for the sensation-mongers present as well as for the press, who dashed off graphic descriptions of him as he left the dock and entered the witness-box. Yet, in reality, there was little sensational about Norman Thorne at that moment. If anything he looked a trifle sheepish; with head averted, pushing the drinking-water bottle a few inches to one side; taking the oath in a quiet but firm voice. For more than two days he had been listening to the intimate details of his life bandied about the court like a common exhibit, to say nothing of his full confessions and the letters which had passed between himself and Elsie Cameron. Now he was to go through it all again, this time confirming it by his own word of mouth.

Once again he began to tell the entire story of his life, this time in answer to Mr.Cassells' gentle questioning. No detail was omitted and when, by degrees, they had reached the early days of his settlement at Crowborough it became clear at once that a main part of the Defense tactics was to involve a concerted attack on the dead girl's mental stability. Beginning with the prisoner, there was in fact to be a gradual build-up of evidence tending to show a particular form of psychosis, and culminating with the purely objective opinion of an eminent psychiatrist who specialized in mental diseases. Thus, referring to those early days, Mr.Cassells asked Thorne:

"What sort of condition of health was she in then?"

"Very nervous condition. Very nervous indeed!"

And again, when they had reached the critical period covering the Summer of 1924:

"What was her condition when she came down upon this visit?"

"She was highly neurotic. Even Mrs.Cosham remarked upon it."

"Did you yourself notice anything strange about her condition during that time?"

"Yes, it was very strange. Mostly during that time she seemed to be practically dazed--or in a semi-trance!"

Much, of course, had been made of the Piper incident; neither was the business of the Alliance of Honour to be omitted by way of a fillip to the prisoner's moral code.

"Why did you get Miss Cameron to join, that day at Wembley?"

"Well...." Thorne began hesitantly, "she had confessed to me some time previously...." Whatever he was about to say, Mr.Cassells saw fit to cut him short.

"I can put it in one word, perhaps," said Counsel. "What was her attitude with regard to you?"

"She was growing very passionate!"

At this bold, smug answer an uncomfortable stir--almost of revulsion--seemed to pass through the courtroom; yet Thorne appeared oblivious to it. He had a part to play, a story to tell, and he was determined to spare his audience none of the trimmings.

When eventually they reached the evening of December 5, Mr.Cassells said: "I want you to tell us in your own way, Thorne, what you found upon your return to the hut that night after leaving Miss C....?"

Thorne gripped the dock-rail, but his voice never faltered:

"Well--I saw to my intense horror Miss Cameron suspended to the beam in the centre of the hut. I rushed in. I took a knife that lay on the table nearby and I cut the cord, holding Miss Cameron with my left arm. The weight fell against me and I twisted her round so that I shouldn't see her face....I struggled to lift her on to the bed. I dragged her legs up and placed them on the bed...."

"What happened during the process?"

"After I dragged her legs up she fell on to the suitcase."

"Where was the suitcase?"

"On the bed--at the head end."

"What part of her fell on it?"

"That would be her face."

Yes, some of the bruises, at any rate, had to be accounted for!

Assuming it had been necessary, Thorne had had weeks in which to think up a detailed story; but it was not so easy to account for his subsequent actions--including the writing of love letters to a girl he had just dismembered and buried--and even with the guidance of Mr.Cassells he could add little to what he had already told Inspector Gillan. Yet, on the whole, Thorne had made a good witness so far, no matter how low his moral character had been assessed by most of those present.

As Sir Henry Curtis Bennett rose to cross-examine, his opening question fell upon a hushed court-room:

"On the morning of December fifth, were you still in love with Elsie Cameron?"

Here, at the very start, was a poser! If he answered NO it might seriously prejudice his case. If he said YES it was a lie.

"Yes," said Thorne.

"On the morning of December the fifth, were you in love with Miss C....?"

Again Thorne was obliged to hesitate. Then:

"Yes," he said, and this time it was the truth.

"On that morning," came Sir Henry's dry tones, "which of those two girls that you were in love with did you desire to marry?"

It was a deadly question, by way of an opening volley. No matter how Thorne answered the inference was there, on a platter for the jury; the damage done; he was a liar!

"I don't know that I was particularly desirous of marrying anyone just then," was all he was able to mutter.

Dealing with the Alliance of Honour, Sir Henry asked:

"You renewed your subscriptions for 1922 and 1923?"

"Yes."

"When you join the Alliance of Honour do you make some sort of written or verbal promise not to have any indecent relations with girls?"

"Yes. That is what it amounts to."

"And being a member in 1922 and 1923, when did you start to have indecent connections with your fiancée?"

"I first became intimate with Miss Cameron in 1923," said Thorne with the utmost calm.

Sir Henry leaned forward slightly: "Do you really tell the jury the reason you got Miss Cameron to become a member of the Alliance of Honour was because she was growing very passionate?"

"Yes."

"Were you growing *less* passionate?"

"As a matter of fact, I was becoming rather alarmed by her conduct, especially when she was in a state of nervous collapse!"

"Passion," pursued Sir Henry, "which had been aroused by you, Thorne?"

"Oh, no, sir!"

"When you say "passionate", are you talking of sexual passion?"

"Yes."

"You had been arousing her sexual passion between 1923 and 1924?"

"Not any more than she had been arousing mine."

Sir Henry waved his brief in the air in an expression of disdain.

"Oh, come now," he exclaimed. "You surely do not put *that* upon this poor girl?"

Thorne shrugged a trifle sheepishly; and once again, amid the murmurs of onlookers, his reply was scarcely audible.

"It was mutual," he said.

Despite the general circumstances of the case, Sir Henry never took advantage of the prisoner. Quite often he would preface a question by saying; "Please think. I do not want to catch you out, Thorne, but I must have an answer to this...."

For the most part, however, the line of probing was deadly, based on cold logic:

"If your story is true, when you went out from the hut at half-past nine that night, she believed you were going to marry her if she was pregnant?"

"Yes."

"Then why should she commit suicide?"

"Why?" Thorne spread his hands. "She left no message behind. I don't think it is safe for me to say any definite reason!" This naive attitude was clearly part of his Defense; seeking whenever possible to put himself forward as a victim of circumstances.

When Crown Counsel finally sat down, Thorne imagined his ordeal to be over, but Mr.Justice Finley leaned forward, clearing his throat.

"Just a few questions, Thorne," said his lordship in a quiet, unemotional voice. "When you came back to the hut that night and found Miss Cameron suspended from the beam, your first act was to cut her down?"

"Yes, my lord."

"Did you make any attempt to resuscitate her?"

"No, my lord. I thought she was dead."

"Did you ever think of going to fetch a doctor?"

"Not until after I got up from the table."

Again the judge cleared his throat. "That was not until an hour later? You never thought of fetching a doctor at once--on the chance of her being revived?"

"No, my lord. I thought at once she was dead," came the dogged reply.

"You have heard, I suppose, that people who are apparently dead are sometimes revived?"

"Yes--I have heard of such things as that."

"Anyhow," said Mr.Justice Finlay leaning back again with an air of finality, "you never thought of getting a doctor and you did not get one?"

"No, my lord." Thorne's voice was scarcely above a whisper.

Much the same ground had been covered both in his examination-in-chief and in cross-examination, but laid bare by the cold, impartial questions of the judge, the truth assumed a much greater significance. Yet, when Thorne finally returned to the dock, it was still his word against the circumstantial evidence and the medical findings in support of it.

Father followed son into the witness-box, Mr.Thorne telling the jury of his own feelings at the prospect of Elsie Cameron as a daughter-in-law; and here the attack on her mental state was carried one stage further.

"There were times," said Mr.Thorne, "when she would sit completely silent, with folded hands. At others, she was quite cheerful. I did not consider her a suitable wife for my son, on account of her nerves."

Referring to the prisoner, Mr.Cassells asked:

"Have you ever known him violent?"

"Never!"

"Have you ever known him lose his temper?"

"Never--except as a child, of course, in a childish way."

Next, by way of corroborative evidence as to the prisoner's good character, a Mr.Samuel H.Robinson was called, who had known Thorne since 1913. Mr. Robinson proved a valuable witness and after Cassells' opening questions, clearly needed no prompting:

"In my opinion he is amiable, courteous, considering others more than himself; absolutely unselfish, and a great favourite with all that knew him. A popular son of a popular father."

"Have you ever known him in a passion?"

"Never!"

"Have you ever known him violent?"

"Never! He is the last person with whom I would credit any act of violence!"

With this high testimonial still ringing in the ears of the court, Sir Henry Curtis Bennett rose, adjusted his wig, and said quietly:

"I must ask you--could you have imagined from your knowledge of the defendant that he would be able to dismember a body?"

It was bathos, combined with brilliance. By this one cogent question, put almost in a conversational tone, all the eulogies of the well-meaning Mr.Robinson were neutralized; and by the time he found voice to splutter, "Certainly not!" Sir Henry had already sat down. Unwittingly, Mr.Robinson had exposed the dangers of over-enthusiasm in the witness-box.

There followed, one by one, three girls of Elsie Cameron's own age who had known her and who now testified to her bouts of nervous disorder. These included the two colleagues who had escorted her home from the office early one afternoon when she had seemed incapable of making the journey alone. In retrospect and taken out of their context the incidents cited by all three assumed a grave significance: the sitting for long spells at a time staring down at her shoes; a haunting fear that people were laughing at her; afraid to cross the road; afraid to enter or leave the Underground train.... Certainly it all added fuel to the fire which Mr.Cassells had kindled early in the proceedings; and he went on to call Dr.Watson Walker, the Cameron's family physician. Dr.Walker admitted that as early as 1921 he was treating Elsie for anaemia and backache. From January to June, 1923, she was under his care for neurasthenia; and again from September 1923 to January 1924 for the same complaint. He also told of her visit on November 18, when she had imagined herself pregnant. If the truth were known, perhaps Dr.Walker resented giving evidence against his own patient for, unlike the enthusiastic Mr.Robinson, he was reserved, confining his answers to the bare facts, never expressing an opinion voluntarily. Yet, of all the witnesses called by both sides of the Bar, Dr.Walker probably knew Elsie Cameron better than any. To him she had confided the most intimate details of her life. To him she had always turned in moments of trouble....

Much was said at the time, and much has been said and written since, denouncing Elsie Cameron as an ingrained neurotic with suicidal tendencies; a girl whose mind harboured few thoughts beyond those of sex, marriage, and babies. That she succumbed eventually to a nervous and mental disorder cannot be denied. Yet nobody--not even the experts--troubled to seek and declaim the cause which was clearly biological and physical rather than a psychological one. Thorne's selfish "practice", indulged promiscuously over a period of two years or more, would have affected nine women out of ten in exactly the same way, and although he made no reference to it in the witness-box, Dr.Walker, alone of all the experts, had diagnosed this cause and had told his patient as much. Elsie Cameron in turn had passed it on to Thorne in a letter:

> *Dr.Walker says it's the way we've been carrying on that's caused it (my nerves), each of us knowing that what we were doing was wrong....*

Yes, the family doctor had pin-pointed the trouble, denouncing it privately if only in a mild, delicate way. Had he offered the same opinion publicly from the witness-box it would have done much towards sparing Elsie Cameron's name and character, both at the time and in posterity....

The unpredictable state of the deceased's mind being an essential contribution to the Defense plea, Mr.Cassells now sought to clinch matters by calling an expert psychologist, Dr.James Cowan Woods, who held appointments at various mental institutions. He had never met Elsie Cameron and the opinions he now offered were based solely upon the evidence which had already been placed before the court and a study of the dead girl's medical history.

"The alternation of elation and depression, of which we have heard so much," pronounced Dr.Woods, "is characteristic, to my mind, of the particular psychosis in which I believe she dwelt."

"How would you classify that psychosis?"

"Sometimes cheerful and talkative--sometimes silent with folded hands--is characteristic of what we call Maniac Depressive Psychosis."

Maniac! The word must have smacked against Thorne's ear as he sat listening intently from the dock, never displaying the least signs of emotion. Yet, if at any time throughout the trial he had allowed his mind to flit back upon Elsie Cameron, it must have been at this moment. And if so, how did the vision of her manifest itself? As she appeared to him in moments of their love-making? Or as her naked body lay butchered and quartered on the floor of the hut, in the hideous glow of the firelight? To which of them could the word "maniac" be more justly applied?

However, the term as used academically in psychology carries a far less stringent meaning than that assigned to it in the dictionary, and under cross-examination Dr.Woods was obliged to expound its limitations.

"Nearly everybody in this world," said Sir Henry, "is sometimes bright and sometimes sad and depressed?"

"Quite."

"Sometimes talkative and sometimes very silent?"

"Oh, quite!"

"There is no magic in that? There is nothing which would cause you to think that a person is going to commit suicide if they show those sort of symptoms?"

"No," said Dr.Woods. "But may I comment on that?"

"Yes," Sir Henry exclaimed, "I am waiting!"

The psychiatrist went on to explain that nearly every mental symptom has its counterpart in normal life. It was the swing from definitely morbid depression to definitely morbid exhilaration that was a characteristic symptom of the particular psychosis in question.

"Is it a definite morbid exhilaration," Sir Henry asked, "that a girl going down to see her fiancée should have done her hair in a different way and bought a new jumper?"

"Only if it shows up in contrast to her general mood," was the ambiguous reply.

"Are you really seriously saying that with a young girl of twenty-six years of age, who is engaged to be married and who is going down to stay with her fiancée, and is having her hair done in a different way and buys a new jumper and a new pair of shoes--that is a symptom of some acute state of neurasthenia?"

"That one thing, no."

"That, in contradistinction from what?...."

It went on like that for some time. Of all the witnesses called on both sides, Dr.Woods fared, perhaps, worst of all. To give the psychiatrist his due, however, he had only been asked to state a purely objective opinion, which at all times would have been open to modification or alteration by personal contact with the subject himself.

Dr.John Smith Gibson was the next witness. A surgeon and Licentiate of the Royal College of Physicians at London and St.Mary's, he had been present with Dr.Bront'e at the second post-mortem on February 24; and he now went on to speak of the bruising on Elsie Cameron's body. The main head injury, he said, might have been caused by a blow, but *not* a violent blow. A violent blow from the Indian Club, said Dr.Gibson, delivered to any part of the head would have fractured the skull. There was no doubt that Dr.Gibson knew a great deal on the subject of extravasation; and at this point the slides made from Bront'e's share of the neck cuttings were produced and put in as exhibits--as Spilsbury had done with his. But Sir Henry was already on his feet, objecting.

"These slides," he said, "could not be used as evidence; they had not been proved! They might have come from anywhere!"

"It will entail calling several witnesses who are not here today," said Mr.Cassells.

"I am sure your lordship will agree," Sir Henry persisted, "that it is essential, in evidence of this sort, that there should be evidence of identification."

"And further upon that," said Mr.Cassells, "I shall make the same request with regard to Sir Bernard's slides!"

"Sir Bernard made them himself. I have only to call him!"

In the end it was agreed that evidence pertaining to Bront'e's slides would be admissible on the understanding that these would be proved later. A storm in a tea-cup and all a trifle petty, but showing nonetheless the high pitch of tension reached between apposing Counsel.

Dr.Gibson thus went on to say that, whilst he was unable to speak as an expert pathologist, in his opinion the slides showed evidence of extravasation in Elsie Cameron's neck; and he was the first of four eminent doctors all sharing the same view.

It was another big moment for the gallery when the name of Dr.Robert Mathew Bront'e was called; and several minutes of the court's precious time sped by as, after taking the oath, the pathologist proceeded to enumerate every post he had ever held, all of which were in Ireland. He concluded by saying that for some years he had occupied the equivalent position in that country to Sir Bernard Spilsbury in England. By complete contrast to the latter, however, Dr.Bront'e was excitable, profusely eloquent, at times even striking dramatic poses in the witness-box. Where Spilsbury had confined his answers to a minimum number of words, Bront'e was not content with merely stating an opinion but must qualify this by citing every known case on the subject. On one such occasion he paused, literally for breath, and added:

"I have brought with me records of between four and five hundred such cases, if your lordship would care to hear them?"

Mr.Justice Finley heaved a deep sigh and said: "There are limits!"

On another occasion, finding his patience at an end, Sir Henry Curtis Bennett rose quickly and exclaimed; "My lord, I am most anxious not to interrupt, but I do not see where we are to stop at this sort of thing!"

"I feel the difficulty," his lordship nodded, "cannot Dr.Bront'e confine himself to cases within his own experience?"

Nevertheless, beneath this somewhat brash exterior Bront'e was a clever pathologist drawing on considerable experience, and his evidence was in direct conflict with that of Spilsbury. From the post-mortem examination on February 24, he was convinced that Elsie Cameron's neck bore the marks of pressure by a rope--not only externally in the form of two lines or creases running across the centre, but also by microscopical examination of internal sections which revealed extravasation. Death, in his opinion, was due to shock, following an unsuccessful or interrupted attempt at hanging. He treated the court to a lengthy discourse on the subject of death from shock and persons attempting suicide by one means but dying from another. Once again Mr.Cassells drew from him the possibility of the heart continuing to beat after every appearance of death; and here the Irish pathologist was in his element, citing case after case--even to that of chickens running around after decapitation. Once again the Indian Club was produced and by way of emphasizing its lethal weight Bront'e struck the edge of the witness-box a resounding blow. As the echo died away in the hushed court-room, Mr.Cassells asked:

"In your opinion, Dr.Bront'e, is it possible to conceive of a bruise such as has been described by Sir Bernard Spilsbury, being produced with that Indian Club, used with the violence of a murderer?"

"In my opinion it is quite impossible."

"What would you say would be the result of a blow--sufficient to pulp the tissues--delivered by that club to the right side of the head between the eye and the ear?"

"It would crush the skull like an eggshell!" was Bront'e's dramatic reply.

In cross-examination he was equally voluble and demonstrative, placing the exhibit cord around his own neck and tying slip-knots to show the many, varying possibilities. Once, when Sir Henry suggested that if the deceased had in fact been suspended long enough to suffer unconsciousness, her neck would have born the marks of the rope externally, not in the form of thin, disputable lines or creases but as ugly red wheals, Bront'e disagreed. Seizing the cord, he took a half-hitch around his forefinger, pulled on it tightly, then released it holding the digit aloft.

"You see?" he said. "It has left a mark on my finger, but soon this will have disappeared!"

Some minutes later he paused in the middle of an answer to observe: "Look--the mark has gone now!"

"It has not gone," Sir Henry contradicted him. "I can still see it from here!"

Nevertheless, despite a long and brilliant cross-examination, Bront'e remained dogged in his opinions, as unshakable as Spilsbury; and by the time he stood down the jury could have been little the wiser.

Had Elsie Cameron been suspended by the neck at any time that evening? If so, her neck would have shown signs of it--if not externally, then internally in the form of extravasation. Bront'e maintained there were such signs; Spilsbury said there were none. Upon this issue Thorne's life hung in the balance. Moreover, as

Mr.Cassells had foreshadowed, a point had been reached where the whole case turned upon a microscopical slide; and the Defense now threw in its remaining reserves.

Dr.David Nabarro, Director of the Pathological Institute at Great Ormond Street Hospital, took the oath and declared that he had examined Bront'e's slides. Like Dr.Smith Gibson he confirmed that these revealed definite signs of crushing of the minute blood-vessels beneath the surface of the skin: the aftermath of pressure. Lastly-- but by no means the least--he was followed by Dr.Hugh Miller Galt, a Master of Surgery and Pathologist to the Royal Sussex Hospital at Brighton. In company with the other three, this distinguished doctor confirmed the presence of extravasation in Bront'e's slides....

How then, did it come about that the opinion of all these experts was in direct conflict with that of a man whom each one in turn, in cross-examination, had acknowledged to be the most experienced pathologist of the day? There was something wrong somewhere!

The answer lay partly in the fact that the Defense doctors had never examined Spilsbury's slides and vice versa. Thus at the end of the fourth day's hearing the court adjourned with the medical evidence still at a complete deadlock; an unprecedented situation arising whereby matters were seemingly out of the hands of learned Counsel and in those of the doctors themselves. It was a Saturday, and over the week-end Spilsbury and his opposing colleagues repaired to Brighton where they held a private conference in the Royal Sussex Hospital. On the Monday morning, when Dr.Hugh Galt was recalled to the witness-box, he disclosed a remarkable state of affairs. It was quite true, he admitted, that Sir Bernard's slides revealed nothing, the specimen matter being completely decomposed! At the same time Dr.Galt upheld his opinion that Bront'e's slides of these neck cuttings showed evidence of crushed blood-vessels. In answer to Sir Henry Curtis Bennett he went further by acknowledging that Spilsbury's slides were the better prepared of the two sets.

From this even a layman might deduce that if extravasation was in fact present in Elsie Cameron's neck, it was to so small an extent that only one half of a minute section of skin revealed it. But was it, in effect, extravasation that Galt, Bront'e and the others could detect under the microscope in that tiny particle of decomposed flesh? Now that Spilsbury had seen both sets of slides, had he altered his opinion? In view of this fresh evidence the Crown was in a position to recall the Home Office Pathologist.

"You have had considerable experience, have you not, Sir Bernard, in looking microscopically at parts of the human body which have been obtained weeks--even months--after death?"

"That is so."

"You have heard the evidence of these doctors as to what they see upon the slides taken from certain sections of the neck? What is your opinion on that?"

"My opinion is," said Sir Bernard slowly, "that what the other doctors have described as evidence of injury and haemorhage are, in fact, the very degenerated remains of what were originally the so-called sebaceous glands, and the hair-roots with which those glands are connected." He paused fractionally, then added: "And I think I can also see slight traces of the remains of the glands cells."

"And you have no doubt about that?"

"None whatever. I should have expected to find exactly what I have found if at the second post-mortem, microscopic slides had been made from flesh taken from any part of the neck--either underneath one of those creases, or above or below it."

"In your opinion, is there any evidence at all upon those slides--of injury such as would be caused by suspension with *that* piece of cord?"

"None whatever."

Thus the bone of contention remained. In the end it fell to the judge to sort out the welter of medical evidence; but not before Counsel had made their final addresses. By calling other witnesses besides the prisoner, Mr.Cassells had sacrificed the right of the last word to the jury and his speech therefore came first. It was a brilliant forensic effort to uphold the truth of Thorne's story.

"Can you really follow, members of the jury," he asked, "that in the mind of a man for whose character of non-violence so many people have spoken, there was indeed so callous, so determined and deliberate a murderous nature that he could calmly and cooly do this crime and then saunter off to Crowborough Station to keep an appointment with the other woman?...."

Dealing with the Indian Club and the Crown's theory that the deceased had been struck on the head with it as she lay on the floor, Mr.Cassells made a telling point with the jury. "Any conscious victim in those circumstances", he maintained, "would automatically try to ward off the blow"; yet there was not a single bruise to be found on Elsie Cameron's fore-arms....

Finally, when it came to the conflicting medical evidence, Defense Counsel had the majority of power to his elbow; but it was still necessary to combat the tremendous reputation for infallibility earned by the Home Office Pathologist. Thus when dealing with Sir Bernard Spilsbury's opinions Mr.Cassells' voice rose in pitch:

"We can all admire attainment, take off our hats to ability, acknowledge the high position that a man has won in his sphere. But it is a long way to go if you have to say that, when that man says something, there can be no room for error!...."

Whatever the outcome, when Mr.Cassells sat down he had the satisfaction of knowing that no Counsel could have done more in defense of a prisoners life. It was now the turn of the Crown.

"My learned friend," said Sir Henry Curtis Bennett, "has referred to the question of deliberation--murder thought out before hand. It is unnecessary for you, members of the jury, to find evidence of long deliberation beforehand in the case of this man. It is only common sense that murders are often committed, not as a result of long deliberation, but as the result of motives which have been in existence for a long time and the motive suddenly coming to a climax...." Sir Henry went on to say that he had not complained about it, but considerable time had been occupied by the Defense in tracing the life-history of Elsie Cameron. In an effort to show that this girl had committed suicide, they had gone back for many years--falling upon certain incidents.

"I wonder, members of the jury, if one went back into the lives of most people one would not be able to find some such incidents as have been pointed out to us in this case! What motive had she for suicide that night? On Thorne's own admission, she had agreed that he should go out and meet Miss C ..., and he had promised to marry her if she was pregnant!...."

Sir Henry played on Spilsbury's reputation and vast experience, concluding: "I submit that on the evidence you have listened to for the last four and a half days, no reasonable man, however responsible the duty cast upon him, could doubt that Elsie Cameron did not die as the result of suicide, but as the result of murder."

‡

Nobody present at a murder trial can fail to be aware of the sense of anti-climax that reigns as the judge begins his summing-up. Coming as this does after the more spectacular oratory of learned counsel, the cold, measured, down-to-earth tones bear steep contrast. Seldom can a judge of the Criminal Court have been faced with a more difficult task than was Mr.Justice Finley on this occasion; yet his summing-up equalled the brilliance of Cassells and Curtis Bennett. Taking every scrap of evidence from the very start of the trial he placed it before the jury, weighing it, and inviting them to form one of two conclusions, but never once imposing upon them his own opinions. In dealing with certain aspects of the Defense hypothesis he said:

"It is this: she is cut down; she is laid on the bed; she gets eight bruises in the process of being laid on the bed, and she then dies."

Mr.Cassells, however, had risen:

"I think I ought at this stage to interrupt your lordship! It is not suggested that the eight bruises were received in the laying down on the bed. There is no knowledge or theory as to how they were caused--only some of them."

Although Mr.Cassells was well within his rights, some judges might have resented the interruption and dealt with it caustically. But not so, Mr.Justice Finley, who at once replied:

"I am obliged to Mr.Cassells and I'm sure he will not hesitate to interrupt me if I mis-state anything!"

Such was the judge whom Norman Thorne was fortunate enough to have presiding at his trial.

In reviewing the vital medical evidence he put the two conflicting opinions and added: "If, as the Defense doctors say, there was some slight extravasation at this girls neck, I suppose this was very slight and very local. I suppose that would be an indication that the injury to the neck causing extravasation was slight...."

When at length the jury retired to consider their verdict the atmosphere in court was still tense; the outcome still anybody's guess. Yet, out of all that gathering, the one person who remained utterly cool, calm and seemingly quite indifferent as the long drawn-out minutes slipped by, was the prisoner himself. Pacing the corridor of the cells below with his solicitor, he spent the time discoursing upon the merits of various breeds of chickens!

For the others, however, the suspense was not to last long. After a trial occupying five full days the jury took just twenty-eight minutes to reach a verdict; and as Thorne was brought into the dock for the last time to learn his fate, the pale, bland features displayed little sign of emotion except that his eyes were fixed upon the foreman.

"Guilty!"

It was a shock to some. At the start of the trial the general public--notorious turncoats--had already condemned Thorne as a monster, long in advance. But the brilliant defense put up by Mr.Cassells, combined with the conflicting medical opinions, had created an unexpected issue and there were many who now found themselves dissatisfied with the verdict. The press too had made vast capital out of the dissenting point of view and continued to do so for days afterwards, backed up by the *Law Journal* itself, as well as by anonymous letters from persons calling themselves "medico-legal experts".

An Appeal, therefore, was a foregone conclusion; and when this came up for hearing before the Lord Chief Justice, sitting with two other judges of the Court of Criminal Appeal, it was Mr.William Jowett,K.C. (later Lord Jowett), who put the case for the prisoner. For the very first time on record, he sought to invoke Section 9 (a) of the Criminal Appeal Act,1907. This in effect provides that in certain cases where the evidence is of a highly technical or scientific nature, a special Commission of experts may be empaneled to sit with the Court and to guide it upon such matters. Thus, in claiming that a jury of laymen were not qualified to draw conclusions from such intricate medical evidence as had been laid before them in this case, Mr.Jowett pleaded for the settling up of such a Commission to review the whole of that evidence and for the Appeal Court to abide by its findings. He also claimed mis-direction of the jury by Mr.Justice Finley; that in his summing-up he had sung the praises of Sir Bernard Spilsbury but failed to draw similar attention to Dr.Bront'e's qualifications. In conclusion he referred once more to the Act of 1907.

"If ever this Act is to be used," said Mr.Jowett, "Your lordships will never find a stronger case than the present one!"

Even in this grave issue the Lord Chief Justice was not without a sense of wit.

"I think," he observed, "that it was George Eliot who said: 'Prophecy is the most gratuitous form of error' !"

To which Mr.Jowett bowed with a smile and replied; "I will confine myself to the past and say your lordships *have* never found a stronger case!"

But it was all to no avail. Without even calling upon Sir Henry Curtis Bennett to answer for the Crown, the three Appeal Judges were unanimous in their opinion. In delivering judgement the Lord Chief Justice concluded:

"Mr.Justice Finley appears to have summed-up a mass of evidence in an admirable way. To put it plainly, there is nothing in this case except the circumstances that it relates to a charge of murder. The application, therefore, will be refused."

That was that! While the press and certain sections of the community continued to smart and to rant. Norman Thorne sat in the condemned cell, his remaining hours in this world spent in writing letters and reading The Bible. A model prisoner, he never once gave way to emotion or despair; and after every effort at a reprieve had failed he went to the scaffold wearing that same incredible mask of reserve which had characterized the latter months of his life.

Yet there are some--even in professional circles--who to this day consider that Thorne, on a show of medical hands alone, was entitled to the verdict; that the jury were prejudiced by the glamour of Spilsbury's reputation.* Sir Bernard's own biographers, however, state the facts less hysterically and more aptly when they say:

"The question is not whether an eminent man, in this case Spilsbury, was invariably right, but whether he was right in the single instance under review, which is the trial of Norman Thorne...."

Miss Helena Normanton, herself a Q.C., who edited the volume† in the *Famous Trials* series, was clearly among those who were not convinced of Norman's guilt. In suggesting a motive for Elsie Cameron's suicide she put forward a theory, no less brilliant because it could only come from a woman, and which Miss Normanton would doubtless have plied upon the jury had she been in Mr.Cassells' shoe's.

"It did not occur to the defense, apparently," she wrote, "to call medical evidence to prove that the onset of menstruation often takes the form of a period of intense and severe melancholy in which the world appears at its lowest and worst....If Elsie Cameron underwent anything habitually like this, and knew the feeling to be her personal precursor of a period, she might logically have concluded that she was not pregnant after all. If Thorne did go out and leave her alone, and she suddenly became aware that her main card had vanished...then her motive for suicide was obvious, because Thorne

---

* 'Bernard Spilsbury, His Life and Cases', by Douglas G.Browne & E.V.Tullett. (Harrop & Co.)

† 'Trial of Norman Thorne', Edited by Helena Normanton, Q.C. -Famous Trials Series

had made it abundantly clear that the prospective marriage turned entirely upon her expectancy of a child...."

Against this may be put a theory based on sound common sense, rather than upon cyclic phenomena applicable to one sex. Of all the mystery surrounding Thorne's movements on the evening of December 5, one factor emerges as a certainty--a factor which was partly laid bare by the judge in a few cogent questions. Namely, that he left Elizabeth C....shortly after 11.15 p.m. that night, returning to the hut approximately ten minutes later. Had he then found Elsie Cameron hanging from a beam; had he cut her down and laid her across the bed; whether she was dead or still breathing, had he run at once to the nearest cottage he must have reached it not a moment later than 11.35 p.m. There was his cast iron alibi, and the law could not have touched him.

Without a doubt, Thorne was guilty. The jury settled that once and for all. They were there; they saw and heard; they judged for themselves--far better than any extraneous critics writing about it afterwards. The basic interest in this story lies, not in the brilliant parts played by Mr.Cassells, Sir Henry Curtis Bennett, Sir Bernard Spilsbury and the rest--but in the unknown quantity, vaguely described as the "Forces of Human Nature", which prompts certain persons, under certain conditions, to commit certain acts. Without this the world would be a bored, indifferent community.

Acknowledgements

"Trial of Norman Thorne" edited by Helena Normanton, Q.C.
Famous Trials Series

"Bernard Spilsbury, His Life and Cases" by Douglas G.Browne &
E.V.Tullett (Harrop & Co.)

National Daily and Sunday Newspapers (January 1924 - March
1925)

Editor's Notes:

1. Norman Thorne was sent to the gallows on April 22nd, 1925 at
Wandsworth Prison (also used to dispatch the "Crumbles" killer,
Patrick Mahon). It was argued that Thorne had copied the same
method of killing.

2. Ironically, April 22nd, would have been Elsie's twenty-sev-
enth birthday!

3. This crime was publicly known as *"The Chicken-Run Murder"*

after nauseating scenes of of pleading, emotional display and
impassioned tears, he had persuaded her to return. She had done so
only for the sake of their three children. Now, it would again mean
leaving them, but ... was determined that this would only be a
temporary expedi... ... the ... a job she
would send for them and, ... matters afoot, nobody could prevent
them from coming. Meanwhile, they would be happy enough with Mary
Rogerson. Dear little ... ... could anyone wish for a better
or more loyal nursemaid? How devoted she was to the children and how
they adored her in return!

Yes, under norm... ... ... have been such a
happy household. Inde... ... ... to it had been a
happy one; but ... ... that; and as
she drove on ... ... speculate as to
what sort of recep... ... ... ry Rogerson and
the children would, of course, be in bed and asleep; but he would be
waiting up for her. Oh, yes......he wouldn't miss a chance like
this to accuse her of having spent the ... with another man. His
imagination knew no bounds. She could scarcely move, nowadays,
without being accused of infidelity. With him this income, wholly
unwarranted jealousy had become a fixation and, in turn, an insidious
form of persecution which had brought her to the end of her tether.

Worse still, Bella Ruxton had seriously begun to fear for
her life........................

A House Of Horror

(Rex v. Buck Ruxton)

*"My wife has been unfaithful and if
it continues I'll kill her!"*

(Dr.Ruxton in the police station
at Lancaster.)

1

At 11.30 p.m. on the night of Saturday 14th. September, 1935, the woman known as Isabella Ruxton waved a final good-bye to her three sisters, Jeanie Nelson, Lizzie Trench and Eileen Madden, at Blackpool. Then she let in the clutch of the Hillman Minx ATC 272 and started off on her return journey to Lancaster. The night was fine and clear, the distance little more than thirty miles. She should be home soon after half-past twelve.

At thirty-four, Bella Ruxton was still an attractive women. She had a full, well proportioned body shapely enough to catch the eye of any discerning male. Her light auburn hair was done in a style which clung to the temples, revealing a high forehead and blue eyes that held a soft, surprisingly youthful expression. The nose was prominent and slightly uneven at the bridge, tending to give a masculine effect, but this in no way seemed to detract from the pleasing aspect of the features as a whole. She had a firm and smoothly rounded chin which bore the merest hint of a dimple. Above this the lips were full and sensuous, the upper one being somewhat short so that the lips themselves appeared permanently parted to reveal an even row of strong white teeth. In fact three of these in the upper jaw were dentures and when she smiled the gold clasp securing them was exposed. Only one factor served to mar the otherwise graceful appearance of Bella Ruxton. Namely, her legs were shapeless, being the same thickness from knee to ankle.

As the little car sped on its way through the darkness now, her thoughts doubtless dwelt on the events of the past few hours. Earlier that evening she had driven over from Lancaster to join her sisters at Blackpool, and the occasion had been a merry one, an annual affair in which the party toured the famous illuminations. As usual it had ended with a light supper at the boarding-house where the others were staying. The others had travelled to Blackpool on a week-end motor coach trip from Edinburgh and would be returning on the Monday. Although Bella was the youngest (the eldest, Jeanie Nelson, was her senior by fifteen years and already a widow with a grown son) the sisters had always been very close. Whereas the others had all led staid, respectable married lives, Bella's had been a turbulent one and it was to Jeanie Nelson that she had invariably turned for help in times of trouble.

Trouble? There had been plenty of it over the past two years; and even tonight, although ostensibly gay and happy, in secret she had felt the desperate need to confide yet again in her eldest sister. Unfortunately the opportunity had not been forthcoming, chiefly because one of the husbands had been among the party. Instead, after a hurried, whispered exchange in the hall before departure she had promised to try to visit Blackpool again the following day, Sunday, if only to talk matters over; for if the truth were known Bella Ruxton had made up her mind to leave Lancaster and the man--the coloured doctor--who for seven years had passed as her husband, this time finally and without any regrets. She had gone away once before, less than a year ago, but he had traced her to Jeanie Nelson's house in Edinburgh where, after nauseating scenes of pleading, emotional display and impassioned tears, he had persuaded her to return. She had done so only for the sake of their three children. Now, it would again mean leaving them, but she was determined that this would only be a temporary expedient; as soon as she had secured a good job she would send for them and, as matters stood, nobody could prevent them from coming. Meanwhile, they would be happy enough with Mary Rogerson. Dear little Mary Rogerson! Could anyone wish for a better or more loyal nursemaid? How devoted she was to the children and how they adored her in return!

Yes, under normal circumstances it could have been such a happy household. Indeed, until a year or two ago it <u>had</u> been a happy one; but Dr.Ruxton's behaviour had put an end to that; and as she drove on through the night, now, she could only speculate as to what sort of reception awaited her upon return. Mary Rogerson and the children would, of course, be in bed and asleep; but *he* would be waiting up for her. Oh, yes...he wouldn't miss a chance like this to accuse her of having spent the evening with another man. His imagination knew no bounds. She could scarcely move, nowadays, without being accused of infidelity. With him this insane, wholly unwarranted jealousy had become a fixation and, in turn, an insidious form of persecution which had brought her to the end of her tether.

Worse still, Bella Ruxton had seriously begun to fear for her life....

2

Isabella Kerr had been born at Falkirk in 1901 of true Scottish descent, her more impressionable years thus coinciding with the period of World War1. She had always enjoyed the society of men and her looks and natural vivacity made her more than popular in that respect. Nevertheless, due chiefly to a strict Presbyterian upbringing, until the age of eighteen her amorous adventures had never graduated beyond a series of youthful romances. At that time, however, she was working as a waitress at Fairley's restaurant in Edinburgh and had met a young Dutchman named Van Ess who, in the full proverbial sense, had swept her off her feet. The courtship had been swift, followed by an equally hasty and disastrous marriage. They had parted after only a few weeks, Isabella completely disillusioned not only with Dutchmen but with men in general. In course of time a divorce had followed, but without any financial benefit to Isabella who found herself once more obliged to earn her own living. She had returned to the restaurant and, for the next eight years, thrown herself heart and soul into the business, working her way up to become manageress. During that time many men tried unsuccessfully to date her. In fact she seemed to have few outside interests other than her family and a daily flutter on the horses.

That was until she met Buck Hakim.

He had walked into the place at lunchtime one day in 1928, a lone and conspicuous figure; so conspicuous that the buzz of conversation ceased abruptly and people turned to stare as he settled himself at a vacant table near the window. That he was of Indian extraction there could be no doubt, although to Isabella his skin did not appear nearly so dark as the ones who called from door to door peddling carpets and shawls. Moreover, she had always imagined that every Indian wore a turban and a beard, whereas he was hatless and clean-shaven, his slim, youthful figure immaculately clad in western style, his linen spotless. It was part of her duties as manageress to approach him, if only to ensure that the food and service were to his liking, and she found herself immediately attracted to this young Indian with the clear-cut features and dark, flashing eyes. He spoke good English with a slight Continental accent; she learned later that in his study of European languages he had mastered French long before he could speak a word of English. His black wavy hair, inclined to be unruly, was brushed back leaving the forehead clear, and when he smiled he kept his lips closed, lifting them slightly towards the right side of his face. But it was his hands that fascinated her; they were slender, almost effeminate with their long, tapering fingers. In fact they were the hands of a surgeon.

He began to lunch there every day and very soon they were exchanging confidences. She learned that his name was Bukhtyar Rustomji Ratanji Hakim, but for brevity he called himself Buck Hakim. He was a native of Bombay where, at that University, he had obtained the degrees of Bachelor of Medicine and Bachelor of Surgery. He had served in the Indian Army Medical Corps and later for a short spell at sea as a ship's doctor. He was now studying at Edinburgh University where he was anxious to secure a further degree in surgery. After that, he told her, he hoped to acquire a practice either in England or Scotland. One thing, however, he failed to mention at that early stage. Namely, that he had a wife living in India.

As the friendship between them ripened, Isabella Kerr, or Van Ess, realized instinctively that her whole life was about to undergo a change. As though from force of habit she repelled his initial advances; but in this case the barrage of reserve was not difficult to overcome and soon they were meeting in the evenings after work. She introduced him to her eldest sister Jeanie Nelson and to other members of her family, who appeared to take no exception to his colour and origin. Possibly to save her from embarrassment he changed his name by deed poll to Ruxton and thenceforth was to be known as Dr.Buck Ruxton.

By the time he confessed to having left a Parsee wife behind him in India it did not seem to matter to Isabella; especially as he explained that the marriage had not been of his own choosing but arranged by the parents of both parties at birth. Nevertheless, she kept the fact a secret from her family and the pair of them drew consolation--perhaps as an excuse for intimacy--from the possibility of securing an annulment of his marriage, if not in India at any rate under English or Scottish law. It was thus that Isabella experienced for the first time in her life the full flood of physical passion. During the ensuing years that passion, mutual between them, was to grow in intensity; but kept alive towards the end only by the sweetness of reconciliation following close upon frequent and bitter quarrels.

It came as a disappointment to both of them when he failed his examinations at Edinburgh University; but he was well qualified for General Practice. Also it was high time he started to earn money, for he was twenty-nine years old and his private funds were not inexhaustible. Thus, when towards the end of 1928 he left Edinburgh to take a post as *locum tenens* in London, Isabella followed a week later and they lived there together as man and wife. Soon enough she had found herself pregnant and in the August of 1929 their first child, Elizabeth, was born.

So far, no attempts had been made to get the Indian marriage dissolved, but the fact did not seem to worry either of them; and when at the beginning of 1930 they returned to Edinburgh to look around for a practice, Isabella imparted her one and only lie to Jeanie Nelson by telling her that she and Ruxton had been married in London.

Several practices were available over a wide area and he finally bought the one in Lancaster, which had a furnished house thrown in. This was a three-storied building of rectangular grey stone slabs and known as No.2, Dalton Square. The ground floor was already suitably laid out for the purpose, having a library or consulting-room on the left of the hall and a waiting-room on the right, the surgery being at the back and adjacent to the kitchen. On the first floor were two large rooms which they decided to use as a lounge and dining-room. Three bedrooms occupied the top landing, whilst a narrow bathroom, evidently added long after the house itself was built, had been squeezed into a vacant space between the first and second floors. The front of the house over-looked a cobble-stone square at the opposite side of which the Town Hall with its clock tower loomed high like a sentinel. At the back of the premises was a narrow yard, bordered on one side by the lofty wall of the County Cinema. On the opposite side it gave access to a small alley known as Friar's Passage through which the dustmen came to collect the refuse.

They were delighted with the place and moved in almost at once.

In 1930 the population of Lancaster was in the region of 40,000 and since coloured doctors were as yet comparatively rare in England it is to Ruxton's credit that his patients eventually numbered over two thousand. In addition he carried out minor surgical operations, whilst his services as an anesthetist were often in demand, particularly by one of the local dentists, a Mr.Anderson, living at Morecambe, a stone's throw away.

There can be little doubt that in those early days Bella Ruxton was ideally happy. The baby and the house occupied most of her time during the day, whilst in the evenings, when he was not out visiting patients, Ruxton devoted all his time to her. To cope with the household chores they had retained the services of a Mrs.Curwan who had acted as cook-general to the previous occupants. Moreover, they were house-proud and had the place redecorated from top to bottom.

After little more than a year their second child, Diane, was born, Ruxton himself having delivered both babies.

Yet, despite this seemingly idyllic set-up at 2, Dalton Square, as time went by something happened to spoil it all.

What was it?

Certainly the quarrels started. At first these can have been little more than "lovers' tiffs", quickly made up and soon forgotten in an excess of physical passion. Nevertheless, in spite of that air of calmness so necessary to a successful doctor and the confidence with which Ruxton instilled his patients, in private life he was both excitable and highly-strung. Over the smallest thing he could display uncontrollable temper and a mental state suggesting deep neurosis. At the same time he would be equally quick to calm down and if his outburst had been directed against Isabella he would show an equivalent sense of remorse. She, in her turn, was of an impulsive nature and also given to excitability at times, though never matching him in this respect. She was inclined to extravagance and liked to have plenty of pocket money, which Ruxton would dole out to her sparingly from a cash-box kept in the bedroom. She also continued to back horses--a practice of which he strongly disapproved--and to gamble on the football pools. Whilst these mildly conflicting traits of character were conducive to minor squabbles from the beginning, they were unlikely to have any serious or lasting effects so long as the sexual harmony remained unimpaired. Indeed, things might never have been otherwise had not Ruxton's neurotic tendencies gradually increased.

Mrs.Jeanie Nelson, Bella Ruxton's eldest sister, had kept in close touch. She was delighted to see her settled down at last, this time happily and, as she firmly believed, respectably married; for still nothing had been done about Ruxton's Indian marriage. By the early part of 1932 Bella was already three months pregnant for the third time and it came as a severe shock to Jeanie Nelson, therefore, when one day, in answer to a telegram, she caught the first train from Edinburgh, arriving at Dalton Square late the same afternoon. Ruxton himself opened the door to her and she could see at once that he was in a high state of nerves. Mrs.Curwan was giving the two children their tea in the kitchen and therefore well out of ear shot as he hustled her into the consulting-room, slamming the door.

"What d'you think," he shouted. "Bella tried to gas herself!"

"I don't believe it!" Jeanie Nelson had gone pale with shock.

"It's true, it's true," he cried, pacing the room and waving his arms about.

"Why?" demanded Jeanie Nelson. "It must be your fault! What have you done to make her like that?"

"I?" he cried. "Nothing! I've been a kind and loving husband, that's all. And now she wants to get me into trouble by gassing herself!"

"The poor girl! I must go to her at once. Where is she?"

As Jeanie Nelson made for the door Ruxton forestalled her. He was breathless, his hair hanging down over a glistening forehead and he spoke incredibly fast:

"Wait a minute! Bella's all right now, she's in bed. What happened was this--she had toothache. It was a bad tooth so I gave her a whiff of chloroform and took it out. She seemed all right when I left her, but the next thing I know--she's on the floor with her head in the gas fire! I tell you, she's trying to get me into trouble! She's trying to ruin my business! I can't afford anything like this!"

"Let me go to her!" Jeanie Nelson brushed past him, flung open the door and went hurrying up the staircase.

Bella Ruxton was sitting up in bed, her eyes red from recent weeping. At the sight of Jeanie Nelson she thrust out both arms, pulling her sister down on the bed.

"Oh, Jeanie," she whimpered. "I want to come back to Edinburgh with you! Please take me back. It was an accident, but he won't believe me!"

"That's a lie!" Ruxton had strode into the room behind Jeanie Nelson and tried to slap Isabella across the face. "Come on, now, tell her the truth! The truth!"

"It was an accident," she moaned. "I swear it! I fell of the bed!"

"Of course she did," said Jeanie Nelson. "What can you expect after giving the poor thing that chloroform? And her in the condition she is in--she should never have been left alone!"

"And who turned on the gas? I tell you--"

"She could well have done it by mistake, what with this chloroform and everything!"

"Please, Jeanie--take me back with you," Isabella pleaded.

"Don't worry, dear, I will. We'll leave the house this very minute!"

"And take the children with us!"

"Before you do that," Ruxton shouted, "I'll cut the throats of all of you!"

"You're not a fit person to leave her with," Jeanie Nelson ignored the threat. Then to Isabella: "Come, dear, I'll help you to get dressed. The sooner we're out of here the better!"

"No, wait!" Ruxton had ceased his pacing of the room. "Don't do that. Please don't go!...." Suddenly he slumped into a chair, cradling his head in both hands. When he looked up again tears were rolling down his cheeks and the expression on his face resembled that of a man coming out of a coma. "I'm sorry, Bella. I believe you--about it being an accident. Please forgive me. I didn't really mean any of the things I said. I must have been working too hard lately. Jeanie--you'll forgive me too--won't you?"

"I suppose so," she said. "All the same, I think Bella should come back with me. She needs a rest and a change."

"Very well." He was completely calm now, but still spoke with his customary speed. "I tell you what, you spend the night here and Bella and the children can go back with you tomorrow morning. I'll come and fetch them in a few days time...."

Soon afterwards he went out to do the round of his patients; and for the rest of that evening he was politeness itself to Jeanie Nelson and had assumed the role of fond, loving husband to Bella. The next morning he drove them all to the station, helped with the children and did not cease to wave until their train was out of sight.

Nevertheless, the "lovers' tiffs" had taken a more sinister turn.

It might be supposed that such a serious incident and lapse on Ruxton's part after less than three years, could well have led to a complete breakdown of the "marriage"--especially as Isabella was under no legal obligation to go back to him. Yet, after ten days in Edinburgh she returned, apparently quite willingly, to resume life at Dalton Square.

Whereas both Elizabeth and Diane had been born in England, it was the wish of Isabella as well as members of her family--who never doubted that she and Ruxton were legally married--that at least one child should be born in Scotland. Accordingly, towards the end of 1932 when the arrival of the third baby was imminent they arranged to go to Edinburgh for this purpose.

On the night before they were due to leave Lancaster, Ruxton awoke in the small hours to find himself alone in the bed. Almost simultaneously he heard a thud on the stairs followed by a sharp cry. Hurrying out on the landing he saw Bella lying half way up the staircase. She had been down to the bathroom for a glass of water and on the return journey had slipped and fallen heavily. By the time he had helped her back to the bathroom he realized she was already in labour; and although on this occasion he called in the help of a fellow practitioner, by morning she had given birth to a still-born child.

‡

Until the middle of 1933 the highly dependable Mrs.Curwan had performed most of the household chores as well as being read-ily available to mind the two children, Elizabeth and Diane, when necessary. Despite the unfortunate accident the previous Autumn, Isabella was once again pregnant and it was at this time that a young girl, Mary Rogerson, was taken on as a full-time nursemaid living in.

Mary Rogerson was then eighteen years old; a girl of simple tastes, devoted to children and with a good family upbringing. She was short, with light brown hair, her otherwise attractive features being marred by a pronounced cast in one eye, which fact, together with certain other physical characteristics, was to become of para-mount importance later. Nevertheless, she appeared in the nature of a divine gift both to the children and to Isabella, for apart from her duties as nursemaid she helped in the house generally and soon became one of the family. Although her mother was dead and Mr.Rogerson had married again, the relationship between the daughter and step-mother was one of mutual trust and affection; and Mary spent every moment of her spare time in their company at nearby Morecambe. If she happened to go with the Ruxton's on a short holiday anywhere she would write home daily.

Although there had been no repetition of anything so serious as the gassing incident the quarrelling persisted, followed as usual by a mutual display of sexual passion. Where these disputes were of a comparatively trivial nature there is no doubt that Isabella derived a certain masochistic pleasure from them; so much so that on occasions she would enter the surgery and approach him in a coquettish manner. Reaching up to straighten his tie, she would whisper: "I wonder how I could pick a quarrel with you!"

Yet, on other, more serious occasions Ruxton's uncontrollable temper clearly showed him capable of violence. Nor did the presence of the servants act as a restraint and Mrs.Curwen recalled a particular Sunday when Bella Ruxton came into the kitchen, crying bitterly and holding her arm which was bruised from wrist to elbow. In front of Mrs.Curwen she had threatened to leave and take the children with her; to which Ruxton had shouted, "You'll do no such thing! You're not a fit person to have the children!"

Before the end of that year Isabella had given birth to their third child, a boy, whom they named Billie, no attempt being made this time to visit Scotland for the occasion.

3

Such quarrels, followed by equally tempestuous reconciliations, might have continued indefinitely had not Ruxton's mental state deteriorated gradually, developing in the process a paranoiac form of jealousy. In the early days of their association, particularly in London, they had lived only for each other, sheer love of the woman blinding Ruxton to all outside influences. By 1934, however, they had become socially acquainted with many people in Lancaster apart from Ruxton's patients. Bella, with her gay, easy-going manner was popular with both sexes and Ruxton clearly resented this--particularly where the men were concerned. If any one of them paid more than passing attention he would be quick to tax her with it afterwards, claiming she had encouraged it; and this inevitably led to further quarrels, at time to further acts of violence.

Was Ruxton, then, reverting to type? Was it in fact a prime case of East meeting West? In India most married women were veiled with the express purpose of discouraging any form of appraisal by the male eye. In addition the Indian wife led a secluded life, subservient always to the husband, seldom venturing into society on her own. Now that they were established, ostensibly as man and wife, Ruxton clearly expected a similar code of conduct from Isabella, if not in actual practice at any rate in theory, and she was not having any of it. Although all thoughts of infidelity were farthest from her mind, there were times when Ruxton managed to persuade himself that she was in fact being unfaithful; and one man in particular he singled out in this respect--a young articled solicitor in the Town Clerk's department, named Robert Edmondson.

Since the Town Hall faced No.2. from the opposite side of Dalton Square, Bobbie Edmondson and the Ruxton's frequently met or waved to each other in course of their comings and goings. In addition, the Edmondson family, consisting of Mr. and Mrs.Edmondson senior and Bobbie's elder sister Barbara, were on friendly terms with the Ruxton's and would often join them in a day's outing to Blackpool or the Lake District. It was quite natural that a young man such as Bobbie Edmondson should enjoy in public the vivacious company of an attractive though considerably older woman such as Bella Ruxton. It was equally natural that she, at the age of thirty-three, should be flattered by even the surface reactions of the young solicitor's clerk. Beyond that there was nothing to it; yet Ruxton's jealousy grew steadily, to become in the end a monster of his own creation....

Soon after the birth of the third child, Billie, the domestic staff was increased by the addition of two persons--a Mrs. Agnes Oxley, who came each morning from 7.15 a.m. until 1.p.m., Sunday's included--and Eliza Hunter, a fully-fledged housemaid who came to live in, sharing a bedroom with Mary Rogerson. Hitherto, the children had slept in Mary's room, but with the advent of Eliza Hunter they were moved into the big bedroom with Isabella, Ruxton occupying the third and remaining room on the top landing. Short of over-crowding, this was the only logical sleeping arrangement and at that time, at any rate, cast no reflection upon the physical relationship. It had one disadvantage, however, in that Isabella had to answer the night calls because the telephone was installed in her room, the only extension being in the consulting-room on the ground floor.

Despite these innovations it was clear to all the domestic staff that the household had by now become anything but a happy one. It was especially clear to Eliza Hunter who was altogether unaccustomed to that kind of menage; the quarrels and bickering's, Ruxton's quick temper and constant threats of violence. She was to stay in fact for less than six months and during that time witnessed many unpleasant incidents, perhaps the most serious of which was the occasion one morning when she heard Bella Ruxton call out to her from the big bedroom. Hurriedly crossing the landing, Eliza had found her mistress lying on the bed fully dressed and Ruxton sprawled across her with his hands encircling her throat. At the intrusion Ruxton had struggled upright to glare angrily at Eliza.

"Get the hell out of here," he bellowed. "And mind your own business!"

Later he apologized to her profusely. Much later still he was to say that the housemaid had surprised them in the prelude to an act of love-making.

However strange this method might seem of arousing a women's erotic instincts, such an explanation could scarcely be offered upon another occasion, when Eliza Hunter was in the back yard and heard her mistress call out to her from the kitchen. As she ran in there she was in time to see Ruxton thrust a hand in his side pocket whilst stark fear showed on Isabella's face.

"He had a knife at my throat!" she panted.

"A lie," cried Ruxton. "A complete lie, I don't possess such a knife!"

Knife, or no knife, when making the beds on one occasion Eliza Hunter had found a revolver under his pillow....

‡

Such a state of affairs could hardly be expected to continue indefinitely. Ruxton's hysterical outbursts, the threats of violence and above all the insane, wholly unjustifiable jealousy--particularly where Bobbie Edmondson was concerned--were fast neutralizing those joys hitherto derived from reconciliation; and one night, shortly after the 'knife incident', matters took an even more serious turn. Until now, when he was in one of his violent moods she had either screamed or called out to the servants for help. On this particular night, however, Ruxton overstepped the mark and she was so scared that she ran from the house, across the Square, and straight to the police station adjoining the Town Hall. Here she came face to face with Detective Inspector Thompson who could see that she was deeply distressed and in a state bordering upon panic.

"I want to leave Lancaster and go to Edinburgh," she gasped. "But Dr.Ruxton won't let me. He's in one of his violent moods and I'm afraid to go back into that house, even to pack!"

The police, notoriously placid and impartial when mediating in cases of domestic strife, can seldom have been called upon to deal with the affairs of a highly respected doctor and his wife. Detective Inspector Thompson, who was shortly to become Chief Constable of Clithero, proceeded to take a statement from her. In the middle of it all he looked up at her and said; "I think, Mrs. Ruxton, it would be best for all concerned if we ask the doctor to step across here."

"Very well," she nodded. "Although I doubt whether you'll get him to come. He was in a terrible state when I left." She had calmed down considerably by now and doubtless drew courage from the official surroundings.

Detective Sergeant Stainton was therefore despatched across the Square, returning in less than ten minutes accompanied by Ruxton.

It was a squalid, sordid scene enacted in the Lancaster police station that night, more worthy of the occupants of a slum tenement dwelling. Ruxton waved his arms in the air, shouted, and actually foamed at the mouth.

"My wife has been unfaithful! If it continues I'll kill her!"

"It isn't true!" Isabella cried. "There isn't a word of truth in what he's saying! I want to leave. I can't stand these accusations a moment longer!"

"She's lying!" Ruxton screamed. "I know very well she's been unfaithful and it's not for the first time!"

Ruxton's hysteria and general condition began to cause the two policemen grave concern. Taking him by the elbow, Inspector Thompson guided him gently towards the door and into a room across the passage.

"Now Dr.Ruxton," he said. "Try to calm down. This kind of behaviour isn't going to get anybody anywhere."

In fact the spasm, the hysteria and the neurotic screaming's were nearly spent and the tears on the way. Ruxton sank onto a hard wooden chair, passing a shaky hand across his forehead.

"My wife is breaking my heart," he said. "I love her dearly and I'm a good husband. She has no right to leave me. Can't you persuade her to stay, Inspector?"

Inspector Thompson left him there and returned to the other room where Isabella sat with Sergeant Stainton. It was now nearly two o'clock in the morning and she looked tired and disheveled; yet her face bore a look of determination. After talking to her for about ten minutes the Inspector went back to find Ruxton now completely calmed down.

"I'm afraid doctor," he said, "Mrs.Ruxton has made up her mind to go. She intends catching the first train to Edinburgh and wants to know if you'll give her the money for her fare."

Ruxton threw his arms wide in a gesture of despair. Then slowly and reluctantly he reached for his wallet, took out three one pound notes and handed them to the Inspector.

"She wished to pack a few clothes," the officer went on, "and since she has asked for police protection I have no alternative but to accompany her to number two, Dalton Square for that purpose."

Ruxton was the first to leave the police station, Isabella and Inspector Thompson following a few minutes later, their footsteps echoing in the silence of the Square. She limped slightly, for she was suffering from a bunion on her big toe and the cobble-stones made the journey painful.

The vestibule light was burning as they entered the house and through the open door of the consulting-room they could see Ruxton pacing the carpet restlessly. Apart from that the house seemed silent; but when they reached the top landing the sound of light snoring reached them from the back bedroom occupied by Mary Rogerson and Eliza Hunter. Isabella knew it was Mary, who suffered from chronic tonsillitis.

Inspector Thompson stood on the landing while Isabella went into her bedroom and began to pack a suitcase. The three children were fast asleep and only Elizabeth stirred and turned over with a grunt of resentment at the intrusion. Some minutes later footsteps sounded on the creaking staircase and Ruxton appeared in the pool of light thrown by the bulb on the landing. He was carrying a folded sheet of paper which he held out to Inspector Thompson.

"Please, Inspector," he said, "will you give this note to my wife? I'll wait in the lounge on the floor below." He turned abruptly and began to descend the stairs again.

Inspector Thompson knocked on the bedroom door and handed the note to Isabella. She took it, sat on the edge of the bed and, thrusting the fingers of one hand into her hair, leaned forward and began to read the contents. After a while she rose wearily and came to the door.

"All right, Inspector," she said quietly. "I'll see him."

As they reached the half-open door of the lounge below she turned to him again.

"Perhaps it would be best,"...she began.

"I quite understand, Mrs.Ruxton," he nodded. "Go ahead. You can always call me if there's any trouble." He held the door wide, then closed it behind her as she went in.

As he waited he could hear the muffled sound of voices on the other side of the door and wondered vaguely how anyone could manipulate the tongue to speak as fast as Dr.Ruxton. He made no attempt to eavesdrop the conversation, but merely looked at his watch in speculation as to how much longer this job was going to take.

When the door finally opened to reveal the pair of them, Ruxton had one arm about her shoulder and was smiling for the first time that night. She too appeared relaxed.

"My wife has changed her mind, Inspector," Ruxton said. "She's decided to stay after all."

"But I want to thank you for all you have done and I'm terribly sorry for the trouble I've put you to," Isabella added quickly.

"That's quite alright, Mrs.Ruxton. Only too glad you and the doctor have made things up between you. Well--if you're quite sure--then I'll be getting along...."

A year later Jeanie Nelson was to say: "My sister was highly impulsive, and excitable up to a point. But she was not one who acted very often on her own. She had to have someone behind her."

Ruxton was to say: "We were the kind of people who could not live with each other and could not live without each other." Then, quoting an old French proverb, "Who loves most chastises most."

‡

French proverbs aside, how much longer could it last?

In an approaching storm each clap of thunder grows louder followed by an interval of comparative silence, each interval becoming shorter. At No.2, Dalton Square the happier interludes were indeed becoming all too short; and in late November of that same year, 1934, shortly before Eliza Hunter left, yet another crisis took shape when Ruxton came home one morning after completing the round of his patients to find Isabella gone. Moreover, such was the air of finality about things this time that she had not only taken a suitcase but a trunk containing all her clothes. True, there had been a bitter quarrel the night before and breakfast had come and gone without a sign of reconciliation; but he had scarcely anticipated such hasty action on Bella's part and the *fait accompli* stunned him. Worse still, she was not present this time to receive the brunt of his hysterical ravings, a frustration which added to their intensity.

"Dead or alive," he shouted, in front of the servants, "I'll have her back here within twenty-four hours!"

Later, in a calmer frame of mind he approached Mary Rogerson. She was nursing young Billie in her arms and her sleeves were rolled right back to the elbows, revealing the huge, unsightly birth-mark which discoloured the greater part of her right forearm. On such an occasion also the operational scar at the base of the thumb on that hand was plainly visible, where in childhood a cyst had been somewhat clumsily removed.

"Mary--" he began, for once hesitant in his speech, "if by chance your mistress should not come back--will you stay on and be a mother to the children?"

She did not answer immediately but looked down at the ground, so that the cast in her eye was hidden from him. Then:

"Yes, sir," she said. "But I'd have to get my parents' consent."

As with almost every other incident, she told Mr. and Mrs.Rogerson about this request by Ruxton and it only served to increase their doubts as to whether she ought to remain in service there at all.

There was only one place, as Ruxton knew, where Bella was to be found and he drove straight to Edinburgh, arriving at Jeanie Nelson's house late that same evening. For once, there were no hysterical outbursts--these had spent themselves many hours ago--but as always he became excited, remorseful, supplicatory. When these tactics failed and Isabella remained coldly adamant he began to demand, to insist upon her return. If she stayed away, he declared, the scandal would ruin his practice. Besides, the children needed her and it was her duty to go back to them.

Strangely enough it was Jeanie Nelson who now took a hand in things, partly siding with Ruxton.

"You should end all this quarrelling," she said, addressing them both, "and learn to live with one another like any other respectable couple!"

"If he leaves Lancaster," said Isabella, "and makes a home somewhere else I'll come back."

"How can I?" Ruxton pleaded. "A Doctor can't just change his practice overnight!"

"That's quite true," said Jeanie Nelson.

Bella Ruxton took several paces backward and forward with hands clasped together.

"Well, leave me a day or two to collect myself--to think things over," she said.

"No, no, that won't do! You must come back at once--tonight! I have to go back tonight, otherwise what will happen to my patients in the morning?"

It went on like that for some time; and in the end, as always, Bella Ruxton capitulated. Ruxton drove back to Lancaster alone that night and she followed by train the next day.

"If he leaves Lancaster and makes a home somewhere else...."

Was she seeking desperately to get away, not only from a house that held so many unhappy memories, but also from young Bobbie

Edmondson? Did she hope to start afresh in some place where there could be no possible excuse even for the mention of that name? For nearly a year now, and without the slightest cause or justification, Ruxton's jealousy over the young solicitor's clerk had increased steadily, to become a basis for most of the quarrels. Their social relationship with the entire Edmondson family made it impossible for her not to meet the son now and again in company with the rest. Nor could she rudely turn her back on him if he waved to her from his car in Dalton Square. He passed their house everyday on his way to and from work at the Town Hall. On a few occasions also he had driven her and Mrs.Ethel Anderson, the local dentist's wife, back from the swimming baths. Yet Ruxton seized upon every little incident to accuse her of having an affair--even of infidelity. It had become an obsession, a cancer too deeply rooted to be plucked out by any logical reasoning.

‡

In the Spring of 1935 Eliza Hunter finally left, not hesitating to give as her reasons that "the house was far too unhappy". Nothing daunted, the Ruxton's replaced her by another regular housemaid, Vera Shelton, who came to live in, also sharing the bedroom with Mary Rogerson. She was to stick it less than three months.

In the middle of June that year the three children, in care of Mary Rogerson, were sent for a fortnight's holiday to a farm-house at Seattle, run by a Mrs.Holmes. Despite the work and added responsibility, this change of environment must have come as a welcome break to the young nursemaid; to be away, for a while at any rate, from the quarrelling, the shouting and at times the screaming of her mistress. Yet she had not left Dalton Square without the consent of her parents, and sent them a postcard every day.

As with Eliza Hunter, the new maid Vera Shelton had been quick to sense the discordant atmosphere reigning at 2, Dalton Square. However, it was not long before she too began to witness various unpleasant incidents, the worst of which was an exact repetition of that experienced by her predecessor. It happened one night while

Mary Rogerson and the children were away at Seattle and she was the only other person in the house. She was in bed and asleep, but was awakened by the sound of voices raised in the big bedroom. She heard a heavy thud and almost immediately afterwards her mistress called out to her by name. As she hurriedly entered the bedroom Ruxton brushed past her in the doorway, flinging over his shoulder the word "Prostitute!". The telephone was lying broken on the floor by the bedside table and Bella Ruxton was crying. Her nightdress was badly torn and Vera Shelton saw a livid mark on her arm that was already turning black and blue....So, in spite of the promises made on both sides at Edinburgh, it was clear that the picture had not changed. If anything, matters were growing steadily worse.

Yet, apart from the children, what kept Bella Ruxton at 2, Dalton Square? What induced her to return there every time she had made up her mind to leave? It was certain that by now the bond of their sexual relationship no longer held her. Indeed, if she still harboured a vestige of love for Buck Ruxton he was fast killing it off. Significantly, whereas she had always addressed him by the endearing term of "Bonnie", she was now calling him "Pa".

A possible answer lay in the fact that she had begun to buy many more clothes than ever before; that material "peace offerings" on Ruxton's part were supplanting physical passion as a means of reconciliation. Other factors were involved too. For years before she met Ruxton, Isabella had been accustomed to earning her own living, to independence; and she was a good business woman. With all the discord and unhappy mode of existence at Dalton Square, she had begun to feel the urge to strike out on her own once more and was in fact trying to persuade Ruxton to set her up in some form of business entirely divorced from his practice. With her flair for backing horses she had in mind a betting shop of some kind, and later her own football pools promotion. Since any undertaking of this nature could scarcely become the wife of a respected doctor, by August she had persuaded him to rent an office in her name at Blackburn, some miles south of Lancaster and where they were not known. Whilst as yet she had not embarked upon any particular line of business, she was optimistically hoping to acquire an exclusive agency in that district for Murphy's Football Pools.

Ruxton could ill afford the outlay at this time; for although the practice was doing well, as with most doctors of the period there were many patients who were either lax in settling their bills or else continued to avoid payment altogether. Ruxton, therefore, was in the process of negotiating a loan with a local firm of solicitors and by way of collateral security had arranged to take out a policy on his life. Among other things he needed a new car. The old one he had been using ever since his arrival in Lancaster had finally disintegrated and he had placed an order for a new model with Mr.Hudson, proprietor of the County Garage, with whom he dealt for all petrol and repairs. Since delivery would take time, he had purchased a second-hand grey Hillman Minx for use in the meanwhile. It was a reliable little car and much easier for Bella to handle than the old one.

By the second week in August, Vera Shelton had had enough and gave notice. Instead of replacing her, yet another daily help was taken on, a Mrs.Mabel Smith, who staggered her hours of duty with Mrs.Curwan and Mrs.Oxley; and these three were to remain until the bitter end.

Negotiations with Murphy's Pools were proving slow and the situation was such, therefore, that Bella had an office at Blackburn but as yet no business to conduct from it. Inevitably, Ruxton's jealous imagination set to work: the office was just a blind, a secret rendezvous for herself and another man--Bobbie Edmondson!

Possibly for a week or two she withstood the accusations--as well as the spying which he carried out on her between Lancaster and Blackburn--with comparative calm, even with disdain. After all, she was more than used to it by now. On Saturday September 7th, however, fate took an ominous hand, providing Ruxton for the very first time with something less abstract. Even so, without the existing groundless jealousy the incident would have meant nothing. As it was, Ruxton's mind magnified things well beyond the point of distortion.

On that day, Bella Ruxton had arranged a trip to Edinburgh with Barbara Edmondson, Bobbie's sister, and obtained Ruxton's permission to go in the Hillman Minx. She had also assured him that she would be staying the night with Jeanie Nelson. At the last minute Mr. and Mrs.Edmondson senior had decided to come along also and persuaded Bobbie to drive them. Thus the party left Lancaster in two cars, Bella and Barbara in the Hillman, and the others in Bobbie's car. Instead of spending the night with Jeanie Nelson, Bella joined them all at the Adelphi Hotel, where Mr. and Mrs.Edmondson occupied Room No.28, Bobbie, Barbara and Bella sleeping in rooms No.44, 49 and 50 respectively. Since Bella had been the first to sign the hotel register the bill for all five was made out in the name of "Ruxton & Party", Mr.Edmondson senior paying.

When Isabella returned to Lancaster the following day, Sunday, Ruxton greeted her affectionately to begin with, even showing concern lest she was tired after the long journey from Edinburgh. Yet, as always, his manner was sly, furtive, as he glanced sideways at her through half closed lids.

"Have a good time, dear?"

"Lovely, thanks," she said.

"Did you stay at Jeanie's house?"

"Yes."

"You lie!" he thundered, swinging round on her suddenly. "You slept with young Edmondson at the Adelphi Hotel!"

"That's not true!" she cried hoarsely.

"D'you think I trusted you, once I knew he was going in the party?"

"But his parents were there all the time. So was Barbara!"

"As if that should make any difference! I know you. I know the pair of you and this time I've got absolute proof! I hired a car yesterday and followed you to Edinburgh. By late last night you weren't at Jeanie's house. I found the Hillman parked alongside Edmondson's car in the Adelphi Hotel garage. I went in and inspected the hotel register. Your rooms were...."

"There was absolutely no harm in it," Bella cried, "except in your vile imagination!"

"Then why tell me you had stayed with your sister?"

"Because you wouldn't have understood. There was a change of plan...."

"I understand only too well!"

"In that case, why don't you see Bobbie and ask him outright? Why don't you ask Mr. and Mrs.Edmondson and Barbara...."

She had scored a point there. What husband, professing such love for his wife and believing her unfaithful, would not face a showdown with the man in question? Yet, in young Edmondson's company Ruxton had always been friendly and hospitable, never by so much as a hint suggesting that anything was wrong. In fact, he had never breathed a word of his suspicions regarding the solicitor to a soul other than to Bella. Even at the police station he had mentioned no names. That was to come later, when it suited his purpose in a very different chain of circumstances.

‡

The bitter quarrel that followed the Edinburgh affair was never entirely patched up; and during the ensuing week, although some form of compromise had been reached and they were again on speaking terms, Bella Ruxton had told the servants that she would be leaving Lancaster as soon as she could make satisfactory arrangements.

By the afternoon of Friday, September 13th, the atmosphere at 2, Dalton Square had become tense and it must have been obvious to all that a crisis of sorts was approaching. Mrs.Oakley, who had stayed on to clean the silver, was the only domestic in the house; Mary Rogerson was out with the children and both Mrs.Curwen and Mrs.Mabel Smith had gone home. During her eighteen months service there Mrs.Oxley had witnessed many quarrels, and now once again she could hear the voices raised. She was in the kitchen when Ruxton came in and asked her to go outside and dust the car over. She had done so often before, but guessed that this time it was merely an excuse to put her beyond earshot of the squabbling. She was only too glad to be free of it and left by the kitchen door, crossing the yard into Friar's Passage where the car was drawn up at the curb. She had not been there many minutes, flicking the paintwork over with a feather duster, when Ruxton appeared. He was in that morbid, lachrymose state which invariably followed the hysterical outbursts. He had been like that, on and off, most of the week. It was in fact a particular psychosis well known to mind specialist's nowadays and accorded a technical name.

"Oh, Mrs.Oxley," he said in a plaintive voice. "She is breaking my heart! Talk to her. Talk to her and ask her not to go, but to stop with her children!"

"Well, of course, it's none of my business," Mrs.Oxley said. "But I'll certainly see what I can do, Doctor."

There was nothing that *Mrs.Oxley* could do!

‡

The following day, Saturday 14th, was something of a red-letter day for the Ruxton children. In the morning they visited the Morecambe Carnival, then in full swing, and in the afternoon there was a party at 2, Dalton Square attended chiefly by Elizabeth and Diane's school friends. This had been planned long in advance to mark the opening of the Christmas term. It was also the date on which Isabella had arranged to join her three sisters at Blackpool for a tour of the illuminations; a primary cause of the altercations the previous day. In fact, only when he had satisfied himself that Bobbie Edmondson was not going to Blackpool also, had he agreed to lending her the car.

She had left the children's party at six o'clock, driving off in the Hillman Minx, and they were enjoying themselves too much to resent her leaving before the end.

Shortly after seven o'clock that evening a neighbour, Mrs.Jackson, arrived to collect her two children. Ruxton opened the door to her and called upstairs to Mary Rogerson, the daily women having gone home. A few minutes later Mary brought Mrs.Jackson's children down already dressed and tidy for the street. She was slightly flushed and seemed to have enjoyed the party as much as anybody. Mrs.Jackson's two were the last to leave.

Mrs.Jackson herself was also the last person, outside the four walls of No.2, Dalton Square, ever to see Mary Rogerson alive....!

‡

That Isabella duly completed her return journey from Blackpool that night is certain from the fact that the Hillman Minx was seen outside the house the following morning. She probably arrived shortly after half-past twelve.

Yet, like Mary Rogerson, nobody ever saw Bella Ruxton alive again!

What happened between midnight that Saturday, September 14th, and the small hours of Sunday morning? Indeed, what unspeakable, obscene atrocities were carried out behind locked doors during the four days and nights immediately following?

Or were they?

Two stories were to run parallel in time: Ruxton's story and that of his accusers. Most of Ruxton's daytime movements and certainly all his conversations are known from the evidence of witnesses. But what of the hours he spent alone in that house, undisturbed, with the run of the place to himself?

Circumstantial evidence can play a terrible part in helping to convict an innocent person. Yet, when amassed in sufficient quantities it can often lead to only one logical conclusion.

In the end, as always, it was to rest with a jury of twelve sane men to decide which of the two stories was true.

Meanwhile, what were those known movements and conversations of Ruxton over the vital period?

4

On the morning after the children's party, Dalton Square was wrapped in its usual early Sunday quietness. A slight drizzle was falling and the Town Hall clock was chiming the half-hour--half-past six--as Ruxton emerged from No.2. Getting into the Hillman Minx that was drawn up outside, he drove the short distance to Mrs. Oxley's house. Mrs.Oxley was due to arrive for work at 7.15 a.m. her usual time even on Sundays. She was still in bed when Ruxton rang and it was Mr.Oxley who opened the door to him.

Ruxton said: "Please tell Mrs.Oxley not to bother about coming today. My wife and Mary Rogerson have gone on a holiday to Edinburgh and I'm taking the children to Morecambe for the day. Tell her to come as usual tomorrow morning."

For Mrs.Oxley, this was an unprecedented occurrence. In all her eighteen months service with the Ruxton's she had never missed a day's work. The doctor had never before been near her house and in any case it was Mrs.Ruxton who always gave the orders to the servants....

At nine o'clock that morning Winifred Roberts arrived at 2, Dalton Square. She was one of two people who delivered Sunday newspapers there and, as she rang the bell, she had removed from the canvas bag slung over her shoulder, copies of the "News of the World", the "People", and the "Sunday Pictorial". When there was no answer to her ringing she returned the papers to the bag and walked away, being reluctant to leave them because two weeks money was owing and the newsagent for whom she worked liked to receive payment on delivery. She returned again in ten minutes and rang the bell three times before the door was finally opened by Ruxton. She was surprised to see him because as a rule either Mary Rogerson or Mrs.Oxley took in the Sunday papers. Ruxton was wearing a white shirt and grey flannel trousers. To Winifred Roberts he seemed agitated and appeared to be holding his trousers up at the waist with his right hand. That was until she noticed that he was wearing braces.

"I'm so sorry to disturb you, Doctor," she said, "but there's two weeks owing."

"That's quite all right," Ruxton spoke rapidly. "My wife and the nursemaid are away in Scotland." He thrust his left hand into a trouser pocket, drew out some change and paid her.

About an hour later Thomas Partridge arrived to deliver the "Sunday Graphic". He knocked hard on the door, also hoping to receive payment. When no answer was forthcoming he stuffed the paper under the door and continued on his round. The copy of the "Sunday Graphic" he had just delivered was what is known as a special 'slip' edition; for circulation only in the Lancaster and Morecambe area and carrying pictures of the crowning of the local Carnival Queen. Thomas Partridge had walked only a short distance across the square when a milk cart driven by a woman pulled up in front of No.2 and Mrs.Hindson alighted, carrying four pint bottles of milk. As a rule one of the servants answered the door and it was her custom to take the milk straight through into the scullery. On this occasion, however, the door was opened by Ruxton. She noticed that his right hand was bandaged and blood was still seeping through.

"My wife and the nursemaid have gone away with the children," he said quickly. "I told Mrs.Oxley not to come today, but since then I've jammed my finger."

"I'm sorry to hear that, Doctor," Mrs.Hindson said. Then she moved as if to take the milk through but Ruxton stopped her.

"Don't bother, Mrs.Hindson," he said. "Just leave the milk here on the hall table."

Around 10.30 that morning Ruxton again left the house by himself and drove to the Midland Station Garage, where he was little known, and bought two two-gallon tins of petrol which he stowed in the boot of the Hillman Minx. Then he went to his usual garage, The County, and had the tank filled up; for Bella's trip to Blackpool had left it almost dry. After that he returned to Dalton Square; and when he emerged from the house again an hour later he was carrying the youngest child, Billie, in his arms, Elizabeth and Diane running on ahead to open the doors of the car.

It was less than ten minutes drive to Morecambe, where they stopped at the Anderson's house. Mr.Anderson, the dentist, was in bed with a touch of 'flu' but his wife Ethel greeted them cheerily. The two families had been close friends for eighteen months and it was Mr.Anderson who frequently called upon Ruxton's services as an anaesthetist.

"Bella and Mary have gone away for a few days," Ruxton said. "I wondered if you'd do me a favour and look after the children for the day. I have several appointments and some calls to make."

"Of course," said Ethel Anderson. "We'd be delighted to have them. But, whatever have you done to your hand, Buck?"

"Well--I was opening a tin of fruit for the children's breakfast and the tin-opener slipped."

"It looks to me as if it's still bleeding quite a bit. Oughtn't you to get it properly dressed?"

"Oh, I'll be all right," he said.

"Where have Bella and Mary gone to?"

"I'm not sure--but they'll only be away for a few days. Well, if you're quite certain you don't mind. I'll--call back for the children this evening."

He seemed in a hurry as he regained the car and drove off.

‡

Mrs.Mary Hampshire had been a patient of Ruxton almost from the time he started in practice at Lancaster. She had a heart condition and was not supposed to do any strenuous work. Certainly she had never done any work at 2, Dalton Square. Yet, on that Sunday afternoon Ruxton called at her house to ask if she would come and help him tidy the staircase as he had pulled all the carpets up in readiness for the decorators in the morning. He had cut his fingers pretty badly opening a tin of fruit and this made things difficult for him.

Mrs.Hampshire was a cut above the ordinary charwoman, nevertheless she agreed to oblige and accompanied Ruxton in the car to 2, Dalton Square. On the way she asked him where Mrs.Ruxton was.

"She's at Blackpool," he said.

"And the nursemaid?"

"Gone away on holiday. Mrs.Anderson is looking after the children today."

As they entered the house two things struck Mrs.Hampshire immediately. The first, that the radio was blaring away on full volume. Secondly, the condition of the staircase. All the carpets on the stairs and landings had been taken up and the bare boards were littered with loose bits of straw from the hall right up to the top story. Mrs.Hampshire knew the consulting-room and the surgery only too well, but she had never before studied the rest of the house and its general condition now surprised her.

"My little Billie has been playing with straw," Ruxton explained. "You know what children are."

After turning off the radio he took her upstairs to the top landing and suggested that she should start there and work her way downwards. The door of the back bedroom where Mary Rogerson slept was half open. She could not see the bed but the room appeared to be in a normal condition, a few oddments of clothing lying across the back of a chair. The doors of the other two rooms on that landing were locked!

Ruxton took her down to the bathroom on the floor below and showed her how to work the geyser.

"Use as much hot water as you want," he said.

Again, Mrs.Hampshire was surprised at the state of the bath. It was coated with a dirty yellow substance which covered the enamel right up to within a few inches of the brim. The linoleum on the floor was of a black and white chequered pattern on which she noticed smears of what appeared to be blood. Against the right hand wall was a built-in bench running the length of the bathroom and the top of which was covered by linoleum of similar pattern. This, too, was smeared with a reddish brown substance.

"The place is in a terrible state!" Mrs.Hampshire exclaimed.

"I know, I know," Ruxton nodded quickly. "But the charwomen aren't here today! Look, Mrs.Hampshire, I don't want you to work too hard. Just do what you can to tidy up a bit. I'll pay you, of course."

Mrs.Hampshire said: "I'll need some help. D'you mind if I ask Mr.Hampshire to come over and lend me a hand? I could get a message to him by telephone."

"By all means," said Ruxton. "The phone is in the consulting-room."

At four o'clock he prepared to go out.

"I have some calls to make," he told her. "Then I have to collect the children from Mrs.Anderson. I'll be back later this evening."

Mr.Hampshire did not arrive until seven; and Mrs.Hampshire was thus left alone in that house for nearly three hours!

She began on the top landing with brush and pan, sweeping up the straw and stuffing it into a bucket. Straw protruded also in large quantities from underneath the two locked bedroom doors, but it was impossible to gather everything up without opening them and she looked around, unsuccessfully, for the keys. Having done all she could to the staircase and landings, she left the scrubbing for Mr.Hampshire when he arrived and turned her attention to the bathroom. Although she worked hard with hot water and Vim she was unable to remove the stains on the inside of the bath completely. There were spots of partly dried blood on the floor by the lavatory seat and she mopped the floor over generally, thing that the Doctor must have cut his hand very badly.

The doors to the lounge and dining-room on the first landing were unlocked and in the latter she found a meal laid for two. It consisted of bread and butter and cakes and fruit salad, none of which had been touched. She left it there, thinking it would do for the Doctor's supper, and went downstairs. In the waiting-room she saw a heap of rolled up carpets and on top of these a blue suit, all of which appeared to be blood-stained. In the kitchen a few items of dirty crockery were piled in the sink, but before setting about washing these up she opened the back door and looked into the yard. It was raining quite heavily now and she saw more carpets and stair-pads heaped up; also a shirt and several blood-stained towels and wads of cotton-wool, all of which had been partly burnt. In fact, under the rain, steam was still rising from a smoldering heap against the high wall of the County Cinema on one side of the yard.

Yes, the doctor must have cut his hand very, very badly....!

It was nearly seven o'clock by the time he returned. He was holding Elizabeth by the hand as Mrs.Hampshire opened the door to him and she saw Mrs.Anderson sitting outside in the car with the other two children.

"Mrs.Anderson has kindly suggested that the children sleep at her house tonight," he told her. "Elizabeth and I are just going upstairs to get the night clothes."

"Can I fetch them for you, doctor?" she said.

"No thanks, Mrs.Hampshire. We can manage."

She remained in the hall as Ruxton and the eldest girl mounted the staircase. She could not tell how far Elizabeth went or whether she in fact entered either of the locked bedrooms because while they were up there her attention was diverted by the arrival of Mr.Hampshire; but when they came down again Elizabeth was carrying a small case evidently containing the night clothes. Before leaving again Ruxton took Mrs.Hampshire into the waiting-room and pointed to the suit and the carpets lying on the floor.

"If these carpets are of any use to you," he said, "you're welcome to them. Also this suit. It's the one I was wearing when I cut my hand this morning, but the blood-stains should come out with cleaning. It's a good suit."

"That's very kind of you,doctor," she said. "It'll do nicely for Mr.Hampshire. You must have cut your hand very badly!"

"I'm afraid I did," he nodded quickly.

At nine-thirty that night Mr.and Mrs.Hampshire left Dalton Square after making sure all the lights were out and locking the house up in accordance with Ruxton's instructions. They carried between them two lengths of carpet rolled up and tied with string;

also the coat, waistcoat and trousers of the blue suit. Later, upon closer examination, Mrs.Hampshire found that one of the carpets was not too bad, but the other piece was so saturated that after pouring more than thirty buckets of water over it the liquid still came away the colour of blood!

‡

On the way back to Morecambe with Mrs.Anderson and the children Ruxton had stopped at the house of Mary Rogerson's parents. They were both out, but Mr.Risby, a guest of theirs, was on the point of leaving by the front door as the car drew up. Ruxton beckoned him over and spoke through the window on the driver's side.

"Will you please tell them," he said, "that Mrs.Ruxton and Mary have gone to Scotland for a short holiday. Mary drew her wages yesterday in advance."

It was shortly after ten o'clock by the time Ruxton returned to 2, Dalton Square, alone. The place was in darkness and wrapped in an ominous silence. He went into the surgery, switched on a strong arc-lamp and proceeded gingerly to unwind the bandage on his right hand. The fingers seemed to be bent in a permanent claw-like position; but it was not until the gauze dressing had finally released its sticky hold that the extent of the terrible injuries was revealed. Starting from high up on the palmar surface of the middle finger a clean gash extended diagonally downwards, finishing right around the back of the little finger. While the slicing of the middle and ring fingers was deep enough, the bone of the little finger was almost exposed.

A tin-opener?

Professor Glaister, Regius Professor of Forensic Medicine at Glasgow University, was to say later:

"When a surgeon is dissecting a human skull, there is a particular spot where the knife is liable to slip and so cause injury...." pg#164

‡

At ten minutes past seven the following morning, Monday 16th. September, Mrs.Oxley duly arrived at 2, Dalton Square. She rang the front door bell several times but could get no answer. She walked round into Friar's Passage where the car was sometimes parked overnight but there was no sign of it; and since rain was still falling quite heavily she decided to return home and try again later.

Wherever Ruxton had been at that time, by nine o'clock he was pulling up outside Mrs.Hampshire's house in the car.The front door was on the latch and, without troubling to knock, he walked strait in. His appearance alone gave Mrs.Hampshire a shock. He was unshaven, without collar and tie, and wore a soiled, crumpled raincoat.

"Good heavens, doctor," she exclaimed. "How ill you look!"

"I feel it," he said, although his manner was excited. "I've been awake all night with the pain in my hand. What did you take away yesterday?"

"Just the suit and two of the carpets."

"Where is the suit?"

"It's on that table over there."

He strode swiftly to the table and picked up the coat. The copious blood-stains, now dried up, were plainly visible.

"I'm sorry," he said quickly. "I had no idea it was so dirty. I'll take it with me and have it cleaned!"

"Oh, no, doctor," said Mrs.Hampshire. "You were good enough to give us the suit and it's only right we should pay for the cleaning."

He became more excited now, as he grabbed at the inside pocket, turning the flap over to reveal a tab which bore both the tailor's name and his own.

"Get a pair of scissors!" he snapped.

As Mrs.Hampshire complied, he took the scissors from her but was unable to hold them properly in his injured hand.

"Don't worry, doctor," she said, taking them from him. "I'll cut out the tab after you've gone."

"No, no, do it now!" Then, as though his anxiety called for some explanation, "It's not dignified for a man like Mr.Hampshire to be seen wearing a suit belonging to someone else."

It took her only a few seconds to cut through the stitches holding the tab.

"Burn it, burn it!" said Ruxton fiercely.

Mrs.Hampshire glanced at him oddly for a few seconds, before dropping the offending square of material into the fire.

"Could you come to the house this afternoon," he went on, "just to answer the surgery door? Also, I have two business gentlemen arriving for tea and I'd be glad of your help."

"Very well, doctor," she said, a trifle mystified.

At a quarter-past nine Mrs.Oxley was again ringing the bell at 2, Dalton Square. There was still no answer, but soon afterwards Ruxton drove up in the car. The charwomen, too, was shocked by his appearance and it was also the first time she had seen the bandaged hand. When she asked him about it he gave the now familiar explanation concerning a tin of fruit, adding: "I lost gallons and gallons of blood and drank gallons and gallons of water!"

"I'll make you some coffee," said Mrs.Oxley, in a homely way. As they went through to the kitchen she halted abruptly in the hall. "Why, wherever are the stair carpets?"

"I took them all up. Didn't you know the decorators are coming today?"

"It's the first I've heard of it," said Mrs.Oxley. "Where are the children?"

"With Mrs.Anderson. They stayed the night there."

Presently, as he was sipping coffee in the kitchen, Mrs.Oxley asked:

"When d'you expect Mrs.Ruxton and Mary to return?"

"I don't know," he said, passing a hand across his forehead, "I don't know. If you ask me, there's something fishy going on between those two. Mary asked for her wages in advance last Saturday and the pair of them left early yesterday morning. They said they were going to Edinburgh."

"Certainly seems strange," said Mrs.Oxley. "Although Madam did say something about going off."

"Exactly, exactly, Mrs.Oxley!"

"What time are the decorators supposed to be here?"

"They should have shown up by now," Ruxton said. "But you know how unreliable these people are. I shall have to get onto them." His dark skin hid much of the haggard appearance which, in similar circumstances, must have shown in a white man's face. Nevertheless, his eyes were hooded, the skin beneath them deeply wrinkled.

He left the house soon after half-past ten, having changed into more presentable clothes. He was unable to shave himself owing to the injured hand and said he would call at Howson's, the barber.

Left alone, Mrs.Oxley wandered around the house. The stairs and landings were passably clean after Mr. and Mrs.Hampshire's scrubbing, but the two bedrooms on the top floor were still locked, with straw protruding from under the doors. She knew that the room in which Ruxton slept was generally kept locked during the daytime because the window in there was very low and thus a danger to the children running in and out; but the key was always kept on a hook just above the door. There was no sign of a key there now. Likewise, the two rooms on the first floor were sometimes locked and the keys kept in a drawer in the hall. One of these, she now discovered was locked but the hall drawer was empty. The meal which Mrs.Hampshire had seen in the dining-room was still there, untouched. Mrs.Oxley put it all on a small table which she left out on the landing.

Downstairs, she looked in the yard and saw the heap of half-burned blood-stained material. A good job, she thought, that the dustmen called on a Monday. She proceeded to do a bit of tidying up generally, and since there was no sign of the decorators, left at her usual time.

Like Mrs.Hampshire, and later both Mrs.Curwan and Mrs.Mabel Smith, such was Mrs.Oxley's simple faith in human nature that no breath of suspicion or hint of anything sinister crossed her mind.

‡

After visiting several patients that morning Ruxton arrived at the County Garage and asked the proprietor, Mr.Hudson, if he would service the Hillman Minx.

"The engine keeps stalling in traffic," he added.

Mr.Hudson glanced at the mileometer and said: "Probably needs de-carbonizing. You've done nearly five thousand, I see."

"If I leave it with you now, can you lend me another car while your doing the job?"

"Well--I've got an 8 h.p. Ford," said Mr.Hudson.

"That's too small!" Ruxton spoke rapidly, holding up his bandaged hand. "My wife's away and I cut my fingers opening a tin of fruit. Haven't you got anything bigger--more easy to handle?"

"Not at the moment, I'm afraid," said Mr.Hudson. "You might try the Grand Garage. Like me to phone them for you?"

"Yes, yes, if you will be so kind."

Mr.Hudson disappeared into his office; and when he returned it was to say that the Grand Garage had a 12 h.p. Austin saloon which they were willing to hire out for a couple of days. Ruxton thanked him, left the Hillman Minx there and went on to the other garage. Having collected a grey Austin saloon, CP8415, he drove back to Dalton Square to find Mrs.Hampshire already there. She had let herself in with a key he had given her earlier that morning and was sitting in the waiting-room, drumming her fingers on the table.

"Why did you ask me to come here, doctor, when there's really nothing for me to do?"

"I asked you," said Ruxton, "because you give me courage!"

"I don't know about that," she said. "What you need is for your wife to return--what with that bad hand. Can't you send for her?"

"No, She's in London."

Mrs.Hampshire looked at him searchingly. Then:

"Doctor," she said, "you're telling me lies!"

"I know I am." Ruxton sat down wearily. "I'm the most unhappy man in the world, Mrs.Hampshire!"

"Why is that, doctor?"

"The truth is, I don't know where my wife is--except that she's gone off with another man."

"Never!" exclaimed Mrs.Hampshire.

"Yes, yes, it's true! You make a friend of a man, you treat him as a friend--and he makes love to your wife behind your back! It's terrible!" He began to cry.

Mrs.Hampshire was visibly shocked; but at least this explained some of the doctor's strange behaviour. Whatever her rejoinder might have been it was interrupted by a load noise coming from the yard. She went and looked out of the kitchen window.

"It's the dustmen," she announced.

Ruxton seemed to pull himself together quickly.

"I want to see them," he said; and hurried through into the yard.

There were four men emptying the dustbins and Ruxton pointed to the heap of rubbish piled against the wall. It was still raining and the amorphous mass of slimy, half-burnt carpets and rags, all blood-stained, was covered by a layer of plaster, evidently scraped from the fire-blackened wall of the County Cinema on that side. There was also a hamper of straw pushed in amongst the dustbins.

Ruxton said: "I want you to take all that rubbish away. I want the yard cleared up completely. I'll pay you for it."

"We can't take that plaster," said Joe Gardiner, who was evidently in charge. "That's the job of the workmen, whoever they are. You had an accident or something, doctor?"

"I cut my finger opening a tin of fruit. My wife's away and I've got three children to look after."

"Then I reckon you ought to send for her, what with that hand!"

"I can't. She's touring with the car and I don't know where to find her. If you clear everything away and sweep the yard I'll pay you."

In the end they obliged, making a good job of things. In the process one of them, Alfred Rutledge, noticed a partly burned women's blouse. It was of blue silk material with glass buttons; but he thought little of it at the time.

Soon after the dustmen had left Ruxton held his surgery, Mrs. Hampshire opening the door to the patients as they arrived. The obliging Mrs.Hampshire also served tea when, later that afternoon, Ruxton's solicitor called, together with an insurance agent from Manchester. It was a business conference connected with the loan he was negotiating on the practice.

Although he had arranged to call for the children at Morecambe that morning, it was after nine o'clock in the evening when he finally set out on this journey. On the way he saw Bobbie Edmondson's car ahead of him and sounded his horn. Edmondson looked round, but not recognizing the Austin car continued driving. Ruxton overtook him, motioning him to slow down, and the two cars pulled up bonnet to tail. Edmondson got out and walked over.

Ruxton greeted him with the utmost friendliness.

"How are the examination studies coming along?" he asked.

"Oh, not too bad," Edmondson said. "I'm finding things a bit tough, but hope to make the grade in the end. Have you changed your car then?"

"No," said Ruxton. "Bella has taken Mary to Scotland for a few days in the Hillman. This is a hired one."

Bobbie Edmondson looked surprised: "She never mentioned anything to us about going away!"

"No, but she gets these sudden impulses, you know. For one thing, she's trying to arrange an agency for Murphy's Football Pool business."

"So she told us."

If Ruxton had ever suspected the slightest form of intimacy between these two, now had been his golden opportunity to mention it. Instead, they parted company on the best of terms; and when Ruxton arrived at the Anderson's house it was to ask if they could keep the children for one more night. They agreed--especially after Mr.Anderson had taken a good look at Ruxton's hand.

"You say you did this with a tin-opener? I wouldn't have thought it possible for a tin-opener to cause a wound like that! I'd be interested to see the offending implement."

"Afraid I threw it away," Ruxton said quickly. "I hated the sight of the thing!"

Thus, for the second night in succession he had the run of 2, Dalton Square to himself.

‡

So far, Ruxton had told a number of differing stories to account for Isabella's absence, including the confession to Mrs.Hampshire that he was in truth completely ignorant of her present whereabouts. When a wife goes off suddenly, with or without another man, it is by no means uncommon for the husband in the early stages, possibly from pride, to try to cover up. In Ruxton's case he was aided by the fact that Bella was known to be impulsive and often made journeys on the spur of the moment. Her absence, therefore, was not likely to cause any undue concern, at any rate for a week or two. In the case of Mary Rogerson it was a very different matter. She had never spent a day away from home without letting her parents know well in advance, and even then kept in touch with them daily. It was necessary, therefore, to suggest a very convincing reason for Mary Rogerson's continued absence; and this Ruxton proceeded to do in a somewhat insidious manner, first with Ethel Anderson and later to the world at large.

On the following morning, Tuesday September 17, Mrs.Oxley duly arrived for work shortly after seven o'clock and was admitted by Ruxton in his pajamas. She cooked him some breakfast; and shortly afterwards he set off to collect the children from Morecambe. It was the opening day of the new term and Elizabeth and Diane were due at school by nine-thirty. He was still unable to shave himself and called the barber on the way, arriving at the Anderson's house a few minutes after nine 0'clock. Mr.Anderson had already begun his dental surgery and Dorothy Neild, their maid, was still getting the children ready. Ethel Anderson, therefore, took Ruxton into the front sitting-room.

"Have you heard anything from Bella or Mary?" she asked.

"No," he said. "Bella seldom writes letters, but I thought Mary might have sent the children a card." He threw her a sidelong glance. "Did you know that Mary was courting a boy from the laundry?"

Mrs.Anderson looked surprised, to say the least.

"But I always thought she had no time for boys!"

"So did everybody else. It was my Elizabeth who told me, several weeks ago. She said one day "D'you know, Daddy, Mary has a laundry boy?" He paused a moment and then went on: "I wasn't going to tell anybody this, but for some time now I've been pretty certain that Mary is pregnant. Haven't you noticed how fat she has become of late?"

Ethel Anderson was flabber-gasted.

"I hadn't noticed anything," she managed to say. "I just can't believe it!"

"Well, I as a doctor know for sure. And d'you know what I think? I think Bella has taken her to Scotland to have an illegal operation. Naturally, she wouldn't say anything to me because I'd have forbidden it!"

"I still can't believe it," said Ethel Anderson.

"It's true all right," he persisted. "I'll tell you what happened. When Bella got back from Blackpool on Saturday night she went straight to bed. She woke me up early the next morning and suggested a trip into the country and I agreed. But at the last minute she changed her mind and said she was taking Mary to Edinburgh. Naturally I was a bit annoyed--being woken up so early on a Sunday, my day off. But you know what Bella is--always changing her mind. Only this time she had a good reason!"

"I still can't believe it about Mary," said Mrs.Anderson.

"Nevertheless, it explains why the two of them went off like that!"

This story, with only slight variations, was the one he was to stick to from that time onwards.

After dropping the two girls at school he drove with the youngest child Billie to the offices of the decorators, where he demanded to know why they had not turned up as arranged. The owner himself was out but his daughter, who handled the books, consulted these and said there was no note of any such appointment. She finally agreed, however, that there might have been a vague arrangement about coming sometime in September, and said they would do this as soon as possible.

Ruxton then drove off again in the hired Austin car.

Exactly where he drove to that morning will never be known for certain. According to his accusers later, he made one of several trips to a place about one hundred miles distant from Lancaster; in which case he must have averaged nearly 60 m.p.h., with an injured hand and a restless child in the car. According to Ruxton, he had driven out to Seattle, where the children had spent a holiday in the Summer, to ask the landlady, Mrs.Holmes, if she could have young Billie for a while; but he had lost his way and been obliged to turn back in order to reach home in time to take surgery. What is certain is that at 12.30 p.m. that day he was in collision with a cyclist at Kendal--well off the route from Seattle--and failed to stop. The cyclist, however, had taken his number and half an hour later Ruxton was halted by a policeman at Milnthorpe. He became very excited and spoke incoherently, telling the officer he had been to Carlisle; that he had not stopped because he could see no damage was done. After taking full particulars the officer allowed him to proceed and he arrived back at Dalton Square more than an hour late for surgery. There were about a dozen patients in the waiting-room, having been admitted by Mrs.Mabel Smith who had born the brunt of their annoyance.

Mrs.Smith had not been there the previous day, Monday, having stayed away to keep a dental appointment. Mrs.Curwan also had stayed at home on the Monday with a bad headache; and the state of the house, therefore, had caused as much surprise to these two as it had to Mrs.Oxley, for nobody had been told anything about the decorators, all three women accepting Ruxton's explanations with bland credulity. He now told Mrs.Smith to fetch the steps and a pail of water and to start stripping the wallpaper from the top landing down as far as the bathroom.

"Try to get finished before the girls arrive home from school," he added quickly. Only then did he turn his attention to the long-suffering patients in the waiting-room.

For the first time since Saturday the three children slept at Dalton Square that night. Despite this, a huge fire was seen burning in the yard of No.2 and neighbours whose bedrooms overlooked the place said it was bright enough to read by.

‡

On the morning of Wednesday, 18th.September, Mrs.Curwan duly arrived for work soon after half-past eight, by which time Mrs.Oxley had already given Ruxton his breakfast. In spite of the dustmen's clearance, the yard was again littered with pieces of material, carpets and other oddments mostly blood-stained and partly burnt. Mrs. Curwan, a stickler for tidiness, began to sweep up. Seeing a pile of sodden but unburnt carpets, she proceeded to scrub these under the tap. A few feet away the remains of a fire still smouldered. While she was thus engaged, Ruxton came out and told her not to bother. He would be putting new carpets down everywhere.

"In that case, Doctor," she said, "perhaps Mrs.Oxley and I could take a few of these strips?"

"Help yourselves," Ruxton said with a shrug.

The two women later shared out the soiled carpets between them; but neither fancied the heavily blood-stained blanket which lay in a recess nearby. Mrs.Curwan put this in a bowl and left it under a running tap in the yard.

Except for surgery, Ruxton generally took time off on a Wednesday, but he had been neglecting the Practice of late and had a good deal of work to catch up with. Thus he was kept busy throughout the day; yet he found time in the late afternoon to drive the three children and Mrs.Anderson over to Morecambe Carnival where Elizabeth was due to take part in a procession. Leaving them there, he hurried home in time to take evening surgery, after which he went back again to collect them. On this second journey he returned the hired Austin car to its owners and retrieved the Hillman Minx, now de-carbonized, from the County Garage. Seeing that he looked so tired, Mrs.Anderson again offered to have the children for the night. Ruxton thanked her profusely, promising to fetch them in good time for school in the morning. Then he slumped into a chair and promptly fell fast asleep. He did not wake up until nearly 1 a.m., after which he returned to Dalton Square alone.

When Mrs.Oxley arrived the following morning, Thursday, he was up and about and seemed anxious to have his breakfast as soon as possible.

"I'm going to see a specialist about my hand," he told her.

"And none too soon, doctor, if you ask me," said Mrs.Oxley.

While she was busy getting his breakfast, Ruxton brought the car round to the side entrance in Friar's Passage. Regaining the house by the back door, he closed the kitchen door in passing, thus virtually shutting Mrs.Oxley in there. *She heard him make several journeys up and down the stairs and out to the car* --and by the time he had apparently finished these excursions his breakfast was ready.

Before leaving the house at eight o'clock he said: "Please ask Mrs. Curwan to tell the afternoon patients that if I'm not back by three o'clock, I'll be there for evening surgery at six."

When he had gone Mrs.Oxley had occasion to go upstairs to the top landing, where she found that the door of Mrs.Ruxton's room was now unlocked and the room itself moderately tidy. The other bedroom door, however, remained securely fastened and she was aware for the first time of a dreadful odour emanating from it. When Mrs.Curwan arrived she, too, noticed the smell which now seemed to pervade the whole house. After some discussion the two women decided that it must be coming from the damp walls of the staircase which Mrs.Mabel Smith had stripped of paper the previous day....

It was nearly half-past three by the time Ruxton returned; and he had not been near any doctor for treatment to his hand. Mrs.Curwan and Mrs.Smith were there, but the surgery patients had given him up and gone home. Although he had promised Mrs.Anderson to collect the children that morning he had failed to do so and the Anderson's maid, Dorothy Neild, had taken the trouble to bring the three of them all the way over from Morecambe.

Despite these shortcomings, Ruxton seemed to be hungry and telephoned a local restaurant, ordering a hot meal to be sent across.

This he ate in the kitchen, attended by Mrs.Curwan, while Mrs. Smith took the children out for a walk, Elizabeth and Diane having missed school that day.

Mrs.Curwan knew the household at 2, Dalton Square better perhaps than anyone, for she had been with the Ruxton's ever since they first moved in. She was thus more in their confidence than many people; and as Ruxton ate his lunch now, struggling to manipulate the knife with his injured hand, he said to her: "Have you noticed how fat our Mary has become lately?"

Mrs.Curwan hesitated, a trifle surprised at the question. Then: "Possibly she has filled out a bit. But that's only natural at her age."

"Did you know she was pregnant?"

"Pregnant?" Mrs.Curwan looked incredulous. "Oh, no, doctor...."

"It's true. Mrs.Ruxton has taken her to a young doctor she knows in Scotland to have an illegal operation. That's where they've gone!"

"I'm pretty certain you're mistaken about Mary, doctor."

Of all people, perhaps Mrs.Curwan was the most risky in whom to have confided this news, if it were in fact untrue. She showed as much now by invoking a subject which she would never have discussed with any man other than a doctor.

"I can tell you for sure that Mary was menstruating when she went away. I've been in her bedroom and seen some recently used, washable sanitary towels which she keeps in a bag. There was also some blood in her chamber-pot."

Ruxton swallowed a mouthful of food which all but choked him.

"Maybe," he said quickly. "But I can tell you from experience--and it's also a well known fact--that some women lose a bit of blood each month even during pregnancy. I, as a doctor, can tell you for sure that Mary was pregnant when she went away from here last Sunday morning."

Like Ethel Anderson, Mrs.Curwan was only partly convinced. At any rate she changed the subject.

"Have you noticed the unpleasant smell in the house, doctor?"

"Yes," he said. "It must be due to the carpets being up and the damp plaster in the walls."

"It's not very healthy for the children."

"I agree, Mrs.Curwan. In fact I was going to ask you to pop out and buy a scent spray."

"I'll do that now, doctor." Mrs.Curwan rose quickly and reached for her hat and coat which hung on the back of the kitchen door.

"And while you're at it--" Ruxton added--"a bottle of Eau de Cologne."

When Mrs.Curwan returned with the purchases, Ruxton sprayed the house from top to bottom; and for a while afterwards the scent, mingling with the original nauseating odour, left an even more fetid atmosphere.

The next day, Friday 20th. September, for the first time in nearly a week the keys were back in all the doors.

5

During the days immediately following, some semblance of normality returned to 2, Dalton Square. Despite this, fires kindled by Ruxton continued to be a nightly occurrence and the three charwomen were kept busy clearing up in the yard. On one occasion Mrs.Curwan had come upon the charred remains of a coat and also a dressing-gown remarkably similar to ones belonging to Mary Rogerson. Yet, still no sinister application seems to have crossed her mind. Certainly she drew nobody's attention to it at the time.

Ruxton went about his daily duties as a medical practitioner; and to cope with the children in the evenings while he was out visiting patients he resorted to various baby-sitters.

Until now he had managed to steer clear of Mary Rogerson's parents, but, inevitably, one evening during that second week her brother, Peter, called to ask if there was any news of her.

"I haven't heard a word yet," Ruxton told him. "D'you know if she's been in any kind of trouble?"

Young Rogerson looked mystified.

"Trouble? None that I know of."

"I paid her wages in advance for last week. Here...you'd better take what's due to her for this week." Ruxton counted out fifteen shillings.

"Thanks, doctor. Could you come and see my father? He'd like a word with you."

"Yes, yes," said Ruxton quickly. "I'll call round tomorrow evening."

True to his word, he arrived at the Rogerson's house in Morecambe shortly after five-thirty the following day and, not surprisingly, walked into an atmosphere charged with resentment and suspicion.

"I came to see you about Mary," he began.

"Well, what about her?" said Mr.Rogerson. "Where is my daughter?"

"All I know is that she went off suddenly with Mrs.Ruxton last Sunday week."

"She's never done such a thing before without telling us!" Mrs. Rogerson flared up.

"Because she's never been pregnant before!"

"*What?*" They both shouted.

"Mrs.Anderson first drew my attention to it several weeks ago," Ruxton lied. "And I, as a doctor, know it to be so."

"I don't believe you," Mrs.Rogerson cried. "I know that isn't true! Mary had no secrets from us. She always told us everything!"

"Did she tell you about the laundry boy?"

"What laundry boy?" thundered Mr.Rogerson.

"She's been going with him for several months now. Even my little Elizabeth knows about it!"

"It's the first we've heard!" Mrs.Rogerson threw her chin up.

"I'll have this fellow produced!" said Mr.Rogerson.

"At any rate you see what's happened," Ruxton went on quickly. "Of course it's none of my business, but Mrs.Ruxton has obviously taken her away to have an operation...."

"It can't be true," Mr.Rogerson shouted, "I want my daughter back here! I'll give it until Sunday. After that, I shall go to the police!"

"No,no!" Ruxton showed the first signs of panic. "Don't go to the police. We--don't want the whole world to know, do we? I'll get Mary back somehow. I promise!"

"By Sunday!" Mr.Rogerson repeated.

By Sunday. It was at least a respite; and the perspiration must have been pouring off Ruxton's back as he left that house. Yet there was worse to come.

By something of a coincidence there had been a sanguinary murder in the district the previous night, in which a women known as Mrs.Smalley had been found stabbed to death. It is doubtful whether the police, at this stage, were even aware of the strange disappearance of Isabella Ruxton and Mary Rogerson; certainly it was none of their business as yet and they were in no way interested. Nevertheless, with so many people such as dustmen, tradesmen--to say nothing of Ruxton's patients--calling regularly at 2, Dalton Square, it was inevitable that certain rumours should have leaked out concerning the general state of the house and yard; and on that afternoon of September 24, Mrs.Curwan was summoned to the police station and questioned by the officer in charge of the Smalley case, whose name, by an even greater coincidence in the light of subsequent events, was Detective Inspector Moffat. Her information could have been of little help to the police in their hunt for Mrs.Smalley's killer; and such was her sense of loyalty that Mrs.Curwan came straight away to Ruxton and told him all about it. She had always known him to be excitable, but his reactions now startled her.

"What did they ask you. What did you tell them?" he cried.

"I told them all the carpets were up and the walls stripped on the staircase ready for the decorators. I also said you'd cut your hand very badly. It was that Inspector Moffat."

"How dare they!" Ruxton screamed. "How dare they question my servants behind my back! I'll have something to say about this!"

He had gained the front door and was hurrying across the Square before she could barely recover from the shock of his outburst.

Detective Inspector Moffat was still in the police station when Ruxton burst unceremoniously through the door.

"Look here, Inspector..." he began in a high pitch of excitement, "what the hell do the police mean by enquiring into my private affairs?"

"Take it easy, doctor," said Inspector Moffat. "We're only making routine enquiries into the death of Mrs.Smalley."

"That doesn't give you the right to question my servants behind my back! Why couldn't you come and see me? I've got nothing to hide. I don't know Mrs.Smalley. I've never met her and I know nothing whatever about her. If I want to take up my carpets and strip the wallpaper, it's my own affair and nothing whatever to do with the police!" He had become breathless, almost incoherent.

"We're satisfied of that now, doctor," said Moffat quietly. "But it came to our notice that certain articles of blood-stained clothing...."

"Blood!" Ruxton cried, holding up his bandaged hand. "You see that....? The fingers are severed almost to the bone! How much blood d'you think I lost? I did it opening a tin of fruit for my children. My wife has gone off and left me with three little ones to care for. I tell you, I've got enough troubles of my own and now you come bothering me about this Mrs.Smalley!" He relapsed into a chair, cradling his head in both hands. His anger was nearly spent. He was beginning to feel sorry for himself.

"As I've already told you, doctor," said Inspector Moffat, "we're satisfied that you were in no way connected with the death of Mrs.Smalley. In view of what we heard it was our duty to make these enquiries."

"Professional jealousy, that's all it is!" Ruxton was on his feet again. "I've got more patients than any other doctor in Lancaster and they're all jealous of me!"

He left the police station soon after that and returned to 2, Dalton Square, to find a letter lying on the hall table. The envelope was familiar, being addressed in his own handwriting to: "Mrs.Ruxton, c/o Nelson, 12, Bothwell Street, Edinburgh," and across the top: "Please forward if away". Jeanie Nelson had re-addressed the envelope to 2, Dalton Square, Lancaster.

He put the letter, unopened, in his pocket. Nobody could say he was not doing his best to trace Bella's whereabouts!

‡

The morning of Sunday, 29th. September, dawned bright, with the promise of a fine day ahead. It was also the dead-line imposed by Mr.Rogerson for Mary's return, but this did not seem to worry Ruxton unduly. If anything, he was in better spirits than he had shown for sometime. The Mrs.Smalley affair had blown over and he had even begun to treat it as a joke. Nevertheless, he was evidently in need of company other than the children, for when he promised to take them for a drive into the country he invited, first the Anderson's who declined, having made other arrangements for the day, and then Mrs.Curwan; but she too had to refuse, on domestic grounds. Finally, he telephoned a Miss Sharples--a patient of his and whom he and Bella had often mixed with socially--and extended a similar invitation. Miss Sharples said she would be delighted but had a Miss Robson staying for the week-end. Would there be room in the car for her too? Ruxton said: "Of course. The more the merrier!"

After an early lunch he picked up the two spinsters and, together with the children, they all set off in a northerly direction, stopping at the first garage to fill up. Ruxton then got behind the wheel and said: "Now! Where shall we go? The sky's the limit!"

They decided on the Lake District and drove through the Lyth Valley to Windermere, then on to Ambleside and Keswick, where they halted for tea at the Waverley Temperance Hotel. Everybody seemed to be enjoying things immensely, particularly Ruxton who cracked jokes with the waitress. Miss Robson had not been in this part of the world for more than twenty years and said she had always wanted to visit Gretna Green but never managed to do so.

"Well," said Ruxton somewhat naively, "I must say it's rather tempting for me to go to Gretna Green with two unmarried ladies! How about it?"

After tea they took the road to Carlisle and from there on to Gretna and the famous Forge, where everyone, except little Billie who was too young, signed the visitor's book. It was then time to start the return journey; and they finally arrived back in Lancaster at nine o'clock. It had been a thoroughly enjoyable day.

It might scarcely have been so enjoyable for Ruxton had he known that on that very afternoon, not many miles from where he had been entertaining the "two unmarried ladies", stark horror had burst upon an unsuspecting society!

A Miss Susan Johnson, on holiday with her brother at a place called Moffat just over the Scottish border, was taking a solitary afternoon stroll along the Carlisle to Edinburgh road. There was little traffic about as she came to a stone bridge spanning a ravine, at the bottom of which flowed a stream known as Gardenholme Linn. The water was shallow and flowing lazily, but the state of the banks suggested that the stream had recently been in full spate, leaving a high coating of mud on the grass and bushes along its route. As Miss.

Johnson looked down over the parapet, admiring the picturesque scenery, her scalp suddenly tingled. Peering closer, she saw what appeared to be a human leg protruding from a bundle lodged half-way down the bank. Her Sunday afternoon walk ruined, she hurried back to the hotel at Moffat and told her brother, who returned with her to the bridge. Clambering down the bank, he reached the bundle to confirm her first, horrified impressions. He immediately informed the police; and when they arrived in force more bundles came to light at intervals along the ravine, more limbs as well as many other atrocious revelations. In all, this terrible harvest of human remains amounted to the following:

Two heads, from which the eyes had been removed and the nose, lips and ears cut off; two trunk portions--one upper portion including the chest and shoulder blades, one lower portion including a complete bony pelvis; seventeen sections of assorted limbs, some with hands and feet attached, the toes and fingers mutilated; forty-three pieces of flesh and soft tissue which included three female breasts with the nipples cut off, and two portions of female external sex organs....

In addition to all this, *one cyclops eye*!

Such were the girls, charnel relics, already decomposing and infested with maggots, wrapped in various bundles of sheet, clothing and newspaper, discovered in that otherwise peaceful ravine. Such was the hideous, complex task that was to face a team of the world's most brilliant pathologists, anatomists and medico-legal experts from Glasgow and Edinburgh Universities.

From a brief preliminary examination by the police surgeon, it seemed evident that at least two human bodies were involved. But they were both female? Was there, perhaps, a third body entailed, only portions of which had so far come to light? Did the presence of the cyclops eye* suggest a monstrous birth somewhere along the line?

---

*   In Greek mythology the Cyclops were a race of one-eyed giants, having a single eye in the centre of the forehead. Their job in life was to make thunderbolts for Zeus. Nowadays the term is applied to a monstrous birth of this nature, much more common to animals such as pigs than to human beings.

Above all, to the layman, what unspeakable horrors, unsurpassed since the heyday of "Jack the Ripper", had gone before, to culminate in these dreadful discoveries?

Late on that Sunday night the editor of every national daily newspaper scrapped the front page make-up and supplanted this with the banner headlines, announcing what promised to be the most gruesome crime, or crimes, of the century.

6

Whilst the greater part of the total "haul" of human remains had been made on the Sunday afternoon, other parcels continued to come to light during the next few days near the banks of the Rivers Linn and Annan. That at least two persons had been murdered was evident, but the Dumfriesshire police could do little at that early stage, other than to check on all persons reported missing before September 19. This date was arrived at by the fact that following heavy rain the rivers and streams were presumably in sufficient spate to carry the bundles downstream and leave them high and dry on the bank when the water subsided. Had the bundles been thrown in after that date they would have been found considerably lower down the bank.

Like every other town in Britain, Lancaster buzzed with the news of the grim discoveries; more so, since Moffat was barely a hundred miles distant. As yet, however, the public knew little beyond the fact that a dreadful crime had been committed, from which the newspapers were seizing the opportunity to put out sensational copy.

Although Mr.Rogerson had threatened to act on Sunday, by the Tuesday he had still made no move. On that evening, however, accompanied by Mrs.Rogerson, he paid a visit to 2, Dalton Square. Ruxton was obviously excited and ill at ease but made an effort to control himself as he showed them into the consulting-room.

"I haven't been able to get a clue as to where they are," he said quickly. "I've tried every place I know. Look at this--" he produced the envelope re-addressed by Jeanie Nelson, "I wrote to my wife in care of her sister at Edinburgh, thinking she was sure to know where my wife was, but she returned it to this address! What can I do?"

"There's only one thing to be done," said Mr.Rogerson soberly.

"I tell you what--" Ruxton tried hard to forestall the inevitable. Instead of continuing to plug his story of Mary's pregnancy he now went out on a different limb. "My wife wanted to go into business on her own and it's my belief that the pair of them have gone away together for that purpose."

"Mary would never dream of doing such a thing without telling us," said Mrs.Rogerson fiercely.

"Nevertheless, she has obviously done so. There's always a first time for everything, you know! What's more, she's taken most of her clothes with her. Oh, there's no doubt about it! Mary has been deceiving us all, in conjunction with my wife! I'll tell you something else--they took nearly forty pounds out of my cash box! You can bet they'll be staying at some slap-up hotel and having a really good time. Don't worry--they'll both be back when the money runs out!"

Mr.Rogerson said: "I know one girl who won't be having a good time. My daughter is not that sort. I'm going to the police!" He took up his hat and, motioning to Mrs.Rogerson, made for the door.

Peering through the window after they had gone, Ruxton must have licked dry lips as he watched them cross the Square making a bee-line for the police station....

Detective Constable Winstanley was on duty when the Rogerson's entered.

Mr.Rogerson said: "I want to report my daughter as missing."

"I see," said Winstanley, pulling a sheet of paper towards him. "Can you give me some particulars, please?"

Mr.Rogerson gave his name and a few other details, and then added, "For two years she has been employed as nursemaid to Dr.Ruxton's children. We know she was at 2, Dalton Square on Saturday, September fourteenth, but she hasn't been seen or heard of since."

"It's most unlike her to go off anywhere without letting us know," put in Mrs.Rogerson.

"I want every effort made to find her!" Mr.Rogerson's voice trembled slightly.

"We'll do our best," said Winstanley. "Now--let's have some fuller particulars...."

That night a detailed description of Mary Rogerson was circulated over a wide area. The cat was out of the bag; the police were now directly concerned with 2, Dalton Square and everything that had happened there since Saturday, 14th, September.

‡

As though to meet them on their own ground, Ruxton himself walked into the police station two days later and saw Officer Winstanley.

"Look," Ruxton said, "I want to help if I can. My wife left home on the morning of Sunday, September fifteenth, and took the nursemaid with her. She said she was going to Edinburgh, but I don't really know where she went and I haven't heard a word from her since. She can't have much love for the children. Not even a postcard to any of them!"

"We are not concerned with your wife, Dr.Ruxton," Winstanley said.

"But they went of together," he persisted. "Wherever my wife is, you'll find Mary Rogerson with her! She's not at her sister's place at Edinburgh, because I wrote to her there and the letter came back unopened. See?...." He thrust a hand in his pocket and took out a bundle of letters. The top envelope was the one re-addressed by Jeanie Nelson. The rest were bills. "And look at these," he went on. "They're all accounts run up by my wife, mostly for clothes. There's one here from a Lancaster bookmaker demanding twenty-one pounds fifteen shillings for horse racing bets! But in spite of it all, I'd take her back willingly if she'd only return!"

"I must remind you again, doctor...." Winstanley tried to get a word in, but Ruxton was well away.

"Ask young Edmondson where she is. I wouldn't mind betting he knows! I've suspected those two for a long time and now I've got proof. Oh, I could tell you a lot of things, Winstanley! Can't the police intercept Edmondson's mail? If so, they're pretty certain to find a letter from Mrs.Ruxton! That would lead them to Mary Rogerson!"

"I'm afraid we have no authority for doing that," Winstanley said. "Now, if you take my advice doctor, you'll just calm down and relax. We'll let you know soon enough if we have any news of Miss Rogerson".*

This interview took place on Thursday, 2nd. October, and by the end of that week a team of experts, headed by Professor John Glaister, of Glasgow University, had begun to make a little headway in the grim task of sorting out the mass of bones, flesh and tissue discovered at Moffat. Their work had been hampered by the necessity of treating each separate component in formalin before it could be examined, such was the extent of decomposition and erosion by maggots. At this stage they were only able to state that the remains constituted those of two bodies, neither of which was complete; and owing to the fact that one set of bones appeared to be larger and heavier than the other, these *might* belong to a man, the other body being definitely that of a woman.

‡

The Scottish police, in turn, had acquired three possible leads. Firstly, among the various newspapers in which some of the remains had been wrapped was a copy of the special "slip" edition of the "Sunday Graphic" dated September 15, circulated only in the Lancaster and Morecambe district and containing pictures of the Carnival. Secondly, one of the heads had been wrapped in a pair of child's woollen rompers; and thirdly, a bundle containing two upper arms and four pieces of flesh had been wrapped in a blouse which, at some time or other, had been patched under the armpit. In due course, the police published photographs of the rompers and the blouse, asking for anyone who could identify either of these articles to come forward.

---

*   During the War the author met one of the officers who had been stationed at Lancaster at this time. He said: "Ruxton was forever running into the police station to ask if there was any news of his wife or Mary Rogerson. We felt pretty sure he had murdered the two women and that the object of these visits was not so much to divert suspicion from himself as to find out, if possible, what progress the police were making in their enquiries."

By now, Lancaster was seething with rumours. Whilst Bella Ruxton had not been officially reported as missing, it was common knowledge that the police were searching for Mary Rogerson and inevitably the two women's names were being linked with the dreadful discoveries at Moffat.

One morning, when Mrs.Oxley took Ruxton's breakfast upstairs, she found him lying in bed reading the morning papers. He was excited and the dark eyes, now slightly sunken in, shone brightly against the oriental colour of his skin.

"Listen to this, Mrs.Oxley," he cried, tapping the copy of the "Daily Express". He then read out a paragraph and added: "So you see--it's a man and a woman! It's not our two!"

"I should hope not!" exclaimed Mrs.Oxley, a trifle shocked. She was evidently not up to date with local gossip.

As she left the bedroom, Ruxton's high-pitched laughter rang in her ears.

His mirth was short-lived, however, for two days later the doctors announced that both bodies were unquestionably those of women!

‡

So far, Ruxton had made no attempts to get in touch with Jeanie Nelson. On October 6th, however, three weeks after Bella's "departure", he wrote her a long-winded letter beginning:

My dear Sister, I am heart-broken and half-mad. Isabella has again left me. She has done this trick again after about ten months. Do you remember she left me bag and baggage last November, when I came to your house?....The most important thing is that she is trying to help our maid who is in a certain condition....The children are asking for her daily and I really cannot sleep without her. Mine is only the temper, but in my heart she is my all in all. She has taken my 30 pounds and two gold coins....There followed a request for the addresses of various people with whom Bella might be staying; and the letter concluded: You must ask

her on your own to come back to me. I am surely coming to
see you on Wednesday afternoon at about four. Till then,
Yours affectionately, Bonnie.

This communication was answered by Jeanie Nelson's son, Jim, who had forbidden his mother to reply to it personally. The letter was scarcely couched in friendly terms, and drew yet another lengthy epistle from Ruxton to Mrs.Nelson. If she would not see him at Bothwell Street, would she at least go to her sister, Lizzie Trench's house in Edinburgh, where he would be at four o'clock the following afternoon? The letter continued, like the first, full of self-pity and complaints about Bella's extravagance and the bills which had come in since her departure.

There was not time for a reply to this, and the following day, October 9, Ruxton went to Edinburgh by train, arriving at Lizzie Trench's house to find Jeanie Nelson had complied to this extent and was already there; although the look of cold reserve on both the sister's faces must have warned him that his visit was anything but welcome. Ignoring this, Ruxton immediately became excited and words poured so fast that at times the two women found them incomprehensible.

"Tell me honestly--" he paused for breath, addressing Jeanie Nelson, "are you hiding her?"

She looked him straight in the eye and said: "Don't you *know* where she is?"

"What d'you mean?" He was momentarily taken aback.

"Have you *done* something to her?"

"Me? I wouldn't harm a hair of her head! I love her too much, you know that! Besides, I don't stand to make a penny by her death!"

Out came the story of Bobbie Edmondson and the Adelphi Hotel; of Mary Rogerson's condition and the laundry boy; of how Bella had suddenly changed her mind that Sunday morning and said she was taking Mary to Edinburgh.

"How could she do that," said Jeanie Nelson, "if, as you say, she took all her clothes with her?"

"Every stitch," Ruxton cried, "except an old leather motoring coat!"

"How could she have taken all that luggage without you knowing about it?"

"She did so once before, remember?"

"On a Sunday morning, she could only have gone by train. Have you made enquiries at the railway station?"

Ruxton paused with mouth agape. For once he was at a loss for words. Then:

"No," he said. "I'll--I'll do that as soon as I get back!"

It was ten o'clock by the time he left the house. He had done most of the talking, Jeanie Nelson and Lizzie Trench being scarcely able to get in a word. At the door, his parting injunction to Lizzie Trench was: "If anyone comes asking questions don't answer them!"

Had he but known, he might have saved himself the breath for this final remark because already the police were dogging his movements. The presence of the "slip" edition of the "Sunday Graphic" amongst the remains at Moffat had brought the Scottish C.I.D. into touch with their colleagues at Lancaster who, in turn, had been able to supply information, not only concerning a woman reported missing from 2, Dalton Square, but also of the fact that a copy of the newspaper had been delivered to that address on the morning of Sunday, September 15. Thus, when Ruxton arrived at Castle Station, Lancaster, in the small hours of October 10, he found himself greeted by the uniformed figure of Inspector Clark. Although the Lancaster police had been notified that Ruxton had boarded the night train out of Edinburgh, there was nothing exceptional about Inspector Clark's presence there, it being part of police routine to meet all trains arriving at that station during the night. Nevertheless, Ruxton seemed embarrassed.

"I've been to Edinburgh to try to find my wife," he said quickly.

"And were you successful?" asked Inspector Clark, who appeared quite friendly.

"No, unfortunately. I saw her sister and she doesn't know where she is. In fact, I saw two of her sisters."

"I've got a car outside, doctor. I'll run you home."

"That's very good of you, Inspector," Ruxton said.

On the way, he became talkative.

"Inspector--young Edmondson knows where my wife and nurse-maid are!"

"You think so, Dr.Ruxton?"

"I'm certain of it. I'll tell you...." Out came all the old suspicions, as well as a falsified version of the Edinburgh trip and the night at the Adelphi Hotel. He was still talking when the car drew up in Dalton Square. Inspector Clark had listened with only a mild display of interest, but later he put down in writing all that Ruxton had said.

As he got out of the car Ruxton repeated once again; "You ask young Edmondson at the Town Hall. He'll be able to tell you where my wife and nursemaid are!"

He did not mention to Inspector Clark, any more than he had to Jeanie Nelson and Lizzie Trench, that two days previously he had received a visit from Bobbie Edmondson and Mr.Edmondson senior during which the latter had asked:

"Are you inferring that my son is in any way responsible for your wife going away?"

"Oh no, no," Ruxton had assured him.

"Well, if I hear of you or anyone else mentioning my son's name in connexion with Mrs.Ruxton there'll be trouble!"

‡

On the same morning as Ruxton's return from Edinburgh, Mrs. Holmes, landlady of the Seattle farmhouse where the children had stayed during the Summer, recognized the pair of child's rompers, from the published photograph, as identical with a pair she had given to Mary Rogerson; and later identified them positively by the very special knot which she herself had tied when putting in new elastic. Almost coincidentally with this, Mrs.Rogerson recognized the blouse, also publicized by the police. It was in fact one she had bought at a jumble sale in Morecambe. More than anything else, she identified the patch under the arm which she had been at pains to sew in before giving the blouse to Mary. Although these two vital clues constituted the first major break-through by the police, the news was not immediately made public. Nevertheless, Ruxton must have felt the net beginning to close in, for his actions over the next two days became increasingly those of a desperate man.

Despite his assertion to Jeanie Nelson that Bella had taken everything except an old leather coat, at lunch-time that same day he was sharing out her wardrobe between Mrs.Curwan and Mrs.Oxley, putting only a few of the better clothes into a suitcase which, he told them, he would be taking to her sister at Edinburgh.

Since the day that Mrs.Hampshire had cut out the tailor's tag from the blue suit, he had only seen her once, when she had called at his surgery as a patient, and he had asked whether the suit had been sent to the cleaners. She had told him yes; although this was in fact untrue. Now, however, the suit seemed to have assumed a major importance once more; and on the afternoon of his return from Edinburgh he called at Mrs.Hampshire's house.

"Where is that suit?" he asked excitedly.

"Upstairs," said Mrs.Hampshire.

"Then, burn it! What about the carpets?"

"Your standing on one of them, doctor."

Ruxton looked down and grunted.

"Not too bad," he said.

"I couldn't do much with the other one. It was in a dreadful state!"

"Then burn it! Burn it, Mrs.Hampshire! What with all these rumours going round--d'you know the police are actually questioning me about Mary Rogerson?" He sat down, passing a hand across his forehead. He had been travelling all night and the dark eyes were heavy with lack of sleep. They also bore a haunted look. "I haven't a friend in the place," he went on, brokenly. "Mrs.Hampshire, will you stand by me?"

"I'll do what I can, doctor."

He rose: "I'm going to see the police and make a statement. They're bound to question you--but promise you won't tell them anything until I've made my statement?"

"Not unless I can help it," said Mrs.Hampshire, guardedly.

At ten o'clock that night Ruxton walked into the police station. He was in his usual excited mood as he was greeted by Officer Winstanley.

"Look Winstanley," Ruxton said, "all this damned nonsense is ruining my practice! Can't anything be done to stop the talk? Why, the newspapers are actually connecting my name with the remains found at Moffat! You've got to put a stop to it!"

"I'm afraid that's impossible,"said Winstanley. "We've no authority over the press, and although we're making enquiries into the whereabouts of Miss Mary Rogerson we're not in a position to make any statement."

"I'm doing everything possible to find my wife," Ruxton went on. "In the meantime, all these rumours are ruining my practice and driving me mad!"

"I suggest, Dr.Ruxton," said Winstanley, "that you give us a full description of your wife. We could then with your permission, circulate her as a missing person."

Ruxton paused before replying. This was the last thing he had wanted, for such a move would impose an air of finality, tending to negative the stories he had already put out about Bobbie Edmondson, and one or two other things besides. Moreover, in spite of Mr.Edmondson senior's stern warning, they had all parted friends and, to account for the return of the Hillman car without Isabella, he had told them she had gone to London. It was indeed the proverbial "tangled web". Yet, he reflected, to refuse the police request might arouse even more suspicion; and there was the added chance that Jeanie Nelson might take matters into her own hands and officially notify the Scottish police.

"Very well," Ruxton said.

Officer Winstanley proceeded to take down particulars in the form of a statement which Ruxton duly signed:

BUCK RUXTON STATES--*I am a medical practitioner and I reside at 2, Dalton Square, Lancaster. The following is a description of my wife. Name: Isabella Ruxton. Age: 35*

years....I would like discreet inquiries made by the police
with a view to finding my wife. She left home on Sunday,
15th. September, 1935, and I have not seen her since....

That night, Ruxton sat down at home and composed another
document, entitled "My Movements". Beginning with the morning
of Sunday, September 15, it recounted, in more detail than hitherto, the story of how Bella had changed her mind and gone off to
Edinburgh with Mary Rogerson. Thereafter it contained a day to day
account of all his movements up to September 29. These were, in
fact, no more than could be checked and borne out by the persons
he had met and spoken with, and gave no hint as to his nocturnal
activities--particularly over the vital period covering the 15th, to
the 18th, September --other than, *Home by 7*, or *Dressed hand. Went
to bed as usual.* Nevertheless, he seemed satisfied with the document
and thrust it in his pocket.

The following day, 11th. October, was one of continued rumours
and press reports. Ruxton went about his normal duties as a practitioner, although to many of the patients his mind appeared to be
wandering and altogether lacking concentration on the important
issue of their own particular ailments. Satisfied that Mrs. Hampshire
would have carried out his request to "burn everything", he did not
see her that day. If he had, she would doubtless have told him that
the police had paid her a visit the previous night and taken possession of the suit, as well as the blood-stained carpet which she had
failed to get clean.

Apart from routine questioning, and a brief inspection of the
interior of 2, Dalton Square, the police had as yet made no direct
approach to him or intimated their highly charged suspicions, and
this seeming complacency on their part played upon Ruxton's
nerves; so much so, that by ten o'clock that night he was again
hurrying up the steps of the police station. This time he found himself confronted by a group of high ranking officers, headed by Chief
Constable of Lancaster himself, Mr.Henry J. Vann. In fact, it was
evident that he had walked straight into a police conference of sorts,
and whilst many a man in Ruxton's situation might have hesitated

at the sight of such an austere, if not ominous, gathering, he went right up to the Chief Constable and shook him by the hand.

"My dear Vann, can't you do something about these newspaper reports?" He held out a copy of a national daily. "It says here that this women--they're trying to make out is Mary Rogerson--has a full set of teeth in the lower jaw, whereas I happen to know for certain that Mary had at least four teeth missing there!"[*]

Glancing around at the deadpan expression on the faces of all the officers, he flew into one of his tantrums, waving his arms in the air.

"This publicity is ruining my practice!" he shouted. "Particularly at a time when I'm negotiating a loan. I didn't want to tell you this, but....here are the papers...see?....It's a loan for eight hundred pounds."

Mr.Vann gave only a cursory glance at the letter heading and nodded: "I know the firm well."

"And all this business may well stop it from going through!" He thrust the documents back in his pocket and perched on the table, putting his feet on an upright chair. With his uninjured hand he began to thump the back of the chair. "This damned Bobbie Edmondson is ruining my home! One day I tapped a telephone conversation when she spoke to this man. It was all in lover's terms!" Tears had begun to run down his face. "Can't you stop all this trouble? Can't you publish it in the papers that there's absolutely no connexion between these bodies at Moffat and my wife and nursemaid?"

Mr.Vann said: "I'll do that, Dr.Ruxton, when we're satisfied that there is no connexion between the two!"

Another officer now approached him. "I'm Detective Inspector Green," he said, "and I'm making enquiries about Mary Jane Rogerson. I've seen her parents and understand that you told them she was pregnant. What reasons had you for saying that?"

---

[*]   This was an erroneous press report. Both the heads had a number of the teeth missing from the upper and lower jaws. Some of these were normal dental extractions, others had been drawn immediately before or after death.

152

"Well, of course, I haven't examined her," Ruxton said. "But then it doesn't need a doctor's examination to tell when a girl is pregnant." Never at a loss for a longwinded story, he warmed to the task. "It's like this--one day we had some friends for tea, and she was passing me to serve at the other side of the table when I noticed she was holding herself in a peculiar way..." here he treated the officers to a practical demonstration--"and it suddenly flashed through my mind that there was something wrong with that girl. I looked again and noticed that her face was pinched--but of course a women can often conceal her condition until she's six or eight months pregnant. I just noticed a slight swelling and, as a doctor, I'd say she was two to three months pregnant."

"You have stated, I think," Inspector Green went on, "that your wife and Mary Rogerson left 2, Dalton Square on the morning of Sunday, September fifteen. What luggage did they take with them and how did they travel?"

"I don't know because I didn't see them go, I was in the bath-room when my wife knocked on the door and said, 'I'm going now, dear'." Suddenly he began to loose control again, flinging his arms about. "I know what they're all thinking! Why don't you accuse me of the Moffat murders? Somebody'll be putting a dead baby on my doorstep and I'll be accused of killing it! My patients keep looking at my hand...."

"How *did* you cut your hand, Dr.Ruxton?"

"After my wife and the nursemaid had left that morning," he said, moistening his lips, "I went downstairs to get a tin of fruit for the children's breakfast. I took it upstairs to the bedroom and put it on the commode. I then inserted a tin-opener and began to hit it with a loose sofa arm. The opener slipped and gashed my fingers. Look...the little finger is completely dead!"

Three weeks and four days had elapsed since the injury was incurred and although the terrible wound had now healed super-ficially, it had left the little finger in a state of numbed paralysis. Hardened as the officers were, most of them looked away as Ruxton took a pin from his lapel and jabbed it into the mortified flesh.

"After that," he went on, "I held it under the tap in the bathroom. Then I went down to the surgery and wrapped a towel round my hand."

"Have you given any carpets away?" asked Inspector Green.

"The carpets on the stairs and landings were so worn that I gave my servants the privilege of taking them!"

"You told the servants, I believe, that the decorators were coming and that was the reason for stripping the walls and stairs?"

"Yes, but they failed to arrive. There was a mis-understanding. What's more--" his voice rose, "I'm glad they didn't come, because if the walls had been re-papered and new stair carpets put down everyone would be saying I'd done it to cover something up!...."

At any rate, nobody could say that Ruxton was not putting up a desperate fight; so desperate in fact that the following day, October 12, he committed two acts of folly. From the very attitude of the police the previous night, he must have known that they were bristling with suspicion; that it could not be long now before they took some decisive action. Whilst he was handicapped by not knowing exactly how many facts were already in their possession, it was essential, if possible, to remove at least one link from the chain of circumstantial evidence. With this object in mind he approached Mrs.Oxley. It was by now common knowledge, even to Mrs.Oxley, that the police were making widespread enquiries, and Ruxton, therefore, had no need of preliminaries.

"Oh, Mrs.Oxley," he said, trying to keep his tone casual, "if the police question you about that Sunday morning, tell them I came to your house about seven o'clock and said there was no need for you to come. Say I came again at nine o'clock and that you came to work here until eleven."

Mrs.Oxley looked at him in surprise: "I couldn't say that, doctor, it wouldn't be true!"

As Ruxton muttered something and walked away, she noticed that he seemed agitated. If it had been true and she *had* gone to the house at nine o'clock on that Sunday morning, what horrifying sights must have greeted her! Not even Mrs.Hindson, who delivered the milk, had been allowed over the threshold; and the police knew it!

Having failed with Mrs.Oxley, he drove to the Anderson's house and saw their maid, Dorothy Neild. Whilst he had accounted, in one way or another, for most of his daytime movements over the vital period, Thursday, September 19, left a blank. It was the morning he had told Mrs.Oxley he was going to see a specialist about his hand and had left the house early, after making several journeys up and down the stairs and out to the car while she was in the kitchen cooking breakfast. In "My Movements" he had stated that he went to Blackburn to look for Bella at the office she rented there, a bare thirty miles away; yet he could produce no proof of this. It was also the day he had promised the Anderson's to collect the children in the morning and had failed to do so, Dorothy Neild bringing them to Dalton Square while Bella was still absent. If, therefore, it could be said that he had called at the Anderson's place during the course of that morning, on a time schedule, it would negative any assertions by the police that he had made a final journey all the way to Moffat.

"Dorothy," he said, "you remember the week immediately after my wife and Mary went away?"

"Yes, doctor. I remember it well."

"I called here every day that week. Didn't I?"

"Yes, doctor, I think so."

"That Thursday, the nineteenth--I looked in that day--sometime during the morning. Remember?"

"Yes, I--I think you did, doctor."

"But are you sure, Dorothy?"

"Yes, I'm pretty sure, doctor."

"Good girl! Don't forget it now, will you!"

"No, doctor, I won't forget."

But she did forget; or rather, she remembered. Soon after Ruxton had gone, Dorothy Neil, thinking back over three weeks, recalled that particular Thursday; how he had been expected to call for the children and had not done so. She particularly remembered having to bring them all the way over to Dalton Square herself. No, the doctor had not been near the house that day! Later, when questioned by the police, she told them as much.

That afternoon the police called upon both Mrs.Oxley and Mrs. Curwan and took possession of the blood-stained carpets. They also took away all the clothes belonging to Bella Ruxton which the two daily helps had been told to share out between them. Somehow into this collection a blue beret had found its way and which Mrs.Curwan recognized as the property of Mary Rogerson. It also matched the coat, the charred remnants of which she had seen when sweeping up in the yard.

‡

At a quarter-past nine that night a Miss Bessie Philbrook sat knitting and listening to the wireless in the lounge at 2, Dalton Square. Upstairs the children were in bed and asleep. Miss Philbrook, a personal friend of Bella Ruxton, was fond of children and had frequently acted as baby-sitter since Bella's "departure". She had also accepted Ruxton's story of Mary Rogerson's condition and the reason for the two women's absence. Ruxton had asked her to come tonight as he was on call and might have to go out. To Miss Philbrook he seemed restless and pre-occupied and she could hear him pacing the floor downstairs. Suddenly the telephone rang. She heard him answer it and a moment later his footsteps echoed on the bare boards of the staircase.

"It was the Chief Constable, Mr.Vann," he told her. "He wants me to look in at the police station. You know there are lots of silly rumours going around about Bella and Mary. Anyway, I shan't be long. If any calls come through say I've had to go out and I'll be back soon."

As Ruxton left the house and crossed the cobble-stoned square in the direction of the Town Hall, did it enter his head that he might be doing so for the last time? Later, Mr.Vann was to be asked:

"When you sent for him that night had you made up your mind to charge him?"

"No."

If there had been a sizable gathering of police the night before, this was now augmented by officers from Dumfriesshire. Whereas Mr. Vann's attitude had hitherto been quite congenial, there was no smile on his face as he greeted Ruxton now.

"I think, Dr. Ruxton," he said, "that you can give some useful information in helping us to find your wife and the nursemaid."

"Of course," Ruxton said. "I'll be only too pleased to tell you anything I can."

"I propose to ask you to account for your movements between the fourteenth and thirtieth of September "

"That's easy! I thought you'd want it sooner or later...you'll find it all there!" With a flourish he produced the document, "My Movements", from his pocket.

Vann took it and flicked rapidly through the sheets, most of the officers present trying to catch a glimpse over his shoulder.

"That should be helpful," he nodded, handing the document back. "However, I should like something a bit more detailed--in the form of a signed statement from you. Of course, you are not bound to give this, but if you do so I must warn you that it may be used in evidence later."

Ruxton shrugged, and splayed his hands: "Anything you say! I'm only too willing to help!"

At Mr. Vann's invitation Ruxton followed him into a room across the passage. They sat on opposite sides of a table and, in the presence of several officers including Detective Inspector Green, while Ruxton dictated, Vann took down every word in long-hand. Whenever he came to the end of a sheet he handed this to Detective Sergeant Stainton who took it into another room to have it typed.

"I would like you to start at the very beginning," said Vann, "from the time your wife returned from Blackpool on the night of fourteenth--fifteenth of September."

Whereas "My Movements" was a day to day account, the statement which Ruxton now proceeded to make was, upon Vann's insistence, an hour to hour treatment. Yet, in all essentials the two were much the same. Parts were manifestly untrue and in conflict with explanations he had already put out to various witnesses; but in the main the statement sought to describe the movements of an innocent man and ill-used husband.

At the very beginning he gave his version of what happened after Bella's return from Blackpool on the Saturday night:

"My Elizabeth had given a children's party prior to school re-opening. Mary was with my children and she stayed in my house. She went to bed roughly about ten p.m. I had gone to my room by the time Mrs.Ruxton got back, after half-past twelve. e wee using separate rooms--last intercourse was Xmas 1934....I heard her come up the stairs and go to her room. As she passed she said, "Good night, Pa"....This is a dirty trick of the woman. She got up a little after six o'clock....She came to my room and in a coquettish manner said. "Want to go anywhere, Pa?" There was no definite arrangement as to place but we would go from the house. She said, "Get up, Pa" and seemed anxious to get me out of the house. I got up...and she said I should go to Mrs.Oxley, asking her not to come today....When I got back to the house Mrs.Ruxton was in the room previous to the kitchen, and Mary was in the kitchen....I went to my room and lay on the couch to await my coffee and toast. I waited nearly three-quarters of an hour in vain, and then went to the children's room where Mrs.Ruxton also sleeps. She was dressing. The children were asleep. I offered to help with getting the children ready, and she said there was no hurry, just to put me off. I went to the bathroom...I took off my coat and waistcoat and sat on the lavatory. I was sitting and thinking. When I was there, Isabel comes into the bathroom to powder and make up....She was making up and talking to me as she had to look in the mirror. The first mean action now. "D'you mind if I go to Edinburgh today instead of tomorrow?" I said, "Have you made up your mind?" because she had made me get up and lose my sleep. Anyone would get sarcastic with her. She then said,

"I am doing all this for your sake." She was referring to a football pool agency of Wm.Murphy which she had proposed to start. She meant as I had certain liabilities to pay off, if she could make money she would wipe them off for me. I said, "You can do what you like, you are not running away with my car again"....I went back to the bedroom. I took my trousers off and vest and put my pyjama trousers on again. My shirt was still on and I lay on the bed. I went again to the bathroom to make water. They were then ready to go and while I was in there she said, "I am taking Mary with me." I was rather glad because she couldn't abscond having Mary with her. She knocked and said, "Toodleoo, Pa. There's a cup of tea on the hall table." That was the only breakfast I got that morning. I heard them go out and the catch of the door fall...."

Whereas he had told Mrs.Hampshire he was wearing the blood-stained suit when he cut his hand, the statement went on to describe the tin-opener incident while he was still in pyjama trousers and the shirt he had put on that morning. The copious bleeding of the wound, coupled with various stained cotton-wool swabs and surgical towels, were put forward as an explanation for the vast amount of blood and burnt trappings seen in the house and yard. The statements seemed to pour from Ruxton, Mr.Vann asking no questions at this stage except occasionally to remark. "Well, we have reached seven o'clock on such and such a date. What happened next?"

Ruxton was clever enough to know that if he were ever to be charged with the murder of the two women in conjunction with the discoveries at Moffat, part of the case against him would be that he had made at least three journeys to the spot to dispose of the remains: during the night of Sunday, 15th., on the morning of Tuesday, 17th., (when in the hired Austin car he had been involved in an accident at Kendal on the way back), and on the morning of Thursday,19th. He had already told the police that he had tried to go to Seattle on the Tuesday but lost his way. Confident that he had an alibi in Dorothy Neild for the morning of Thursday,19th, he now told Vann:

> *"I went to the Anderson's late that morning and I did not go for my usual shave because it was late….I wanted to go to Blackburn to see the room which Mrs.Ruxton had furnished for the betting business….I intentionally went on Thursday because she would not be expecting me to spy on her on a Thursday. She would expect me on a Wednesday or a Sunday, my days off…I thought Mrs.Ruxton and Edmondson were meeting at this address in Blackburn….I thought this was a rendezvous for Bobbie Edmondson and her….I did not want them to know I had been there…."*

When it came to accounting for his nocturnal activities, particularly during the nights when the children had slept at the Anderson's, his story was almost naïve. Except where he could safely quote the exigencies of the Practice, it was, *"I was aimless. There was nothing to do--"* Or, *"I read a little and made out my bills, and went to bed as usual soon after midnight…."*

At twelve o'clock Miss Bessie Philbrook telephoned the police station to enquire how much longer Dr.Ruxton was going to be there. One of the officers spoke to her and said the Doctor was busy and would be unable to get away for a while. Would she mind remaining to look after the children?

By 2 a.m. Ruxton was still at it. He was feeling tired now and unable to concentrate. He told the Chief Constable as much and asked to be allowed to go home.

"All in good time," said Vann. "We shan't be long now."

It was in fact 4 a.m. by the time Ruxton finally completed his statement. It took him another hour and a quarter to read through the typewritten sheets, make corrections in ink, and sign it.

He had by then been detained at the police station for more than eight hours, but if he had hoped to be allowed to go home after signing the statement he was in for a disappointment; for Mr.Vann proceeded for the first time to put various questions. This interrogation lasted a further three-quarters of an hour, after which the Chief Constable left the room. His object was to confer with the officers from Scotland, and the consultation dragged on for more than an hour, while Ruxton was kept waiting in the adjoining room. Elsewhere, the police station was filled to overflowing with newspaper reporters who had got wind of a sensational development.

It was 7.20 a.m. when Mr. Vann finally returned and his face wore a grave expression.

"Listen very carefully to me Ruxton," he said. "I wanted to prefer a very serious charge against you. You are charged that between the fourteenth and twentyninth September, 1935, you did feloneously and with malice aforethought kill and murder one Mary Jane Rogerson. I must warn you that anything you say may be taken down and used in evidence at your trial."

Ruxton swallowed hard. He looked tired and bedraggled, his dark skin the colour of old parchment. Yet a certain fire still showed in the black, hooded eyes.

"Most emphatically not," he exclaimed. "Of course not! The furthest thing from my mind. What motive and why? What are you talking?"

Even these clipped sentences were taken down in writing and his signature demanded. He had been in the police station for exactly ten hours.

Poor Miss Bessie Philbrook! There is no record as to how she had spent the night.

Had the police taken a risk in charging Ruxton before the medical evidence was anything like complete.

Two women had disappeared from the same house on the same day. The mutilated remains of two female bodies had turned up in a ravine one hundred miles away. There was the evidence of the 'slip' edition of the "Sunday Graphic", the child's rompers and the blouse. These three items connected the Moffat remains with 2, Dalton Square; although, if Ruxton's account of the two women's departure was in fact true they could have taken all three items with them. There was evidence of vast quantities of blood in that house which Ruxton had been at pains to remove; the taking up of the stair carpets and the stripping of the walls; the nightly bonfires in the yard which involved the burning of much of Mary Rogerson's clothing. He had told obvious lies as well as conflicting stories to account for the two women's absence. In addition, he had tried to persuade at least two witnesses to make false statements.

All this evidence, though mostly circumstantial, would seem to provide a formidable case against the prisoner. Nevertheless, Article 768, Sect.9, of Halsbury's "Laws of England" states:

> "Where no body or part of a body has been found, which is proved to be that of the person alleged to have been killed, the accused person should not be convicted of either murder or manslaughter unless there is evidence either of the killing or the death of the person alleged to have been killed. In the absence of such evidence there is no onus upon the prisoner to account for the disappearance or non-production of the person alleged to be killed."

In other words, unless the remains found at Moffat could be proved, beyond the bounds of possibility or reasonable doubt, to contain at least part of the body of Mary Rogerson, the police case against Ruxton would automatically collapse.

Another three weeks were to go by before the full medical findings were made known.

7

The distinguished team of doctors who had undertaken the night-mare task of sorting out, examining, and re-constructing the mass of severed limbs and mutilated flesh was led by Professor John Glaister, Regius Professor of Forensic Medicine at Glasgow University, and included, among others, Professor J.C.Brash, Professor of Anatomy at Edinburgh University.*

The job fell into two categories: firstly, the thorough examination of all the remains by Professor Glaister and his colleagues; secondly, the re-construction of the two bodies by Anatomist, Professor Brash. From the start it was clear that the dis-articulation, or severing of the limbs, as well as the rest of the dreadful work had been performed by someone with a fair amount of surgical skill; each joint hav-ing been cleanly separated with a knife, as opposed to anything so crude as a chopper or saw. It was also evident that the mutilations had been carried out with a dual purpose: (a) to void subsequent identification, and (b) to hide the cause of death. Professor Glaister began by taking the two heads, which differed greatly in shape and size, and calling the smaller one Head No.1, and the larger, Head No.2. From the general characteristics, including the absence of any beard-growth, it was ascertained that both heads were undoubtedly female. In the case of Head No.1., both eyes had been removed and a large area of the face had been skinned. The right ear had been partly severed, the left ear completely so, as well as the nose and lips. Part of the scalp had been removed but a few hairs of a medium brown colour remained above the temples. On the crown of the head was an irregular shaped wound which took the form of the letter Y; and just behind this there was a cut, suggestive of a slicing operation. This *might* have been an unsuccessful attempt to

---

*   See "The Trial of Buck Ruxton", edited by R.H.Blundell and G.H.Wilson. (Notable British Trials)

cut out the wound.* There were also present two small fractures of the skull, one much deeper than the other, and the brain was congested. The two central incisor teeth in the upper jaw had been removed immediately before or after death, while six others--three in the lower jaw and three in the upper--were missing as a result of normal dental extraction over a period. There was evidence of bruising to the cheek and jaw, the former having been sustained during life, the latter probably after death. One further point: The tonsils were found to have a "craggy" appearance, as often occurs from chronic inflammation. In fact, under the microscope, definite signs of old inflammation were visible.

Head No.2. (the larger one) had been completely scalped and all the skin of the face removed except for a few tags left hanging down. Yet, one or two hairs of a light auburn colour were still clinging to the tissues. As with Head N0.1., the eyes, nose, ears and lips had been removed. In addition, the tip of the tongue had been cut off, while the tongue itself was swollen over and protruded beyond the margin of the gums. Only a few teeth remained in this head, most of them having been extracted after death, as evidenced by the hollow and fine edges of the sockets, the absence of blood clots, and the failure of any sort of contraction by the gums. There was also a space in the front of the mouth which *might* suggest that a dental plate had been worn. In the neck, the hyoid bone was found to be fractured on the outside; the hyoid being a small bone shaped like a horseshoe and situated just below the level of the floor of the mouth. This bone is so well protected that it is seldom damaged other than by the application of violence, such as strangulation. Although the brain matter in this head was soft through de-composition, there was evidence of congestion also.

It must be stressed that these eminent doctors carried out their examination without reference to any sort of "blue print" such as the known features and physical characteristics of the two missing women. They merely applied their skill and knowledge objectively,

* See page 119: Professor Glaister's evidence as to how Ruxton may have sustained the injury to his hand.

elucidating the facts and tabulating them. If, therefore, interested parties such as the police were anxious to attribute Head No.1. to Mary Rogerson, and Head No.2. to Isabella Ruxton, how were they doing so far? Details were as follows:

MARY ROGERSON: HEAD NO.1.:

Had brown hair	Strands of brown hair remaining.
Had freckles	Skin of face removed.
Had a cast in one eye	Both eyes removed.
Had at least six teeth extracted, by dentist	Eight teeth missing, two of which extracted after death.
Suffered from chronic tonsillitis	Strong evidence of tonsillitis.

ISABELLA RUXTON: HEAD NO.2.:

Had large, rather masculine shaped face	Similar shape.
Had light auburn hair	Traces of similar coloured hair.
Bridge of nose slightly undulating	Nose removed.
Had three teeth missing in upper jaw and wore dental plate	Most of teeth removed after death. Some evidence of dental plate having been worn.

‡

So complex was the medical evidence as a whole, that the average layman is apt to wince at the knowledge and brilliance of these experts, while the mind struggles to absorb the welter of detail. In order to understand the final, overall picture, therefore, it is prudent to leave Professor Glaister and his colleagues for the time being and move ahead to the work carried out by Anatomist, Professor Brash.

The task facing Professor Brash resembled that of two mammoth jig-saw puzzles, the pieces of which were all mixed up together in a single box. Some of the bones had flesh on them, others had the flesh and tissue removed or otherwise mutilated. Some were missing altogether. He, too, began by taking the two heads and calling them Body No.1. and Body No.2. He then sorted the limbs into pairs, forming a longer set and a shorter set; and, allowing for the missing parts, was satisfied that he had not more than two bodies to contend with. He fixed the two heads, side by side, to a platform which resembled a giant school blackboard.

Among the remains were two portions of trunk; an upper portion including the chest and shoulder-blades, and a lower portion containing the skeleton of a pelvis with a section of the vagina attached. The upper part of the trunk contained two lumbar vertebrae (individual bones and sockets forming the spinal column) and two cervical, or neck, vertebrae; the lower trunk portion embodying three lumbar vertebrae. These two trunk portions fitted together perfectly in the lumbar region; and Professor Brash now had a complete trunk. But which head did it belong to?

Head No.2. had been severed at a point which left five cervical or neck vertebrae still attaching to it. There are, in all, seven cervical vertebrae in the human body, and since the upper portion of trunk contained two of these it seemed likely that the trunk belonged to Head No.2. Professor Brash tried it and found a perfect fit, even to a small splintering of bone caused during decapitation. To make doubly sure, he tried the same assembly with Head No.1. but with negative results; especially since this head had only four cervical vertebrae, with a fragment of the fifth, attached. As though to clinch matters, X ray photographs were taken; and in addition Professor Brash cited fourteen other reasons to show that the assembled trunk and Head No.2. were part of the same body.

Since there was no trunk for Body No.1., he concentrated on the assembly of Body No.2., on the basis that whatever was left over must belong to Body No.1.

Taking the longer set of limbs he found that they fitted perfectly, not only at such joints as the elbows and knees but at the major junctions of the hips and shoulders. Again he carried out similar tests with the shorter set of limbs and found that with one exception--the humerus or upper arm--they did not fit. The socket into which the humerus fits to form the shoulder joint is not nearly so deep as those at most other main points of articulation, being chiefly formed by the overhanging portions of the shoulder-blade together with certain ligaments. Thus, while the larger set of arms fitted perfectly into the shoulder sockets, the shorter set fitted also, but nothing like so convincingly. In order, therefore, to remove any possible doubt, the ligaments, tendons and other soft parts were dissected, and with the aid of the microscope and X ray photographs it was shown conclusively that the longer set of arms belonged to Body No.2. and therefore the shorter ones could not.

In the end, Professor Brash had almost a complete body fixed to the "blackboard", with the flesh and tissue adhering to some bones and missing from others. Moreover, he was satisfied, by every means including the diametrical measurements of various bones, that they all formed part of one and the same body. Only the right foot was missing.

He then turned to the pieces that were left over in the double human jig-saw puzzle. In the absence of a trunk, or any part of one, he could only try re-assembling the limb joints, which were found to fit together perfectly; but again the absence of the trunk made it impossible to state with certainty that the limbs all belonged to the same body. Nevertheless, they formed a consistent pattern; and when age and sex were taken into consideration the general characteristics of the head, bones, and the flesh that remained on them left very little doubt that the shorter set of limbs all belonged to the same body as Head No.1. The same characteristics also showed that the body was unquestionably female.

When he had completed the re-construction of Body No.1., there was not a single bone left over, and the giant "blackboard" now displayed two female bodies assembled to the extent to which available parts permitted. Body No.1. consisted of the head, both upper arms and forearms with hands attached and both thighs and legs with feet attached; but no trunk. Body No.2. presented a much fuller picture with the presence of the trunk. All the limbs were present and attached, with the exception of the right foot which was never found.

Professor Brash's work, however, was not yet done. He had to determine the ages of the two women and their approximate heights during life. Again without any guide to the originals and using certain medical formulae, he gave it as his opinion that Body No.1. was between eighteen and twenty-five years old--probably between twenty-one and twenty-two, while the living stature he put at 4 ft. 10 ins. to 4 ft. 11 1/2 ins. In the case of Body No.2., the condition of the bones suggested a much older woman and, taking everything else into consideration, he estimated the age to be between thirty-five and forty-five, and the living height approximately 5 ft. 3 ins.

Mary Rogerson was twenty years old and 5 ft. tall; Isabella Ruxton was thirty-five years old and 5 ft. 5 ins. tall.

Although no bones were left over by the time Professor Brash had finished, forty-three pieces of flesh and soft matter, including three female breasts, still awaited allocation to either one body or the other. Among these also was the cyclops eye. Bearing in mind the de-composition and maggot activity present when the remains were first discovered, it is not surprising that the task of assigning this lot with any degree of certainty was found to be impossible. Of the three breasts, two were a pair and slightly pendulous, suggesting that the subject had born children. They probably belonged to Body No.2. The remaining one was round and firm, but in the absence of the nipple it was not possible to state if it was a virgin breast. Also amongst the soft matter left over, was a complete uterus and two portions of external female sex organs representing the genitals of two separate bodies. The uterus showed no signs of pregnancy, nor was this condition present in any of the other genital parts.

Despite the fact that pains had been taken to remove or mutilate most of those parts which might have indicated the cause of death, such as eyes, nose, ears etc., with Body No.2. the swollen tongue, the fractured hyoid bone together with signs of lung haemorhage, left little doubt that death had resulted from asphyxia by strangulation. In the case of Body No.1., however, the only signs of violence during life were the bruising and the two fractures to the skull; and whilst these fractures would have led to unconsciousness, they were insufficient to have caused death by themselves. It was, therefore, not possible, particularly in the absence of the torso, to assign the cause of death in this case.

Professor Glaister and his colleagues were of the opinion that both bodies had been drained of blood almost immediately after death.* This fact was determined by the absence of any clotting when they came to dissect certain vessels. It would also have enabled dismemberment and mutilation to be effected much sooner.

Looking at the remains of the two bodies now affixed to the "blackboard", what was the overall extent of those dreadful mutilations?

The right forearm of Body No.1. was not present when the remains were first discovered at Moffat. This had turned up some time later, with the hand attached to it, wrapped in newspaper. All the fingernails had been removed and were lying loose in the package. Now, from the "blackboard", it could be seen that the skin of this right forearm had been sliced off over a wide area, as had also the skin of the lower part of the thumb. In addition, the middle finger was completely denuded of skin and the finger-tip cleanly severed. By contrast, both the upper arms as well as the left forearm and hand of this body were almost free of mutilation. This also applied to both thighs, both legs and both feet.

Body No.2. was a different story. Most of the flesh had been cut away from the shoulders and upper arms, the forearms being left almost untouched. The tops of all the fingers of both hands had been cut off at the first joint and were missing. Practically all the flesh had been sliced from the thighs and both legs, but the left foot (the only foot present) was untouched in this respect. The toes,

---

*   See condition of bath at 2, Dalton Square when Mrs. Hampshire first saw it on the Sunday (Chapter 4 page 116).

however, had all been severed at the middle joint and were missing.

It has already been seen how the two heads compared with the known physical characteristics of Mary Rogerson and Isabella Ruxton, and how most of these had been deliberately removed by mutilation. How, then, in addition to the remarkable similarity in heights and ages, did this apply in the case of the two bodies? As follows:

MARY ROGERSON: BODY NO.1.:

Had 4 vaccination scars on left upper arm	4 vaccination scars present on left upper arm.
Had extensive birth-mark on right forearm	Right forearm denuded of flesh.
Had operational scar at base of right thumb	Base of right thumb denuded of flesh.
Had appendix operational Scar	Trunk missing.
Was a domestic servant	Left hand suggested that of manual worker.

ISABELLA RUXTON: BODY NO.2.

Had conspicuously bev-elled finger-nails	Tops of fingers all missing.
Her legs were same shape from knee to ankle	Flesh from both legs removed.
Had humped toes	Toes all missing.
Suffered from a bunion on big toe of left foot	X ray photo's of severed joint of big toe showed inflammation indicating presence of bunion during life.

Together with the two heads, the similarities in each case were blatant. Moreover, the mutilation or disposal of all those parts by which the two women might have been readily recognized had merely served to create an even stronger presumption of identity.

The cyclops eye? All the experts, including Professor Brash, were of the opinion that this was something quite extraneous to the rest of the matter submitted to them. In the first place, it was in a different state of preservation altogether; secondly, they deemed it more likely to belong to an animal as opposed to a human being. Nevertheless, a significant theory was to be put forward on this later.

The welter of medical findings, of which the foregoing is a mere peripheral sketch, were finally delivered during the last week in October; and on the 5th.November Chief Constable Vann, accompanied by Detective Inspector Green, saw Ruxton in the presence of his solicitor and further charged him with the murder of Isabella Ruxton, to which Ruxton replied: "No, certainly not!"

‡

Soon after Ruxton's arrest in October, Professor Glaister and his colleagues had carried out a thorough examination not only of the interior of 2, Dalton Square but of the carpets and stair-pads which had been given away to Mrs.Hampshire, Mrs.Curwan and Mrs. Oxley; also the blue suit. These were all found to have absorbed human blood in vast quantities. While drops of dried blood on the bannister of the staircase could have been caused by an injured hand, the clots discovered in various crevices on the side of the bath and elsewhere could only have found their way there by the pressure of a cold mass of flesh still in the process of bleeding. In his examination of the drains, Pathologist Dr.Miller also found traces of blood and human protein.

While Ruxton was in Strangeways Gaol awaiting trial, the prison medical officer, Dr.Shannon, carried out a close scrutiny of the injured hand. His conclusions were that such a cut could only have been caused by a very sharp-edged instrument such as the blade of a knife; a tin-opener could not have produced such an injury when used in the manner stated by Ruxton. He was also of the opinion that although a fair amount of bleeding would result from such a wound, this could easily be controlled by a doctor.

It had been possible to take finger and palm prints from the left hand of Body No.1. (Mary Rogerson) and identical prints were found in numerous places at 2, Dalton Square. In addition, Professor Brash had made plaster casts from the left foot of each body and these, allowing for the missing toes of Body No.2., fitted perfectly into shoes belonging to the two women respectively.

As though all this evidence were not sufficient, a final damning link connecting the remains at Moffat with 2, Dalton Square now came to hand. Some of the remains had been wrapped in a cotton sheet, which had been sent to the Testing House of the Manchester Chamber of Commerce for examination. On the bed in the room lately occupied by Isabella Ruxton only one sheet had been found--the lower one. This had also been sent to the Testing House and under microscopical examination by an expert, Mr. F.W. Barwick, it was found that the two sheets were exactly similar in composition, weave, weight, thread per inch, and in every other respect. Furthermore, Mr.Berwick was able to say that by a chance in a million the selvedge, or seam, of both sheets had been woven on a loom which had a faulty warp. This would not have affected the entire factory output because the fault would have been quickly spotted and the warp changed. Thus he could state that the two sheets were an identical pair, manufactured on the same faulty loom.

In view of this mass of evidence collected by the police it is small wonder that when Mr.Norman Birkett, K.C. (the late Lord Birkett of Ulverston) accepted the brief for Ruxton's defence, he saw little hope of obtaining a verdict. Nevertheless, like all brilliant men of his calibre, he was a fighter and at his best when faced with the heaviest odds. Years later, in a television interview, he was asked whether he had ever defended a person on a murder charge whom he knew to be guilty. The question clearly irritated Birkett as shown by his reply: "How can you defend a man you *know* to be guilty? The answer is, you never do. You are not permitted to do so. A barrister may *think* his client guilty; but that is a different matter." When asked about the Ruxton case, he said: "Nobody could read, as I read, all the facts the prosecution were going to prove, without thinking that, well, this is a very difficult case. But it didn't make me any less anxious to do everything that I could for Dr.Ruxton."

8

The trial opened at Manchester Winter Assizes on Monday, 2nd. March, 1936, before Mr.Justice Singleton. The Director of Public Prosecutions was taking no chances and had instructed Mr.J.C.Jackson, K.C. to lead Mr.Maxwell Fyfe, K.C. (later Lord Kilmuir) and Mr.Hartley Shawcross, K.C. (later Lord Shawcross) for the Crown. Mr.Norman Birkett, K.C. led Mr.Philip Kershaw for the Defence. Although Ruxton had originally been charged with the murder of Mary Rogerson, the indictment against him now only embodied one charge: that on a day between the 14th. and 29th. days of September, of 1935, at Lancaster, he murdered Isabella Ruxton. To this Ruxton pleaded not guilty.

From Mr.Jackson's opening speech it was clear both to on-lookers as well as the all-male jury that the case for the Crown was not only formidable but meticulously well prepared. In fact, long before he reached the end of his preliminary address many persons in court must have found themselves wondering why the prisoner bothered to put up any sort of defence, so heavily did each factor, as disclosed by Mr.Jackson, fall upon the hushed, tense gathering: the unhappy household at Dalton Square, the quarrels, the violence and threats of violence…the quantities of blood found in that house and the prisoner's suspicious behaviour, the buying of petrol on a Sunday and the burnings in the yard…to say nothing of the grim and significant evidence that would be given by the doctors.

Then came the witnesses in corroboration of all these damning facts. Starting with Mrs.Jeanie Nelson and followed by all the servants at 2, Dalton Square as well as Mrs.Hampshire, they passed through the witness-box like a cavalcade of accusing fingers; though most of them did so with obvious reluctance. So many things which had seemed of little importance at the time now assumed a horrifying significance. Poor Mrs.Hampshire fainted in the witness-box and as she was being carried out of Court, Ruxton leaned far over

175

the dock-rail, following the procession closely and exclaiming in a load, re-assuring voice: 'She'll be all right!"

Birkett could do little in cross-examination of these witnesses, other than to establish from each one of them the fact that Ruxton was normally a good husband, but excitable, highly-strung, and given to violent outbursts from which he would very quickly calm down. Nevertheless, he <u>had</u> scored a point with Mrs.Hampshire. It was the case for the Crown that throughout that first Sunday the bodies were lying dismembered, in the two locked bedrooms on the top landing. Yet, at seven o'clock that evening Ruxton had returned with Elizabeth to collect the children's night clothes and they had both gone upstairs together. Therefore, Birkett put it to Mrs.Hampshire:

"Did you hear him go into the children's bedroom to get their clothes?"

"No, I did not."

"It is quite clear that with this child the doctor went upstairs, and must have gone into the room of Mrs.Ruxton to get the children's night things?"

"He must have gone into one of the rooms, because he came down with the nightdresses in a case."

"How long do you think he was up there?"

"About three minutes."

"It would have been a very simple thing for Dr.Ruxton to say to the child, 'Stay here with Mrs.Hampshire while I go upstairs?' "

"Yes."

"But he did in fact go up with her?"

"Yes."

Mr.Justice Singleton then took over.

"Do you know," he asked, "whether they went right to the top of the house?"

"I don't know, but the fact that Elizabeth came down carrying the case herself...."

"Rather points to the fact that she had been to the bedroom to get the case herself?"

"Yes, I thought so," said Mrs.Hampshire.

It was a point in the prisoner's favour; though rather as if the smooth stone from David's sling had struck the shield of Goliath.

In his fight for Ruxton, Birkett was quick to pounce upon any such evidence as he thought inadmissible. For instance, whilst the prisoner was charged only with the murder of Isabella Ruxton, evidence relating to Mary Rogerson was admitted so far as it had a direct bearing on that charge. When it came to the identification of her clothing, Birkett was on his feet, demanding to know how far this was going to go. The Prosecution, he declared, was treating the matter as two indictments of murder instead of one! After giving Mr.Jackson a chance to reply, the Judge ruled that since the two women had disappeared from the same house, and particularly since parts of the two bodies had been found intermingled in at least one of the bundles at Moffat, the identification of Mary Rogerson had a direct bearing on the indictment for the murder of Isabella Ruxton.

Again, when the Chief Constable, Mr.Vann, began to tell the Court how, after Ruxton had completed and signed his statement, he had gone on to put further questions to him, Birkett was quick to object to this evidence. Citing Archbold's 29th. edition of "Judge's Rules", he quoted rules 1 and 7. Rule 1 stated: "When a police officer is endeavouring to discover the author of a crime there is no objection to his putting questions in respect thereof to any person or persons, whether suspected or not, from whom he thinks useful information can be obtained." Rule 7: "A prisoner making a voluntary statement must not be cross-examined and no questions should be put to him about it, except for the purpose of removing ambiguity in what he has actually said. For instance, if he has mentioned an hour without saying whether it was morning or evening...." Birkett maintained that since Ruxton had been detained in the police station since half-past nine the previous night he was virtually in the position of a prisoner and therefore Rule 7 applied.

After listening to lengthy arguments on both sides Mr.Justice Singleton finally gave his ruling: "The officer has said that the prisoner was not then under arrest. Notwithstanding that fact, I do not think evidence ought to be given about those questions. Under Rule 7 it may be that, technically, it was right the questions should be put, and that, technically, the questions and answers are receivable in evidence; but if it be the fact that the prisoner was there the whole night, even though he had not actually been taken into custody and charged, I think he was virtually in the same position, or ought to be regarded for this purpose as in the same position."

Ruxton was certainly getting a fair trial.

‡

Wisely, perhaps, Birkett refrained from disputing the bulk of the medical evidence. These eminent doctors knew their stuff much too well to be shaken or caught out in cross-examination. Moreover, they were scrupulously fair, never once stretching a point against the prisoner. Unless they could answer with absolute certainty, the tenor of their replies was, "This *may* be so and probably is so." Beyond that they would not go. On three issues only, therefore, did Birkett seek to strike back.

Among the many gruesome exhibits was a life-size photograph of the left hand of Body No.1. (Mary Rogerson). Upon close scrutiny a faint mark or line could be seen at the base of the third finger, such as might be found on a person who wears a ring all the time. It was now clear why Birkett had been at pains to extract from every witness who knew her the fact that Mary Rogerson never wore a ring, except occasionally on her day off. If it could be shown that this was indeed the mark left by the constant wearing of a ring it would cast serious doubt as to whether this was in fact the hand of Mary Rogerson, in which case there must have been the remains of three bodies present. The doctors, however, asserted that the mark in question was due, either to decomposition changes or else to shadow in the photograph itself. They were certain that no such mark was present on the original when they had first examined it.

Still on the subject of photography, in the lounge at 2, Dalton Square had been found a cabinet picture of Isabella Ruxton wearing a tiara, which had given a useful guide to the shape of her head.

This had been blown up to life-size and a similar negative of the skull of Head No.2. superimposed upon it. The result was not only horrifying and macabre, but showed a complete conformity both in size and shape. The process, known as Photomontage, was first practiced in Germany shortly after World War 1, particularly by the artist John Heartfield. The pictures took the form of grotesque caricatures and were used chiefly for the purpose of political propaganda. Today it is a recognized form of art. Such a process, however, had never before been introduced in a British Court of Justice and Birkett was quick to object to its admissibility on the grounds that this was "constructed evidence" and therefore liable to error. After much deliberation, the Judge expressed himself unable to exclude the evidence; at the same time he suggested that the Jury should bear in mind the liabilities to error.

"You may get a false value from a photograph at any time," he added, "and you may get a doubly false value if one photograph is superimposed upon another. On the other hand, it may be of use in some way."

Finally, there was the cyclops eye. How this had found its way into the remains at Moffat was something of a mystery, for (as already seen) the doctors declared it to be something quite apart from the rest of the matter submitted to them and in a different state of preservation altogether. They were also pretty sure it was an animal cyclops as opposed to anything human. Birkett, on the other hand, was ready to clutch at any straw. If it could be shown that this was indeed a human cyclops eye, the possibility of a human monstrous birth would immediately suggest itself and thus do much in support of Ruxton's story of Mary Rogerson's pregnancy. The advocate was also well known for scanning text books at a moment's notice and then confronting an expert on his own ground; and although the cyclops eye was not entirely within the province of the anatomist, it was to Professor Brash that Birkett now applied his smattering of hastily acquired knowledge.

"Did you recognize it as being a cyclops eye, either human or mammalian?"

"I formed the opinion that it was a specimen of that nature."

"Do you agree that in the animal cyclops eye the tapetum is always present?"

"That I cannot answer."

"In the present cyclops eye, is the dark pigment of the retina well developed?"

"It seemed to be."

"The dark pigment of the retina, which is well developed in this eye, as I suggest to you, shows it to be human, because you do not find that dark pigment well developed in the case of the animal cyclops?"

"That I do not know."

"No test was ever carried out to determine whether it was a human monstrous birth or an animal monstrous birth?"

"A section was made of it, but to my knowledge no test such as you mention was made."

It all sounded highly technical and no doubt the jury would have been duly impressed had not the Judge stepped in and rather spoilt things.

"How many of you," he asked Professor Brash, "have considered that cyclops eye altogether?"

"Four or five of us have all spoken together about it."

"Have you any reason to doubt that this is an animal and not a human cyclops eye?"

"I myself have no reason to doubt, but I do not claim expert knowledge of comparative anatomy of the cyclops eye."

"I am not sure that anybody else does," said Mr.Justice Singleton; and there the matter rested.

Such was the vast sum of evidence for the Crown that it occupied eight full days and was not concluded until early on the morning of the ninth. Birkett was then faced with the usual dilemma: whether to put the prisoner on oath in the witness-box and thus lay him wide open to the devastations of cross-examination. Failure to do this was always apt to create an impression that the prisoner was unwilling to face such questioning. Ruxton, however, was an unusual prisoner, emotional, highly-strung and unpredictable. How would he stand up to things? It was a gamble; yet one which Burkett was clearly willing to risk, for in a note to Ruxton's solicitor's the previous night he had offered three lines of defence, the third of which was to let the prisoner give evidence on his own behalf and by confining the evidence to this, so exercise the right of the final word to the jury. This course, Birkett emphasized, was in his opinion the best one possible in the prisoner's interest.

"*I entirely agree with you,*" Ruxton wrote back via his solicitor. "*I wish to give evidence on my own behalf and I also note that it is not in the interest of defence that further evidence should be called.*"

Thus, when Mr.Jackson at last rested the case for the Crown on the morning of the ninth day and Mr.Birkett rose and said: "My Lord, I call the prisoner," there was a tremendous stir in the court.

Ruxton was spruce, immaculately dressed, and looked surprisingly young as he stepped into the witness-box and took the oath. Apart from the dark skin and oriental features as a whole, it was difficult for onlookers to believe that this was the man and these the hands responsible for the unspeakable atrocities which, for more than eight days, they had listened to and at times seen for themselves.

Under Mr.Birkett's sober questioning he told the story of his life from the time he came to this Country; his meeting with Isabella Kerr (or Van Ess) and their subsequent life together at Lancaster.

"What do you yourself say about your relations with Mrs.Ruxton in general during the years from 1930 to 1935?"

"If I may be permitted to put it in appropriate English, I can honestly say that we were the kind of people who could not live with each other and could not live without each other...."

"You have added something else. Will you tell us what it was?"

"Forgive me the interruption, but my mind works in French. I just used the French proverb, 'Who loves most chastises most'".

"Were there quarrels between you during that time?"

"Not often."

"When quarrels arose how long did they last?"

"Oh, hardly two or three hours."

"After the quarrel had passed, what were your relations then?"

"Oh, more than intimate."

Often when a short answer would suffice Ruxton launched out on a virtual narrative. This drew a plea from Mr.Birkett: "I have a great deal to ask you, Dr.Ruxton, and I'm sure you will forgive my saying this: perhaps you will just deal only with the questions I put to you."

The kind of questions that he put, in fact, dealt for the most part with incidents alleged by Crown witnesses such as Eliza Hunter. Ruxton either denied these completely or, if they applied to words he had used, maintained that the witness had not heard him correctly. In dealing with events immediately following the night of Bella Ruxton's return from Blackpool, he stuck closely to the statement he had already made to the police. Wherever the evidence of Crown witnesses tended to incriminate him his answer was a complete denial of the facts. For instance, he denied that he had ever asked Mrs.Hampshire to burn the suit or to cut out the label. He had given her the suit on the Monday--not on the Sunday, as she had deposed--and never mentioned it to her again. Similarly, he denied the evidence of both Mrs.Hampshire and Mrs.Oxley that he had been out and about without collar or tie on the morning of Monday, September 16th. Mrs.Oxley was quite mistaken in saying he was not there when she first arrived for work at ten minutes past seven that morning. He himself had opened the door to her at that time.

"Mrs.Hampshire has said that you called at her house about nine o'clock on that Monday morning?" said Mr.Birkett.

"Yes, I heard her say that, without a tie and collar."

"Were you at Mrs.Hampshire's house at that hour on that Monday morning?"

"Never, never in my life!" He began to cry.

"She said that you were without a tie and a collar and that you were wearing an old, dirty raincoat?"

"That is ridiculous! I am so fastidious about my looks, especially as 40,000 people in Lancaster know me, and could anyone imagine I would allow them to see Dr.Ruxton at nine o'clock in the morning without a tie and a collar and wearing a dirty raincoat? It is ridiculous! It is a lie!"

He had an answer, or a denial, to everything, including his assertion to Jeanie Nelson that Bella had taken all her clothes with her. By this, he maintained, he had meant all her best and newest clothes; she had bought over a hundred pounds worth during the previous few months. The ones he had given to the charwomen were merely "cast-offs".

How did he explain the blood-stains on the stair carpets? They were old ones, incurred at the time when Bella had fallen on the stairs and had an immediate miscarriage.

The examination-in-chief lasted several hours and among the final questions put by Mr.Birkett were:

"It is suggested here by the Crown that on the morning of the Sunday after your wife had come back from Blackpool you killed her?"

"That is an absolute deliberate and fantastic story; you might just as well say the sun was rising in the west and setting in the east!"

"It is also suggested by the Crown that upon that morning you killed Mary Rogerson?"

"That is absolute bunkum with a capital B, if I might say it! Why should I kill my poor Mary? That child was dear to my heart. She was always treated as one of the family. I called her "My Mary". Tears were again streaming down his cheeks.

Nevertheless, it left an immediate opening for Mr.Jackson, as he rose to cross-examine.

"I understand that Mary was very dear to your heart and you were always very good to her?"

"Yes."

"And she was a very loyal girl?"

"Yes, I could stake my reputation on it."

"One who would never allow any harm to come to her mistress?"

"Yes, loyal to everybody. Mary was a good girl altogether, a 100 per cent girl."

"Was Mary the kind of girl who would stand by her mistress and defend her if she were attacked?"

"Yes, and would have stood by her master as well, or the children."

"Why is she not standing by you today if she is alive?"

The bolt went right home and Ruxton could only mutter, "I am very sorry I cannot fathom the workings of Providence. I cannot answer that."

Yet, on the whole he stood up to the searching cross-examination very well that day. Although circumstances made him an easy target, Mr.Jackson never once took advantage of this and his questions, though deadly, were always to the point.* When dealing with Ruxton's fanatical jealousy in the matter of Bobbie Edmondson, he asked:

"You believed her unfaithful. Did you believe her unfaithful with young Edmondson?"

"I will only say I am on oath in this box, and therefore I can only say that which I can prove, but certainly Isabella did give me strong cause to suspect."

"Do you believe it now?"

"Well, at no time actual misconduct, but I do believe her affections were transferred."

Pressed further by both the Judge as well as Counsel, Ruxton said that the mere thought of committing adultery was, by his moral code, just as wrong as the act itself and when he spoke of infidelity he meant just that.

Throughout the whole of that first day of cross-examination Ruxton had weathered the ordeal better than Birkett had dared to hope. In fact, he had shown himself to be a good witness, if at times giving extremely long answers and bringing in all manner of things

---

* "There can be nothing in the experience of an advocate at the Bar more distasteful than to have to cross-examine a prisoner who is being tried on a charge of murder...." Mr.J.C.Jackson in his closing speech to the jury.

irrelevant to the question; but seldom faltering and never at a loss for an explanation.

Many people were even of the opinion that if the cross-examination had ended there and then at the conclusion of the ninth day, it is possible that the jury might have given Ruxton the benefit of the doubt, so convincingly had he stood up to Counsel for the Crown.

When the court re-assembled on the tenth day, however, a marked change seemed to have come over the prisoner. He was jumpy, excitable, and appeared incapable of controlling his emotions.

Miss Roberts had been the first person to call at 2, Dalton Square on the fatal Sunday morning, to deliver newspapers. Dealing with her evidence, Mr.Jackson asked Ruxton:

"Do you remember Miss Roberts calling?"

"No."

"She says she rang three times before she got a reply?"

"I have no knowledge of that. I might have been upstairs."

"She tells us you opened the door just a little way and she apologized for disturbing you?"

"I do not recollect that."

"She says you were very agitated. What had you got to be agitated about at nine o'clock in the morning?"

"At nine o'clock in the morning? It could not be, because Bella left pretty well after nine. I am telling you, I never saw Miss Roberts!" He was beginning to lose his temper.

"May I suggest a reason why it took you so long to answer that door; that you were busy cutting up the bodies of your wife and Mary Rogerson?"

"May I respectfully say that my three children were in the house with me at that time!"

He was again in trouble when Mr.Jackson dealt with the blue suit. Ruxton had maintained that the vast amount of blood found upon it was the result of minor cases of surgery and attending numerous confinements over a period of years. He never wore a white coat. Mr.Jackson asked:

"Was that suit sent to the cleaners in August of last year and returned to you on August seventeenth perfectly clean?"

"My Bella does all the sending to the cleaners. I know nothing about it."

"Are you denying that this suit was cleaned in August and returned?"

"I could not answer it one way or the other."

"If it was cleaned, as I say, the whole of this blood has accumulated since August seventeenth?"

"I shouldn't put it that way. I don't know how to answer that question."

"Did you attend confinements in that suit?"

"Yes, many a time."

"Did you hear Professor Glaister say that no respectable doctor would ever wear a suit in that condition?"

This hit Ruxton where it hurt and he was beside himself with rage.

"Out of two hundred and thirty cases of confinement in Lancaster," he shouted, "Dr. Ruxton has never signed a death certificate, and you can go and see the Lancashire County Council who gave me five hundred guineas for my allowance! We go by results!"

"You would not agree with Professor Glaister when he said that suit..."

"May I say one word?"

"...would be a potential source of infection?"

"Just listen to the question," put in Mr.Justice Singleton; but Ruxton went on, unheeding:

"Has my learned friend read the life of Jonathan Hunter, the great surgeon?"

"Just attend to me for a minute," said the Judge.

"It is a disgrace! It is a reflection on my professional capabilities!"

"It will be better for you and for everyone in this Court if you will listen to the question."

"Forgive me; I'm sorry. I humbly beg your pardon." Ruxton had burst into tears. "Can't you see how I'm feeling? Everybody is cornering me and trying to get me in a corner!"

"Will you remember this," said Mr.Birkett. "I am watching the case for you and will deal with all these matters."

"I am grateful to you," Ruxton sobbed.

And so it went on, each question becoming more deadly, Ruxton constantly bursting into tears or else throwing fits of temper and hysteria. He was good at evasion too, as in the case of Mr.Jackson's final question, which concerned the sheet:

"If that is a sheet from off your wife's bed, can you explain how it got round those bodies at Moffat?"

"How could it be, sir? There is no such mention in the Court. You have made only a statement that some portion of the linen is the same fabric."

"If that romper, which has been identified, with the head of one of those bodies in it, was Mary Rogerson's romper….?"

"It couldn't be Mary Rogerson's romper! I respectfully submit how could it be? And why should Mary Rogerson have that romper? Would you expect my children to put on that sort of romper?"

But Mr.Jackson had already sat down.

In his re-examination of the prisoner, Mr.Birkett could do little more than clarify one or two points where Ruxton's hasty and lengthy replies might have left a wrong impression with the jury; also to emphasize once again his plea of innocence:

"Did you at any time do any act of violence at all to Mrs.Ruxton?"

"No. I honestly say so, as God is my judge."

"Did you make any journey on either of those days, or at any time, to Moffat to dispose of any remains?"

"No, sir, I say as God is the judge above."

‡

Because no witness other than the prisoner had been called for the Defence, Mr.Jackson's closing speech to the jury came first. The case, he said, had aroused enormous interest throughout the country and there had been many rumours and much gossip. In fairness to the prisoner the jury were to wipe out of their minds everything they had heard and read, and to judge the case entirely on the evidence which had been placed before them.

"What I am going to suggest to you is this," he went on. "That the evidence in this case is such that it must drive you irresistibly to one conclusion only--that the prisoner is guilty of the murder of Isabella Ruxton. In coming to a proper conclusion in this case, one of the things you will have to satisfy yourselves of is this: were those two bodies which were found at Gardenholme Linn on September twenty ninth, the bodies of Isabella Ruxton and Mary Rogerson? Because once you are satisfied of that, I submit you can have little doubt as to how they met their deaths...."

Once again there followed a recapitulation of all the damning evidence, stressed by Mr.Jackson in calm, deadly tones. On one occasion only did he seek to castigate the prisoner's character as a man. This was in the case of Mary Rogerson.

"Do you think for one moment," he asked, leaning far forwards in the direction of the jury-box, "that this doctor ever thought Mary Rogerson was pregnant? We have heard of the sanitary towels; we have heard the mother's statement that the girl was unwell in August; we have heard of the menstrual stains on the chamber in her bedroom. You have heard of the doctor putting forward this story as an explanation as to why Mary Rogerson went away. If it is not true, it is a most dastardly thing to say about a girl who is dead and not here to protect herself. But desperate needs often lead to the doing of desperate things and he had a desperate need to try to shut the mouths of Mr. and Mrs.Rogerson and keep them from going to the police...."

The speech was not a lengthy one, but Mr.Jackson evidently could not rid his mind of the fact that the brilliant oratory of Norman Birkett was to follow; and as though in anticipation of this he added in conclusion:

"You are not to decide this case on anything that I have said; you will not decide it on anything that my learned friend says, however eloquent he may be; you will decide it on the facts that have been proved."

The warning was not without justification, for the speech which followed was calculated to turn the heads not only of the jury, but many of the onlookers who had already convinced themselves long ago of Ruxton's guilt.

"This is the first moment," Norman Birkett began, "that a voice may speak on behalf of the prisoner...." The opening words at once tended to create sympathy for one who hitherto had been fighting a lone battle against heavy odds. Nor were certain aspects of Mr.Jackson's charge allowed to go un-reproached.

"I was astonished," he said, "to hear my learned friend say to you in his closing speech that if you were satisfied that the bodies found in the ravine were in fact the bodies of Mrs.Ruxton and Mary Rogerson, then your task was nigh completed. It seems scarcely necessary to have to say to you that if you are satisfied of the fact that in the ravine on that day were those two bodies, identified beyond a shadow of doubt, it does not prove this case. If, for example, the word of the prisoner is true, 'They left my house', there is an end of the case. Even though their bodies were found in a ravine, dismembered, it does not prove the case against the prisoner. The Crown must prove the fact of murder; and you may have observed how much of this case is conjecture....Mrs.Ruxton had gone away before and, it is surmised, came back on account of her affection for the children. It is beyond the bounds of possibility that she had finally determined to leave that unhappy household and that Mary Rogerson went with her?"

Without ever disputing the identity of the two bodies, he went on to stress that most of the evidence of murder was circumstantial. Whilst the medical evidence had indicated that Mrs.Ruxton died of asphyxia as the result of manual strangulation, the Crown had maintained that this took place on the top landing, in which case there would be no blood.

"With regard to Mary Rogerson," he went on, "the medical testimony says, *We cannot assign the cause of death,*" but my learned friend did not hesitate to tell you that on that top landing Dr.Ruxton probably used a knife. There has been no evidence of it. Nobody except my learned friend in his opening speech has appeared to suggest it."

Most of the evidence upon which the Crown relied, he emphasized, was based on events recalled at a much later date, and the human memory can be a very faulty and dangerous thing. An amazing feature was that immediately after the alleged murders Mrs. Hampshire, Mrs.Oxley, Mrs.Curwan and Mrs.Smith had been in that house day after day, without expressing the least signs of suspicion or doubt. Now, after a long lapse of time, they could recall any number of things giving rise to the gravest suspicion. It was part of the Crown's case that the prisoner had murdered the two women, drained their bodies of blood in the bath, and, having dis-membered them, made a journey to Moffat on the night of Sunday, September 16th, to dispose of some of the remains. It had rained heavily that night, especially in the Moffat district, *yet the car was seen to be perfectly clean on the Monday morning*--after an alleged journey of two hundred miles; nor was there any evidence that the slightest trace of blood or tissue was ever found either in the Hillman Minx or the hired Austin car. If there had been, the carefully prepared case for the Crown would undoubtedly have included any such evidence. As for the discolouration of the bath, this had been caused by rust from the dripping geyser.*

In much the same way as Ruxton had done, though more convincingly and without the hysteria, Norman Birkett put forward an answer to much of the incriminating evidence. Where this was not possible, or perhaps inadvisable, he threw the onus back on the Crown whose duty it was to "prove facts and not offer theories, however great the suspicion attaching". For instance:

"On the theory of the Crown he has murdered Mrs.Ruxton, but on September nineteenth, he goes to Blackburn to see if by chance he can discover her whereabouts, and all the Crown can do is to say," "*We do not think you went to Blackburn. We cannot prove, of course, that you did not, but we shall tell the jury that in our view you did not go*

---

* There was in fact a permanent but entirely localized rust stain at the foot of the bath, due to a leak in the geyser.

to Blackburn. We think you went somewhere else, where, we do not know, to do something we do not know but which we think had something to do with the murder on the previous Sunday...."

In all, it was a magnificent speech and might well have succeeded in implanting that tiny seed of doubt in the minds of the jury which calls for an acquittal. But the summing-up was to follow; and no matter how impassioned a plea has been made on either side of the Bar, the judge's cold, down-to-earth assessment of the evidence invariably infuses a sense of reality. In this case Mr. Justice Singleton's charge to the jury was no exception. It began first thing on the morning of the eleventh day and was delivered with that impartiality which is the keynote of British Justice. He made due allowance for Ruxton's highly-strung nature and his displays of emotion in the witness-box, and stressed that every consideration should be given to his evidence as much as to that of the Crown. Only when he came to deal with the state of the house at Dalton Square did the judge emerge momentarily from his calm, unruffled dignity. Pointing to Exhibit 37 which was one of the blood-drenched carpet, he said:

"Can you think from what you have seen in this case that either the miscarriage of 1932, wherever it happened, or the cut hand on the fifteenth of September, 1935, can account for that blood?"

In paying tribute to the doctors, his Lordship said: "No one could sit in this Court and listen to the evidence of Professor Glaister, without feeling that there is a man who is not only master of his profession, but who is scrupulously fair, and most anxious that his opinion, however strongly he may hold it, shall not be put unduly against the person on his trial; and the same applies to the others. Again, I should like to say that I find it difficult to imagine greater care and greater skill being used than was used by these distinguished Professors of Edinburgh and Glasgow Universities in the putting together of these pieces, in their examination, and in arriving at their conclusions."

Whilst Birkett had not pursued the matter of the cyclops eye, the Judge now made passing reference to this:

"No doubt you wondered at one time in this case what was coming about the cyclops eye; a most unusual thing to find....Has it anything to do with this case now?....I think I am right in saying on behalf of Professor Glaister and Professor Brash that they have no doubt it is animal....All I ask you is, has it anything to do with this case? If it has, give weight to it; but do not let flimsy possibilities take your minds off the evidence."*

The summing-up lasted until 3.50p.m. and concluded: "Let me end as I began by saying, if there be any doubt in it, the prisoner must have the benefit of that doubt. If there be none, let your verdict be equally clear and let justice be carried out. Will you consider your verdict?"

‡

It was a tribute to the defence that the jury took as long as one hour and four minutes to reach a verdict of Guilty; yet the result could have come as a surprise to few, least of all, perhaps, to the prisoner himself. When asked the usual question whether he had anything to say why sentence of death should not be passed upon him, Ruxton appeared perfectly calm. Gripping the dock-rail firmly, he said: *"I want to thank everybody for the patience and fairness of my trial. I have never attempted to pass any restrictions. I should like to hear what his lordship has to say about it."*

What in fact his lordship had to say was, of course, the time-honoured, ritualistic pronouncement, uttered from beneath the square of black cloth and with the Prison Chaplain at his elbow ready to intone "Amen".

It was all over.

---

*   A generally accepted theory later was that Ruxton had possessed a cyclops specimen preserved in formalin; that he had needed formalin when coping with the viscera of the remains, and in hastily poring the liquid from the bottle, had jettisoned the specimen as well.

9

Apart from the horrific nature of the medical evidence with its two hundred and thirteen dreadful exhibits, the Ruxton trial has left little to posterity; certainly no grounds for eternal controversy. The jury's verdict has never been in dispute. Yet, one or two points emerge.

In the first place, nobody, it seems, took any serious trouble to study the state of Ruxton's mind, the Prison Doctor being almost entirely pre-occupied with the injured hand which, in view of the welter of other evidence, was not all that important. Nowadays, the psychologists would be quick to swarm around a man like Ruxton and to probe the depths of his subconscious, not so much in an endeavour to explain away the crime itself and its shocking after-math (he was sane enough during this latter period and fiendishly clever), but to examine his whole conduct over the five years imme-diately preceding. The excitability, the fits of violence, the periods of high elation followed by morbid bouts of self-pity and tears.... All these symptoms pointed to a certain mental illness known to the specialists, whilst the unwarranted jealousy fixation would undoubtedly be put down to a paranoia; a paranoia, as defined by the psychologist Emil Kraeplin, being; *"The insidious development of a permanent unshakable delusion system, with complete preservation of clarity and order in thought, will and action."*

Even this and a lot more Freudian mumbo-jumbo would scarcely have altered the outcome of the trial in Ruxton's case. At best, it might have helped in some measure the subsequent but unsuccess-ful petition for a reprieve which was signed by no less than eight thousand people in Lancaster alone.

Again, it is strange that no reference was made on either side at the trial to one significant line in Ruxton's statement to the police: *"Last intercourse was Xmas 1934...."* If true, how came it that they had not lived together as man and wife for nearly nine months? Had Ruxton grown tired of her? Or had Bella refused him--as well she may have in view of his general behaviour? If the former was the case, why had he been at pains to get her back every time she left or threatened to leave? If the coldness was on Bella's side it could only have added fuel to the existing jealousy, driving him in the end completely out of control.

Such are the anomalous procedures of Law and Justice in England, that a person may be charged with several murders but only stands trial for one, the other charges being held in reserve in case of an acquittal. If an acquittal does ensue, the other charges are seldom proceeded with. Ironically, therefore, it is almost certain that the death of Bella Ruxton, for which Ruxton stood trial, was an accident, whereas the death of Mary Rogerson, for which he was *not* indicted, was cold-blooded murder. The prosecution which, quite rightly, pulled out every conceivable stop, tried to make capital out of the fact that on the previous Friday (the day before the children's party) Ruxton had told Mrs.Curwan not to come again until Monday. It would seem little short of childish to suggest that the two killings were pre-meditated. Far more likely that Ruxton, seeing Mrs.Curwan was not feeling any too well, and with the solicitude of his profession, told her to take the week-end off and have a good rest. She even stayed away on the Monday also, with a bad headache. In fact, it is not hard to picture the scene upon Bella's return from Blackpool that fateful Saturday night. The old row had cropped up and he had accused her of spending the evening with Bobbie Edmondson--or perhaps some other man, just by way of a change. His hands had been around her throat before, but this time he went too far, unable to control the fierce emotional drive. Her screams and dying struggles awakened Mary Rogerson who, when she burst in upon the scene, found her mistress already dead. Panic then took over.

Short of giving himself up to the police, Ruxton had no recourse other than to silence this only living witness; and the few moments which followed were undoubtedly the most dramatic and terrible of this whole story. What exactly happened will never be known for certain. Even the doctors could not tell. It was a secret which Ruxton took with him to the grave. Therefore, however, with the two women lying dead at his feet, the rest of the story was made only too clear by the brilliance of Professor Glaister and his colleagues.

Without seeming in any way to condone the atrocious work, it must be remembered in all fairness that Ruxton, like Crippen, was a doctor, and doctors undergo a long and arduous course of training during which they are taught to regard the human body with complete objectivity. Visit the Dissecting Room at any big hospital where students are attached, and naked corpses of both sexes and in every stage of butchery can be seen lying around on tables. Students take pieces back to their digs for homework. In order to keep up morale, they laugh, joke and sing bawdy songs at the expense of Human Anatomy. Once a student shows signs of being squeamish, he may as well give up hope of becoming a doctor--least of all a surgeon.

On this basis only, the work carried out by both Ruxton and Crippen is more understandable by far, than is that of a man like Norman Thorne who, without any previous knowledge or experience, merely hacked and sawed Elsie Cameron's body into convenient portions for disposal.

ACKNOWLEDGEMENTS

"The trial of Buck Ruxton", edited by R.H.Blundell & G.H.Wilson.

(Notable British Trials Series) Published by William Hodge.

National Daily and Sunday Newspapers - September 1935 to April 1936.

"Lord Justice Birkett" by Dennis Bardens (Robert Hale).

"Norman Birkett. The Life of Lord Birkett of Ulverston" by H.Montgomery Hyde (Hamish Hamilton).

Editor's Notes:

1. A petition and appeal for clemency was dismissed on April 27th, and Ruxton was subsequently **hanged** at "Strangeways" prison, Manchester on the morning of May 12th, 1936.

2. Mary Rogerson's remains were buried at Overton churchyard, near Morecambe.

3. Ruxton disposed of the body parts in Moffat, in an area now known as "Ruxton's Dump".

4. 2, Dalton Square, empty for decades after the murders, was eventually gutted and remains non-residential. The bath, Ruxton used to dismember his victims was later used by the mounted police as a horse trough.

5. This crime was publicly known as *The Jig-Saw Murders*.

"Chief Inspector Chapman would like a word with you," he
said. "Can you come to headquarters right away?"

Manton displayed no signs of alarm at this request. Perhaps
he had been expecting it. He knew that the eldest girl had been
questioned by the police; but so, for that matter, had half the
population of L... over a period. This, he told himself, was
purely routine. [...] sure that the
police had been in and out of the Fire Station most of the day, or
that he himself was the subject of their enquiries.

Then, [...] awaited him
he appeared calm and confident. The Chief Inspector was seated at
a table and motioned his visitor to a chair opposite. This was the
first time Chapman had [...] what he now saw
surprised him. He was [...] nt and this mild-
mannered, [...] rm was his
No.1. Suspect. [...] both
Inspector Fin[...] n the room
as Chapman add[...]

After introducing himself (somewhat unnecessarily, it would
seem but no less in strict accordance with police procedure), he
went on: "I'm investigating the murder of an unknown woman whose
body, unclothed and trapped in sacks, was found in the River Lea
on Friday, November 19, last. In this connection I'm also enquiring
into the whereabouts of certain missing women." He paused and
looked closely at Manton. "I understand your wife is not with you.
Can you tell me where she is?"

Four Sacks for a Shroud

(Rex v. Manton)

"We had a quarrel and she slung her hook. I havn't seen her since."

(Manton to Chief Inspector Chapman, of New Scotland Yard.)

1

Thursday, November 18th.1943, was the last of Bertie Manton's four days leave from the National Fire Service and on the morning of that day relations between him and his wife, Rene, were passably cordial. On the surface, at any rate, things appeared that way, though he could never be certain nowadays that she was not about to erupt in a tirade of complaint and abuse. Matters had been like that for some time now and he had learned to live with it for the sake of the children--two girls and two boys. Soon they would all be home for lunch and Rene Manton was preparing a meal in the kitchen of their modest home, No.14, Regent Street, Luton.

Manton was forty years old; short, but sturdily built. In his youth he had been something of an amateur boxer, though his manner was anything but pugnacious. Rather he was of a quiet, unassuming disposition and always ready to help other people. The present Chief of Luton Fire Service, who had been a colleague of Manton at that time, recently described him as, "One of the nicest, quietist and most helpful persons you could hope to meet." He was one among several sons of a much respected working-class Luton family who were connected with the green-grocery business, and such was their continued unity that even now Bertie Manton seldom let a week go by without visiting his elderly parents on the other side of the town.

Of his own four children, the eldest girl, aged 17, and the two boys, 16 and 14 respectively, had left school and were working; only the youngest girl, aged 8, still attended the local Council School. Whilst all the children displayed some family likeness, the eldest daughter was a complete replica of her mother. She had the same dark brown hair, bobbed and parted in the middle; the same brown eyes with the thick brows above them; the same strait, rather prominent nose and an identical smile. Together, the children were the biggest factor in Manton's life and everything he did was aimed at the furtherance of their welfare and happiness. If he could earn a bit extra in his spare time by helping out behind the bar of the local "Plume of Feathers", the money was not spent on beer and cigarettes but in providing a few more home comforts, particularly where the children were concerned. In return, they thought the world of him. Although he was not serving with any branch of the Armed Forces, they were proud of the job he was doing with the National Fire Service. In fact, he was something of a hero in their eyes, cutting a dapper figure in his uniform with its silver buttons, the huge buckle of the belt, the steel helmet and the respirator slung over his shoulder. Sometimes he would come off a spell of night duty with his face begrimed and the fumes of smouldering timber still exuding from his clothes. He was also a driver of the fire engine and on occasions they had been thrilled to see him thundering through the streets of Luton at the wheel of the massive vehicle. There was the added fact that during the past year or so the children had seen much more of their father than of their mother, for twice she had been away from home for long spells at a time and, with the help of the eldest girl, Manton had kept the house going, looking after them all with meticulous care, never spending an unnecessary moment out of their company.

In all the circumstances, therefore, "Bertie" Horace William Manton would seem to be just about the last person likely to become involved in a murder.

‡

As with most families in Britain, the conversation at lunch that day inevitably drifted towards the latest war news: The bombing of Berlin, the success of the Allied Armies in Sicily and the resignation of Mussolini, despite the smug bleatings of Lord Haw Haw. Soon enough it was time for the children to return to their various duties, but not before they had all helped to clear the table and stack the dishes neatly in the kitchen. There had been no sign or hint of the dreadful tragedy that was to follow. One moment the house had echoed to the clamour of young, happy voices; the next it had resumed its former, somewhat uneasy quietude.

Outside, it was a raw November day, but the parlour was cosy enough with a bright coal fire burning in the grate. Manton drew up two armchairs, one on either side of the fireplace.

"Sit down and have a rest, Rene," he said. "Don't worry about the dishes, I'll see to them presently. Would you like a cup of tea?"

"That would be nice," she nodded. Before easing herself into the chair, she smoothed down the heavy creases in the dress about her waist and thighs, for, after a lapse of eight years, Rene Manton was once again pregnant, five and a half months....

2

Before World War II the population of Luton was in the region of 70,000; an industrial town just north of London, noted chiefly for the manufacture of straw hats and Vauxhall cars. As with almost every other town in England the outbreak of hostilities brought sweeping changes. New factories sprang up, many existing ones being converted and geared to the war effort. Troops were stationed in the vicinity, flooding the town's bars and cafe's, and congesting the roads with lorries and heavy armoured vehicles. More than anything else, however, the upheaval and disruption was to hit everyday family life. Husbands left home to serve with the Forces. In every strata of society women abandoned either their plush drawing-rooms or the kitchen sink to go out and work in offices and factories, many experiencing for the very first time the company and daily intimate contact of men other than their husbands. The result was inevitable: Serving men who had torn themselves away from a clinging, weeping wife, returned home on leave to find a subtle change, a chilly response, in some cases even an ill-concealed lack of welcome. If they, too, had succumbed to the many similar temptations thrown in their path they did not expect it of their wives. The cost of human life and limb was bad enough, but the toll of broken marriages as a direct result of the war has never been listed.

In a simple way the marriage of Bertie and Rene Manton was a typical example and one which would never have echoed beyond range of their immediate friends and relatives but for the tragedy that accompanied it.

In 1926 Manton had married a local girl, Irene Caroline Seagrave Bavister, the wedding being something of an occasion within the social sphere of the two families concerned. After the honeymoon, and the novelty of the first year of married life had worn off, they settled down into a pleasant if somewhat commonplace groove, children being born at varying intervals. Rene proved herself a good wife and mother, Manton an equally dedicated family man. Money had always been tight, but they had managed somehow and for more than sixteen years were reasonably happy.

That was until the war came and in 1942 Rene Manton went to work in a local tobacco factory.

The change did not take place overnight, of course. After sixteen years as a tied housewife it would take most women time to become used to the new daily routine, the new friends and environment, above all the newly found freedom. In Rene Manton's case, however, the roots of domestic life were to prove remarkably frail. Her hours at the factory were from 9 a.m. until 5.30 p.m. and soon enough she began to get home late from work; later each day and often smelling of drink. Whereas she and Manton had always enjoyed a moderate session together in one or other of the many "locals", it was now clear that Rene was dropping in on her way home. More-over, in addition to her friends from the factory the pubs were full of soldiers eager for feminine company. She had also learned to use foul language and if Manton ventured to ask where she had been, he was told in suchlike terms to mind his own business.

Although tolerant to a degree, Manton was not prepared to see the children neglected. His own, far more important job with the Fire Service made it impossible for him to be there every day when they returned home from work or school and, as a result, there were quarrels.

"I kept calm as long as I could," he said later, "in order to avoid trouble in front of the children."

Nevertheless, matters could scarcely continue in this way and a crisis was reached one night in November of that same year, 1942, when, according to Manton, Rene did not return home until after 11.30 p.m., the worse for drink and in one of her more truculent moods. She was wearing a two-piece dress, the back of which was covered in what appeared to be brick dust. He also noticed a stain on the front of the skirt. In answer to his inevitable question, she replied in a slurred voice:

"It's none of your business, but if you must know I've been to the Alma Dance Hall!"

"Who with?"

"Ha! Wouldn't you like to know!" Then, seeing his gaze fixed on the front of her skirt, she unhitched the waistband, stepped out of it and flung the garment across the back of a chair.

"What's more," she added defiantly, "I had a bloody good time!"

Wisely, Manton refrained from pursuing matters that night, but in the morning, after the children had all gone off, he made it clear that he had had enough. During a sleepless night he had reached the conclusion that as a wife and mother Rene had ceased to be of use. Worse still, she was a bad influence on the children--or would become so if they got to know the half of what was going on; and at this rate the truth could not be kept from them for much longer.

Perhaps he had hoped, in the sober light of day, to make one last appeal to get her to mend her ways, but the effort mis-fired and only blew up into a monumental row in which he told her to clear out. It seemed she needed no second bidding, for, by the time the children returned home for lunch that day, Rene Manton had packed her bags and repaired to her mother's house in Church Street.

Mrs.Bavister was in poor health and almost blind. It was easy, therefore, for Manton to explain to the children the reason for their mother's sudden departure: She had "Gone to look after Grannie for a while." Just how long this vague term implied Manton had no idea. He only knew that, as matters stood at present, Rene was better out of the way.

Somehow they managed between them, the children all lending a helping hand about the house and taking it in turns to go out in the evenings so that the youngest girl was not left alone if Manton had to be on duty at the Fire Station. When Christmas came it was scarcely the usual happy family affair; and by early Spring Manton had begun to have second thoughts. This was no kind of life for the children; they needed their mother--not the women he had virtually thrown out of the house, but the old Rene he had known and loved. Perhaps after all these months she had grown weary of the gay life and complete freedom from responsibility. Perhaps she, too, was missing the children and her home and would like to return; but it would have to be on his terms.

He went to see her. Surprisingly, she agreed; and by March, 1943, Rene Manton was back at No.14, Regent Street.

‡

Some estranged couples who effect a reconciliation enjoy a second and better honeymoon, followed by a life of continuing compatibility. Others are not so fortunate. Although the Manton's resumed full marital relations they failed to recapture the old, original harmony. In Manton's own words: "Somehow, things were not the same." She had kept on her job at the tobacco factory, but now, to begin with anyway, returned home in good time to see to the children and the house. Yet, there were quarrels and she was forever complaining about something. To give Rene Manton her due, she had at least two good grounds for grievance. In the first place she had never approved of his going to work in his spare time as a potman at the "Plume of Feathers", chiefly because she disliked the barmaids there, denouncing them as an immoral lot. Perhaps in the early days she had even been a bit jealous of them; although Manton's sole interest lay in earning something extra for home comforts. During her absence he had found little time to indulge in this added occupation, but soon after her return he began going there again. Secondly, if a reconciliation is to succeed the past must be forgiven and forgotten. Yet, whenever there were rows between them Manton was in the habit of bringing up her former conduct, never allowing her to forget it. Fortunately, the children were unaware that anything was wrong. For them, at any rate, life had returned to normal.

The leopard, however, does not readily change its spots. Having once had a taste of independence--and goaded no doubt by the many bickering's in private--by the middle of June, Rene Manton had again begun to stay out late at night. Further rows were inevitable and once again she walked out, this time of her own accord, and went back to her mother in Church Street.

For Manton, the wheel had thus turned full cycle and he was again left to cope with the house and the children.

Just how long this state of affairs might have lasted will never be known, for this time providence took a hand in things. Either by co-incidence or else because it ran in the family, Rene had a younger married sister who was also at loggerheads with her husband and three weeks after Rene had left home for the second time the sister did likewise, also parking herself on old Mrs.Bavister. The little house in Church Street, however, was not large enough to accommodate both of them, and since the sister had come from some distance away, it was Rene who had to give up her room. Short of going to her brother as far off as Grantham, she had no option other than to return home like a prodigal.

However much it may have cost in the way of pocketed pride to go back to Regent Street, there was an added reason for doing so: She was pretty certain by now that she was pregnant. Although she did not confide this to Manton in the beginning, he went out of his way to make her welcome and for the first time for nearly a year they settled down to a life of comparative harmony. Yet, even this was not to last.

Despite everything, including the night she had returned from the Alma Dance Hall, he could not bring himself to believe that Rene had never been unfaithful in the ultimate sense, although the possibility had always preyed on his mind. It was not until the middle of August, by which time she had again become disgruntled and complaining, that she told him of her pregnancy; and since conception must have taken place during May, well before she had started going out again, he was unquestionably the father and was overjoyed at her news. She, on the other hand, made no bones of the fact that she did not want the child.

"She was very nasty to me about this," Manton said later.

To a women advanced in pregnancy the smallest grievance is liable to be magnified tenfold. When she does not want the child she is expecting the emotional disturbances may be greater still. Although Rene Manton exercised some restraint in front of the children, during the weeks that followed the atmosphere between herself and Manton became increasingly volcanic and one in which she was liable to erupt under the slightest provocation. At other times she could be reasonable, docile and quite pleasant. Manton withstood these tirades and vicissitudes with stoical patience, hoping that after the baby was born, things would be better.

And who knows? Perhaps they might well have been. Yet, these were the conditions prevailing at No.14, Regent Street on that fateful afternoon of Thursday, November 18, 1943....

3

Manton came through from the kitchen carrying two steaming cups of tea which he placed on a low table in front of Rene. Before settling himself in the armchair opposite, he kicked aside a wooden stool that stood in the way. It was an old article of furniture, already broken once and somewhat clumsily repaired. Rene looked up from the paper she was scanning, her thin lips parted in the semblance of a smile as she nodded her thanks. She was in the habit of keeping those lips closed, particularly when not wearing her dentures, for she was a trifle self-conscious of having lost all her teeth at the early age of thirty-five. In fact, many of the roots still remained in her jaw, for she had refused to have these extracted and the shrinkage of the gums, therefore, was comparatively slight. The thick black eyebrows tended to give her a severe expression, but when she smiled--all too seldom nowadays--this seemed to melt and she could appear quite attractive.

It was some weeks since Manton had been to the 'Plume of Feathers', not wishing to upset her or cause any added rows. Owing to her condition, she too had given up her job at the tobacco factory and they were thus relying solely on Manton's salary from the National Fire Service and the few shillings which the three eldest children contributed from their wages towards the house-keeping each week. All this was barely sufficient, especially with the new baby coming along, and Manton was eager to avail himself of the extra money that was there for the earning; for the proprietor of the place, whom he called 'Eric', was only too glad of his help and there was a standing agreement that he could go there at any time.

Manton had been thinking things over while making the tea. He was not due back at the Fire Station until the following day. Rene had been in a good mood all morning. Perhaps she would not mind if he put in a few hours at the 'Plume of Feathers' that evening. At any rate, she must know that the extra money was needed.

He had barely seated himself in the armchair before he came out with it, keeping his tone as casual as possible.

"Well, Rene," he said, "I think I'll go and help Eric out tonight."

He could have said nothing worse. They were the very words needed to spark off an explosion and he was totally unprepared for what followed.

"All you think of is those bloody cows!" She had risen and a shower of abuse and foul language poured from her lips. Before he could stop her she had seized her cup of tea and flung the contents straight into his face. His left eye received the bulk of the scalding liquid, the remainder splashing across his face and into the other eye. He was momentarily blinded, shock and pain adding to his confusion. He stood upright, clawing at his face as she came at him with fists flailing. He could still scarcely see and in self-protection thrust out an arm. His hand connected tightly with her throat and, using all his weight, he sent her staggering backwards. She hit the wall hard and rebounded, lumbering forward until she was at the table again. He was still half blinded but could see enough to know that she had seized the other cup of tea and was about to throw it.

He could not stand a second dose; the excruciating pain from the first was bad enough and his vision remained blurred. He had put up with a great deal during the last year, this normally quiet, docile man, but there is always a breaking point somewhere and a fierce, uncontrollable anger now took over as he grabbed the nearest weapon for protection. It was the wooden stool and he swung it crazily from right to left like a battle-axe. He felt the dreadful crunch of bone and flesh as it connected at the first swing. Before he could stop the momentum it had connected a second time, though with much less force. The piercing scream which had risen in Rene's throat was stilled on the instant and she hit the floor with a sickening thud. After that there was only a dead silence in the little parlour.

Manton stood by the fireplace, panting. The whole ugly business had occupied only a matter of seconds and his vision was still blurred from the effects of pain, shock and the fierce anger that had assailed him. The temper quickly subsided and, as his vision cleared, he glanced down as though in a nightmare at the bloody mess on the floor. A moment later he was on his knees beside her, cradling the mashed head and face in his lap. He had even begun to cry with fear and remorse; remorse, because even he could not excuse himself for the terrible blows inflicted on a defenceless, pregnant woman. The severity of these was born out by the very state of the room, for her blood was spattered everywhere, on the floor, the walls--even on the ceiling.

Whatever Manton's thoughts and emotions during those grim moments of silence, they were quickly replaced by a new fear, a new panic: the children! They must never see this. They must never even know....

He glanced down again at the dreadful thing in his lap. Already the features were swollen and distorted out of all recognition. Not a breath stirred in the nostrils; not a nerve or a muscle twitched. She was dead, he told himself, and there was nothing he could do--except from the children....

In fact she was still alive!

‡

When the children arrived home for their tea that afternoon they appeared to notice nothing amiss. If their father was looking pale and his hands a trifle shaky they did not remark upon it. Only the youngest girl asked:

"Will Mummy be back tonight?"

"I doubt it," Manton said. "You know how poorly Grandma has been lately. She had to go over there again."

He could not bring himself to look at the eldest girl. It was as though Rene had come back to life, rejuvenated. The likeness was uncanny and had already begun to haunt him. When she told him she had a date that night he seized the opportunity to suggest that the other three should all go to the pictures. They were delighted, especially when he thrust a hand in his pocket and gave them the money.

By six o'clock that evening Manton was once again alone in the house.

4

In the early morning of November 19, Luton was wrapped in a thin veil of fog. On the outskirts of the town, along a path bordering the River Lea, hundreds of people, some walking and some on bicycles streamed towards the Vauxhall Motor Works. If any of them had glanced down the bank at the river below they could see very little at that early hour, owing to the mist and semi- darkness. Thus, all of them filed unwittingly past a certain spot where there was a gap in the bushes on the bank and the ground fell steeply away, allowing fishermen and others to scramble down to the edge of the water. It was not until 2.30 p.m. that day, by which time the fog had lifted and pale Autumn sunshine was seeping through, that two sewer men employed by the Luton Corporation arrived at this spot to carry out a daily routine check on the level of the river. Immediately, they spotted a bundle of sacking lying in a few inches of water close to the bank. It was caught and held there by overhanging branches, the current not being strong enough to carry it downstream. However, it had not been there the previous day.

At first they thought it must be an animal of sorts, for in war time, with the scarcity of food, many people disposed of domestic pets in this manner. Soon, however, as the two men grabbed the sack and hauled it to the bank it became clear that this was no domestic pet. Indeed this was no animal, but something much more sinister. Only when they had half lifted and half dragged the heavy, partially sodden bundle to the top of the bank and laid it on the grass did they realize the full horror and enormity of their "find".

She was completely naked and wrapped in four sacks split open at the seams to form an improvised shroud. Her legs were drawn up in a pre-natal position and tied tightly together above the ankles with string which had bitten into the flesh. It was the terrible injuries to the head and face, however, which convinced the two sewer men that they were gazing at the victim of a brutal murder.

215

‡

When the police arrived at the scene, immediate investigations were taken over by Detective Inspector Thomas Finch, of Luton C.I.D. Clearly, the killing had taken place elsewhere and the body conveyed by some means to this spot and allowed to roll down the steep bank into the water, where it had lodged in the silt. The fact that the bundle was only wet to the extent of a few inches, precluded any possibility that it had entered the river higher up and floated down; and since the two sewer men were certain that it had not been there the previous day, this operation must have been carried out during the twenty-four hours elapsing between their two visits, probably sometime during the night.

Footprints were out. The soft mud of the tow-path and its surroundings had been churned by a myriad of feet and bicycle wheels-- chiefly from the early morning cavalcade of workers approaching the nearby Vauxhall car factory. Further downstream a bridge spanned the river and at the foot of this were the single tyre marks of a car which at first looked like a promising lead. Later, however, these were traced to a milk van using the same route daily and were thus eliminated. Of the four sacks in which the body was wrapped, two were nondescript; the remaining two were potato sacks bearing the name of FRANK REDMAN. This was a firm of wholesalers, distributing potatoes all over Luton and the surrounding district, and although strictly speaking the sacks were returnable in war time, the company, it transpired, kept no records. The string binding the women's legs together, as well as that used to truss up the body, could have been obtained anywhere.

Inspector Finch was quick to realize, therefore, that the case must hinge largely upon identification of the victim and that this was likely to present a problem. There was not a stitch of clothing with the body; no rings or jewelry and no distinguishing marks other than an appendix operational scar--and how many women had that? Moreover, the severe head and facial injuries had caused so much swelling and distortion that this poor women's death-mask could bare small resemblance to the original during life. Perhaps the medical evidence would help.

After a preliminary examination by the police surgeon, the body was taken to the mortuary at Luton and Dunstable Hospital to await an official autopsy.

Meanwhile, news of the discovery had spread rapidly throughout the Town and, as always in the absence of any constructive details, wild rumours and theories were in circulation, supplanting for the time even the latest war news as a topic of conversation.

On the following day, November 20, instructed by the Home Office, Dr.Keith Simpson, the well known pathologist, carried out a post-mortem examination and although his findings were of little immediate help to the police, in the light of subsequent revelations his deductions and theories were to prove remarkably accurate.

The body, said Dr.Keith Simpson, was that of a well-proportioned young women aged between 30 and 35 years. She was 5ft.3ins. tall with very dark brown, bobbed hair and brown eyes. *Lineae gravidae* scars (lines or creases across the base of the abdomen) showed that she had born at least one child; and at the time of death she was again five-and-a half months pregnant. Slight chafing and swelling of the gums denoted that she had worn dentures, but these were missing; whilst X-rays of the jaws showed that the roots of several teeth had been left behind after extraction. There were no deformities of any kind and no distinguishing marks upon the body other than an appendix scar. When he examined the body *rigor mortis* was fully established but had not yet begun to pass off. This would place the time of death at somewhere during the afternoon or evening of November 18 -19. She was certainly dead when placed in the water.

There was bruising about the throat, said the Pathologist, that suggested an attempt at strangulation by the application of a right hand from the front. This grip had been released and then re-applied a second time and there were signs that she had struggled violently, whilst bruising of the elbows, hips and spine showed that she had been either flung or pressed hard against the floor or a wall during the process. Although there was evidence that a fair amount of strength had been used, no neck bones were broken and neither of the two grips had been fatal or near-fatal. Death was in fact due to a single violent, crushing blow delivered to the left side of the head and face with some blunt-edged weapon (possibly a rifle stock). This had split the ear open, crushed both the upper and lower jaws as well as the cheek bone and loosened the skull bones on that side, causing congestion of the brain. A second blow, much less severe, had been sustained on the right side of the head either from the same weapon or else by striking her head on a piece of furniture when falling.

Although the first blow would have caused immediate unconsciousness, said Dr.Keith Simpson, death had not supervened for a further half to three-quarters of an hour. *She was still alive when the legs were tied together, but dead when the string had been tightened around the sacking....*

‡

After a post-mortem examination of this nature there are generally a number of minute clues found during the process, such as hair fibers from the assailant's clothing, or tiny particles of skin under the victim's finger-nails, all for microscopical study later in a forensic laboratory. In the present instance there was nothing whatever, other than the body itself and the story it told. Even the nail scrapings yielded no more than a few particles of coal dust. Either the killer had taken ultra- precautions or else good fortune was on his side.

The blood group 'O' was established, samples of head and pubic hair retained and the dead women's fingerprints taken. Most macabre of all, the feet were preserved in the hope that shoes might be found to fit these at some future date

‡

In all the circumstances, Luton police felt the case to be beyond them, particularly with their reduced war time strength, and the Chief Constable, Mr.G.E.Scott, applied to London for help. On the day after the post-mortem, therefore, Chief Inspector William Chapman, of New Scotland Yard,* accompanied by Detective Sergeant Judge, arrived to take charge of investigations.

Like his Luton colleagues, Chief Inspector Chapman was quick to see that identification of the victim was the only key to the whole business and his very first step was to create what must have been something of a precedent in modern British crime detection by publicizing a close-up photograph of the corpse. This was a profile shot of the face and neck taken from the right side where the injuries were less severe and thus less likely to horrify or offend; even so, the swelling and distortion were sufficiently pronounced. The picture was flashed on the screen at all local cinemas and displayed in many shop windows, with the following caption:

Murder

The police are anxious to establish identity of
this unfortunate woman. Here is her picture....
If any person can help please communicate
with POLICE IMMEDIATELY.
Her description is....

Details supplied by Dr.Keith Simpson as to age, height and colouring, together with the five-and-a-half months pregnancy was the best that could be mustered.

Thirty-nine people came forward, thinking they could help, and were shown the body. Thirty of these failed to recognize it; the remainder made various identifications, all of which were later shown to be wrong. In the general round-up, four hundred-and-four missing women were either found or else eliminated from the case; and while this mammoth task was in progress a squad of foot-slogging detectives tramped from house to house in Luton, showing the photograph of the corpse and asking two questions: (1) Is anyone missing from this house? (2) Do you know this woman? Two hundred-and-fifty lorry drivers who had called at the Vauxhall

---

* The late Chief Superintendent (C.I.D.) William James Chapman, who died in 1956 whilst still serving with the Metropolitan Police.

car works on November 18th. and 19th. were traced to various parts of the country and questioned. None of them could help the police. Every dentist in the area was visited, all of whom failed to recognize either the photograph or the dental chart drawn up by Dr.Keith Simpson. Somewhere, somehow, Chief Inspector Chapman argued, the killer must have disposed of the victim's blood-stained clothing and every rubbish dump, every bit of waste ground--even private dustbins--were scoured in a search for garments or pieces of garment; for, with the tight rationing of clothing nobody threw out the smallest strip that could be used for patching or "making-up". In all, it was one of the biggest murder hunts ever laid on by the police in time of war.

It got them nowhere.

‡

Meanwhile, at No.14, Regent Street life continued on much the same lines as it had during the past year or so when the mistress of the house was absent. By now, the Manton children were more than accustomed to their mother being away, "looking after Grandma". Manton's time was fully absorbed between his duties with the N.F.S. and the demands of the house and home, but whenever possible he continued to lend a hand behind the bar at the "Plume of Feathers". Nobody, in fact, noticed the slightest change in his manner or appearance.

Bertie Manton was certainly "playing it cool".

There had been a big round-up of Redman's potato sacks, particularly in clubs and institutes such as the N.A.A.F.I., and the canteen at Luton Fire Station was no exception. Here, although records were supposed to be kept, a number of these sacks could not be accounted for. The answer lay simply in the fact that many of the members (Manton included) were in the habit of buying potatoes through the canteen at a reduced price, taking them home and failing to return the sacks. In addition, one enterprising fireman who ran a side line in cooked meat and pies had also supplied his colleagues with Redman's potatoes, thus aggravating the general muddle. However, beyond a tightening up of regulations all round, nothing was done and the matter soon blew over.

Unlike London, in provincial towns people are apt to make it their business to know as much as possible about their neighbour's affairs. Living next door to No.14, Regent Street were a Mr.and Mrs.Parr, and although this couple were remarkably un-inquisitive and thus an exception to the rule, Mrs.Parr had been on friendly terms with Rene Manton and would often drop in for a chat. She had, in fact, done so on the morning of November 17th, when the two had talked together for some time. On the day after the finding of a woman's body in the River Lea, Mrs.Parr again looked in and Manton told her that Rene was with her mother in Church Street. Mrs.Parr called yet again on November 21st. and this time Manton said that she had gone to stay with her brother at Grantham. Mrs. Parr was thus effectively deterred from calling again for a while.

Nevertheless, in all Luton the breath of suspicion seems to have crossed the mind of only one person. This was Mrs.Parr's husband, who said to her one day: "You know, that woman found in the river could be Rene Manton! The description fits her perfectly--and five-and-a-half months pregnant--d'you think I ought to tell the police?"

"Nonsense," said Mrs.Parr. "You'll only make a fool of yourself if you do!"

Some days later, when a detective called as part of the house to house canvassing, Mrs.Parr failed to recognize the dead woman's photograph. The same detective called next door at No.14 and the door was opened by one of the boys, who was the only person home at the time.

"Is your mother in?" the officer asked.

"No, she's away looking after my Grandma," said the boy.

"Is anybody missing from this house?"

"No."

"Do you recognize this woman?"

The boy studied the grim photograph for some seconds then shook his head.

How close can you get? How often do the hunters all but tread upon a fugitive hiding in the undergrowth and pass on?

Police enquiries continued unabated, but by Christmas they had made no headway whatsoever.

‡

For the second year running the Manton children spent Christmas without their mother. On Christmas Eve, however, Manton received something of a jolt. All the children were out and he was thus alone in the house when he answered a ring at the front door to find Rene's mother, Mrs.Bavister, peering at him through her thick lenses. Making one of her rare excursions nowadays she had brought the family a rabbit to help out with the Yuletide fare and it came as an equal shock to the old lady to find her daughter absent.

"She's in London," Manton said, quickly recovering from his confusion at the unexpected visit. "Staying with friends. Hasn't she written?"

"I haven't heard a word!" Mrs.Bavister was both mystified and a trifle annoyed. "I do think she might have dropped me a line!"

"Don't worry," Manton went on hurriedly. "She's quite well and I'm sure you'll be hearing from her soon!"

Mrs.Bavister had to be content with these assurances for the time being. Moreover, it was not long before they were seemingly justified, for, during January of the New Year she received four letters signed "Rene". Owing to her failing eyesight these had to be read out to her and the contents of all four letters ran on similar lines: the writer was staying at Hampstead (spelled "Hamstead"), was quite well and hoped to be returning home in time for the birth of the baby. Two of the letters bore a Hampstead postmark, the remaining two had been mailed from St.Pancras, the London Main Line station serving Luton. The dates of posting, in fact, corresponded with Manton's leave days from the Fire Service.

As with Mrs.Parr, old Mrs.Bavister was thus discouraged from pursuing matters, at any rate for a while.

Nevertheless, from two other sources enquiries were being made as to Rene Manton's whereabouts: by the local Food Officer regarding her ration book and by the District Nurse who wanted to see her in connection with the pregnancy. The latter had called at the house on February 2, and, finding nobody at home, left a note. Manton told the Food Officer that she was at present living at Grantham and in a written reply to the mid-wife he gave the same explanation.

Although an immense amount of time and public money had been spent on police investigations into what had become known as the *"Luton Sack Murder"*, by the middle of February they were no wiser than on the day the body had been found in the river; and in the absence of any such developments local interest in the case had long since petered out. Chief Inspector Chapman, however, was not yet ready to admit defeat and ordered a complete review of all the facts and clues in the case. Clues? There *were* no clues, other than the four sacks and the string used to truss up the body. At police headquarters, however, a heap of rags and other oddments of material retrieved from various refuse dumps had piled up, and although these had already been subjected to a cursory examination, each bit of tattered cloth was now scrutinized more carefully.

On the face of things it would seem that the heap of nondescript rubbish could hardly be expected to yield any constructive information. Yet, as the detectives worked laboriously at their task, for what it was worth a pattern of sorts did emerge. In the pile was found a number of pieces of black material, all of exactly the same texture and quality. Some of the fragments were badly singed as though they had been on the very edge of a fire and thus escaped the main conflagration. There were no manufacturer's tabs or other markings on any of the pieces, yet when all placed together they appeared to form part of a garment of some kind, possibly a woman's coat. Nothing sensational about this discovery, but the material was placed on one side while the officers continued their probing.

Then, a day or so later, Fate or Coincidence--or perhaps a combination of the two--came up with one of those uncanny tricks, the kind of trick that no author of fiction would dare to try out, even on the most gullible of readers. A detective engaged on the case was walking home and took a short cut which led him across a patch of waste ground. There, he was amused at first to see a mongrel puppy playing with a dirty piece of rag. The dog was growling and shaking the object violently in the manner of its natural predatory instincts. Then something about the piece of material caught and held the officer's interest and after a good deal of coaxing he managed to retrieve it from the animal's reluctant jaws. As he examined it closely, despite the mud and the dog's saliva he felt sure that this was in fact a piece of black cloth remarkably similar to those segregated from the pile of rags at police headquarters; the more so, since it bore signs of having been partially burnt. Most important of all, inside the sack part of the lining some letters or numbers were faintly visible which could be a cleaner's code mark.

So impressed was he by the coincidence, that the officer turned and went straight back to headquarters with his "find". There, when all the dirt and grime had been removed, the piece of black material was found to match up in every respect with the other pieces which had been placed on one side. Moreover, under a magnifying glass the code marks left by a firm of cleaners or dyers were plainly legible.

Still nothing sensational, but at least here was something to bite on, something to follow up; and Chief Inspector Chapman bestowed a well deserved pat on the back to the detective responsible, if only by way of encouragement.

It took the better part of a day to trace the firm of cleaners involved and less than an hour for them to consult their records. The article in question, they said, was a lady's coat, handed in by a customer eighteen months previously to be dyed black.

And the name of the customer? *Manton, 14, Regent Street, Luton.*

A sensational development at last! A woman's coat had been dyed black eighteen months previously, subsequently burnt and the remnants thrown away. It could mean everything or nothing.

A glance down the list of addresses already visited by the police in the house to house canvass with the photograph showed that 14, Regent Street was among them; but this time Chief Inspector Chapman was taking no chances. He went there himself and in answer to his ring the front door was opened by the eldest girl. Chapman had long since formed in his own mind what he thought was a fairly accurate picture of how the dead woman must have looked during life--*and here, confronting him, was the complete but youthful replica!*

In that second Chapman knew that the case was as good as broken wide open.

‡

Even the strongest "hunch" of a high ranking police officer falls far short of the evidence necessary before taking any definite action. It was a matter of enquiries and still more enquiries; and not until two days later, at 11.45 p.m. on February 22, did Inspector Finch call at Luton Fire Station where Manton was on duty.

"Chief Inspector Chapman would like a word with you," he said. "Can you come to headquarters right away?"

Manton displayed no signs of alarm at this request. Perhaps he had been expecting it. He knew that the eldest girl had been questioned by the police; but so, for that matter, had half the population of Luton over a period. This, he told himself, was purely routine. At the same time, he was quite unaware that the police had been in and out of the Fire Station most of the day, or that he himself was the subject of their enquiries.

Thus, when Manton entered the room where Chapman awaited him he appeared calm and confident. The Chief Inspector was seated at a table and motioned his visitor to a chair opposite. This was the first time Chapman had set eyes on Manton and what he now saw surprised him. He was engaged on a murder hunt and this mild-mannered, stockily built character in a fireman's uniform was his No.1. suspect. Somehow, Manton did not look the part. Both Inspector Finch and Detective Sergeant Judge remained in the room as Chapman addressed his quarry.

After introducing himself (somewhat unnecessarily, it would seem but no less in strict accordance with police procedure), he went on: "I'm investigating the murder of an unknown woman whose body, unclothed and wrapped in sacks, was found in the River Lea on Friday, November nineteenth, last. In this connection I'm also enquiring into the whereabouts of certain missing women." He paused and looked closely at Manton. "I understand your wife is not with you. Can you tell me where she is?"

Manton gave a short laugh. It could well have been a nervous laugh, but the fact was duly noted and referred to at a later date.

"We had a quarrel," he said. "And she slung her hook. If she's not with her mother in Church Street she's probably staying with her brother at Grantham. She's very fond of her brother," he added naively.

"On what date did she leave you?"

"It would be November twentyfifth."

"Was she pregnant at the time?"

"Yes."

"Five-and-a-half months?"

"Something like that. She didn't want the baby, but I did."

Chapman knew that next door neighbor Mrs.Parr had last seen Rene Manton on November 17; that she had called to see her on the 20th. and again on the 21st. and was told she had gone away. He could find nobody who had seen her after November 18. He now opened a file in front of him and took out two photographs, handing them to Manton. They were mortuary shots of the dead woman, but Manton displayed little or no emotion as he studied the gruesome pictures.

"Is that your wife?" Chapman asked.

"No," Manton said, shaking his head vigorously. "It's nothing like her! I tell you, my wife is alive!"

"I should like," Chapman said, returning the photographs to the file, "to take a statement from you, giving all the facts right from the beginning. Of course, you are not compelled to make any statement…."

It was the usual caution, but Manton seemed unimpressed.

"Certainly", he said, almost patronizingly. "I'll help you all I can." He was still fairly sure of his ground, although the police appeared to know more than he had bargained for; and as he began the statement one of the officers present took it down word for word. In answer to a few preliminary questions by Chapman he gave a brief picture of his married life up to the outbreak of war and then went on:

> *"In March 1942 my wife went out to work. She got into bad company, started drinking and smoking heavily and stayed out late. If I asked her where she had been and who with was told to mind my own business. This led to quarreling between us as I did not think it right she should behave like that when there were four children to look after.... Matters came to a head in November that same year, 1942, when my wife did not get home until after 11.30 p.m. one night. She was unsteady on her feet and told me she had been to the Alma Dance Hall....The following day we had a row about this and I told her to clear out. She went to her mother's place at 28, Church Street....The following March I persuaded her to return home for the children's sake and to mend her ways....She came back and although we lived together things were not the same. We were very happy...."*

So far, it had been plain sailing and Manton had no need to draw upon his imagination or to lie his way through...until it came to the events of November, 1943.

> *"For some time past," he went on, "I have been working in my spare time as a potman at the 'Plume of Feathers'. My wife objected to this as she disliked the barmaids there and this led to further quarrels....it was on November twentyfifth, after lunch when the children had all gone off, that I said I intended going to the 'Plume of Feathers' that night....My wife flew into a temper and threw a cup of tea at me....Later, she packed her bags and left. I have not*

seen her since--that is, not to speak to--but I did think I saw her once at Christmas, in a crowd coming out of the Alma Market....My wife was still with me when the woman's body was found in the River Lea. She read about it in the papers and I distinctly remember her saying, "Some poor bugger has got caught out!...."

To most people the statement would have appeared genuine enough. There was just sufficient detail to make it sound convincing. Chief Inspector Chapman's feature's, however, remained impassive. When Manton had read the document through and signed it Chapman rested both forearms on the table and leaned forward.

"I believe," he said, "that on November eighteen last you were on leave from the Fire Station?"

"Yes," Manton replied after a short pause. "I did have a few days off around that time."

"When your wife went away, did she take all her clothes with her?"

"Most of them."

"Including a black coat?"

"A black coat?" Manton appeared puzzled. "She had a light brown or a grey coat. I don't remember a black one."

Had he but known it, he was in deep water and there was no need to lie about the coat. He must have remembered a death in the Bavister family some eighteen months previously when Rene had had the coat dyed black, especially for the funeral.

Chapman again opened the file in front of him and took out an envelope, handing it to Manton. It was one of the four received by Mrs.Bavister.

"Is that your wife's handwriting?" he asked.

Manton studied the envelope and nodded.

"Yes, that's her handwriting all right."

Chapman pushed a plain sheet of paper across the table together with a pen.

"I would like you," he said, "to write down the following words." He had no need to refer to the file, for he had as good as memorized the contents of all four letters and each of the words he now mentioned was contained in one or other of them. The last was the word "Hampstead".

Manton wrote laboriously at Chapman's dictation. When it came to the final word he paused fractionally before writing: "<u>Hamstead.</u>"

Only then did Chapman look in the file and compare Manton's scrawl with the contents of the letters. When he looked up again the Chief Inspector's face was grave, his manner entirely official.

"I am not satisfied with your explanations, Manton," he said. "I'm going to take you into custody and charge you with the murder of your wife sometime during the eighteenth--nineteenth of November last year. I must warn you...."

Manton was still seated but he swayed visibly in the chair, putting one hand up to his forehead. In Chapman's own words: "He seemed to go all to pieces."

So it had come at last--as he must have known it had to sooner or later. He could scarcely have kept up the lies and deception for very much longer. Yet, he had given no thought to the future, living only from day to day with his terrible secret. For Manton this was the 'Moment of Truth' and his world had already begun to crumble.

For some reason a prisoner's very first words after being charged are taken down and quoted later. Sometimes they may be incriminating, at others they may suggest innocence. In Manton's case it was partly an admission of guilt, at the same time leaving no doubt as to his uppermost concern.

"I don't mind for myself," he managed to say in a hoarse voice, "I know I am done for. It's the children. I have tried to protect my children. Will you please do what you can for them?"

Chapman nodded. Perhaps he even felt a trifle sorry for Manton at that moment. Yet, when he spoke his voice was devoid of all sentiment.

"Now--would you like to make another statement?"

"Yes," Manton said almost eagerly. "I'll tell you what happened."

After the usual caution he proceeded to make a second statement and--as will be seen later--in so doing virtually sealed his own fate.

"I'm sorry I have told you lies," it began, "but I love my children and have only tried to protect them and their future. I have always worked hard and been an honest man and I don't deserve the trouble my wife has brought on me. I killed her, but it was only because I lost my temper. I never intended to kill her...."

There followed a recapitulation of events leading up to that fateful November afternoon. Once again he told of the bone of contention between them over his part time job at the 'Plume of Feathers' and how he had announced his intention of going there that night.

"My wife jumped up from her chair, using foul language, and threw a cup of hot tea straight into my face. I was blinded....As she continued to come at me I pushed her back and she hit the wall by the window....She came at me again, picked up the other cup of tea and was going to throw it. I lost my temper then and seized a heavy wooden stool...I lashed out with it, scarcely knowing what I was doing...."

He rubbed his forehead, striving to recall the dreadful details of that now far off nightmare. Yet it must have been a merciful relief to share with someone--even the police--the horrifying secret he had been carrying around for more than three months.

"When I came to and got my senses again, I saw what I had done. I saw she was dead and decided to do something to keep her away from the children....I undressed her and got four sacks from the cellar, cut them open and tied her up in these. I then carried her down to the cellar and left her there....I had washed the blood up before the children came home for tea....After it was dark I brought the wife up from the cellar, got my bike out, lifted her across the handlebars and wheeled her down Osborne Road to the river...."

Of a necessity, any statement given to the police and read out later sounds cold, factual and entirely dispassionate. Yet it requires little imagination to picture the macabre scene of Manton, with the heavy bundle balanced precariously across the handlebars of his bicycle, trundling it through the black-out. As though by way of an accompaniment to this funeral journey the air raid sirens were wailing at the time.

> *"I lifted her onto the edge of the bank and she rolled down it into the river...."*

It was as simple as that. He had achieved his object: to get the body out of sight of the children. Thereafter, beyond telling a few lies and forging a few letters, he had merely sat back while the entire police force scoured the countryside for clues.

> *"The next day, I burnt all the blood-stained clothing in the copper and some more besides....I also threw in her false teeth which I found in a glass of water. I was afraid the children might see them as they knew she wouldn't go out without them....After Grandma Bavister brought the rabbit I was afraid she would become suspicious, so I wrote the letters to make out that Rene was living in London... .I have now told you the whole truth and I know what it means to me. I am terribly sorry. It was done on the spur of the moment and if it had not been for the children, I'd have given myself up...."*

Just how the all-important piece of black material showed up as and when it did is something of a mystery. Obviously Manton had not disposed of the ashes from the copper all at once, but over a period. Refuse is apt to scatter on the wind, especially during the process of removal and tipping by the dustmen, thereafter moving from place to place; and the fact that this vital clue bearing the dyer's mark revealed itself three months later between the playful jaws of a stray dog can only be dismissed as "one of those things".

‡

It might be supposed that with Manton's full confession and the various witnesses to his deceptions the police had sufficient evidence. Nevertheless, many prisoners have been known to retract a confession later, claiming that it was obtained under threats or duress; and although Manton was scarcely the type to adopt such tactics it was essential to secure positive identification of the body.

Seldom can that time-honoured proverb "Easy to be wise after the event" have been more forcibly born out than in the case of two Luton dentists, both of whom had treated Rene Manton and both of whom had failed at the time to identify either the mortuary pictures or the dental data supplied by Dr.Keith Simpson. Now, when confronted with a photograph of the woman taken during life, both immediately recognized her as a former patient. In fact, the one who had fitted her with dentures was able to produce from his files a mould of both the upper and lower jaws which corresponded in detail. It was just one among the many simple errors which, for more than three months, had conspired to conceal the truth.

In a search of the house at No.14, Regent Street faint bloodstains were found on the walls of the living-room, on the plaster of the ceiling and on the door jamb. These were established as Group 'O', the same as that of the victim. Not content with this further evidence, Superintendent Cherrill, the Scotland Yard expert, was called in to scour the house for fingerprints; but either Manton was inordinately house-proud (which in fact he was known to be) or else he had gone to extreme lengths to obliterate all possible clues, for not a stick of furniture in the place revealed any fingerprints such as the police were hoping to find.

The search extended to the cellar where, earlier, a blood-stained envelope similar to those used by Manton to send the letters from London had been found. Yet, with all the grime and coal dust this seemed an unlikely place for fingerprints; and such was the case until Superintendent Cherrill spotted a row of bottles tucked away on a shelf in a darkened recess. Each was coated in a thick layer of dust and yielded nothing…until he came to the last one of all, an empty pickle jar. Here his thoroughness and tenacity were rewarded. The pickle jar revealed part of a single left thumb-print, identical with that of the body taken from the River Lea three months earlier.

Finally, the gruesome and by now seemingly unnecessary business of trying the preserved feet for size with shoes found in the house was effectively carried out. The authorities then had sufficient evidence to indict a judge........But was it *Murder*?

5

The trial began at Bedford Assizes on a Friday afternoon in May before a jury of ten men and two women, Manton pleading "Not Guilty" to a charge of murder. Mr.Richard O'Sullivan,K.C., led for the Prosecution, whilst the prisoner, having been granted legal aid, was ably defended by Mr.Arthur Ward,K.C., who fought hard to obtain a verdict of manslaughter. Once again the judge was Mr.Justice Singleton who, almost exactly eight years before, had sentenced Dr.Ruxton to death at Manchester. Despite the urgencies of war, the public gallery was filled to capacity.

Mr.O'Sullivan's outlining of the case for the Crown held all the ingredients of a first rate detective story, with the difference that these were grim, realistic facts as opposed to commercialized fiction: the discovery of the body by the two sewer men, its condition and the fatal injuries as disclosed by the post-mortem examination--above all, the total absence of any clues to the victim's identity. There then followed a gap of three months in the narrative, which learned Counsel filled in with an account of the prisoner's conduct over the period: his "campaign of lies and dissemination", the sending of the letters from London, ending finally with his two statements to the police which, for some reason, both Mr.O'Sullivan and, later the judge himself, seemed to regard as of the utmost importance.

It is difficult to see why. The first statement was merely a continuation of the "lies and dissemination" and was natural enough in the circumstances; but once he knew the game was up, Manton had made a full confession, giving Chief Inspector Chapman as many details as his distressed mind could recall at that time. Yet the Prosecution were to make capital out of this second statement which, in fact, had saved the police a good many further enquiries. Moreover, without it Mr.O'Sullivan would not have been in a position to present the completed picture which he was now unfolding to the jury. To cite but one detail, the actual weapon used would never have been known; the stool, already broken once before, had again come apart in the fracas and had long since been chopped up for firewood. Yet, an exact replica was put in as an exhibit, doubtless by way of a constant reminder to the jury of the violence of the assault.

Of the eleven witnesses who came forward to corroborate the case for the Crown, the evidence of Dr. Keith Simpson told most heavily against the prisoner: the preliminary marks on the throat, the appalling injuries received by at least two blows from the stool and the callous treatment of the body afterwards. Even so, Dr. Simpson was quick to tell the jury that although the victim was still alive when the legs were tied together, there would have been every appearance of death and the prisoner might well have thought her dead at the time.

Mr. Ward made little attempt to dispute any of the evidence in cross-examination of the witnesses, for Manton had already admitted it all. He made it quite clear, at the same time, that the main line of defence was that there had never been any *intent* to murder; and when at length Manton moved from the dock and stood in the witness-box, Mr. Ward's opening questions served to press the point home.

"Did you intend to kill your wife on November eighteen, last year?"

"I never had any intention of killing her."

Manton was looking pale, but calm and somewhat resigned. More than two months on remand in a prison cell had wrought changes in his appearance and he had lost weight. Nevertheless, he seemed to realize that Mr. Ward was fighting to save his life and that the least he could do was to co-operate. In fact, he made a good witness, seldom faltering in his evidence.

Aided by further questions from Mr. Ward he went on to tell once again, this time in greater detail, of events covering the last two years of his life with the deceased. It was a sordid tale of domestic strife, of frequent quarrels.

"She was always kicking up rows," he said, "but I did my best to keep calm for the sake of the children."

"Throughout all these rows, did you ever lift a hand towards your wife?"

"I had never struck my wife before."

In fairness to the prisoner, Mr.O'Sullivan had made two points clear. Firstly, that Manton was obviously very fond of his children. Secondly, there was no suggestion that he had been in any way familiar with the barmaids at the 'Plume of Feathers'.

"In fact," Mr.O'Sullivan had added, "all the evidence points to the contrary."

Yet, this was the fuse which had sparked off the final and fatal explosion.

"I had only been going there," Manton now said, "for the sake of her and the children, to give them more comforts."

He went on to describe, again in much greater detail than in his second statement to the police, the tragic events of that November afternoon; how he had made tea in the kitchen and brought it through to the parlour, pouring out two cups.

"As I sat down I said, 'Well, Rene, I think I'll go down and help Eric out tonight.' By this I meant I would go to the 'Plume of Feathers'. I had not been there for some time, in order to please her and keep the peace. My wife flew into a temper, shouted and used bad language. At the same time she jumped out of her chair, picked up her cup of tea and threw it in my face. It had only been poured out a minute or two and was very hot. It went into my eyes....I was practically blinded and it was very painful. The whole thing was very sudden....As she threw it in my face she rushed at me, shouting and swearing. I was getting up out of the chair, wiping the tea from my eyes and face when she knocked me backwards....I got hold of her throat with my right hand and pushed her violently across the room. She struck the wall, but came back at me again, shouting and swearing--something about blinding me. She made an attempt to pick up the other cup and in my temper, and frightened to death of having another cup of hot tea flung in my face, I picked up the nearest thing handy--the wooden stool....I hit out blindly. I couldn't see clearly where I was hitting. I was in great pain--I had no inten-

Austin Stone

tion of killing her--I had no intention of harming my wife....When I saw her lying there I fell on my knees beside her and called out, Rene, Rene, what have I done?...."

This poignant story must surely have held the ring of truth, for the mild, short little man in the witness-box did not look capable of inventing such details. Nor, it must be truthfully added, did he appear the type capable of disposing of his wife's body in the manner he now went on to describe--*unless it was entirely for the sake of the children.*

Mr.O'Sullivan's quiet, deadly tones in cross-examination, however, seemed likely to dispel any sentiment which might have begun to build up in the minds of the jury:

"She was quite a small woman?"

"About my size, sir, a shade bigger."

"She was no match for you in strength?"

"No, I should not say so."

"Did you hear Mr.Keith Simpson tell the jury that there were marks upon the neck of the application of a hand and re-application of a hand?"*

"I remember taking hold of her throat and pushing her against the wall."

"And the marks showed that the hand had been applied with very considerable force?"

"I may have grabbed her twice. That was in my temper."

"You said nothing about that in your statement to the police?"

"No, Sir."

At the time Manton had made that second voluntary statement he was under great mental strain, striving to recall for Chief Inspector Chapman's benefit an episode which, for three months, he had been trying hard to forget. The terrible blows with the stool must

---

* There is no verbatim account of Dr.Keith Simpson's evidence from the witness-box, but in an article appearing subsequently in the "Police Journal" he wrote, of the so-called attempted strangulation injuries: "Bruising was present behind the voice-box to give evidence of the strength of the grip, but there were no fractures. Asphyxia had not followed and it was clear that the grip had not been fatal or near fatal."

clearly have been uppermost in his mind and if he had remembered all the secondary details of the struggle at that time it would have been remarkable.

"You took hold of that stool with both hands?" Mr.O'Sullivan went on, relentlessly.

"Yes."

"And you struck her twice with it?"

"I think so."

"What did you think was likely to happen if, taking that stool in both hands, you hit your wife with it twice?"

"I had lost my temper and was not thinking of what I was doing."

"What do you think now is likely to happen if a man strikes a woman with a stool using the strength of both hands?"

"I know what it means now, but I didn't realize it then. I was in such a temper."

"It must cause grievous bodily harm?"

"Yes, but I had no intention of harming my wife."

No intention. Manton was certainly upholding his Counsel's main line of defence; and the argument could have gone on indefinitely.

All the evidence, as well as the closing speeches, was completed on that Friday afternoon. Mr.O'Sullivan addressed the jury first, once again putting the principle points for the Crown and stating in conclusion:

"Even if she did throw a cup of tea in his face, that can be no warrant or excuse for doing her to death. In my submission it is a clear case of murder."

In an eloquent speech Mr.Ward claimed that the Prosecution had failed to prove either motive or intent and certainly no pre-meditation. Nobody could deny, on the other hand, that there had been extreme provocation. In his submission, manslaughter was the only possible verdict.

On the following morning Mr.Justice Singleton delivered his summing-up. The jury retired and were absent for two hours and-a-quarter before finding the prisoner "Guilty of Murder".

Manton was duly sentenced to death.

‡

The verdict was received with mixed feelings locally. True, the crime had been a shocking one, steeped in horror from the start to finish, but the public had now heard the prisoner's side of the story for the first time in full detail and there were many who felt that in all the circumstances, in particular the amount of provocation, the verdict should have been one of manslaughter. Still more people thought that at the very least the jury should have added a strong recommendation to mercy.

At a conference between Mr. Ward and Manton's solicitors on the Monday following the trial it was decided to appeal; and this came up for hearing on June 19, in the Court of Criminal Appeal before the Lord Chief Justice, Lord Caldecote, sitting with Mr. Justice Oliver and Mr. Justice Humphreys.

It must be something of an ordeal, even for a King's Counsel, to confront the deadpan faces of three of the most senior judges on the Bench for the purpose of criticizing one of their colleagues. Yet, such was Mr. Arthur Ward's lot on that June morning. It was "D" day plus fourteen and Hitler's flying-bombs were doing their best, unsuccessfully, to scare the populace of London into submission. Manton had been brought from Bedford Gaol for the hearing. He looked pale and seemingly devoid of emotion as he sat, listening to this renewed fight for his life. It was almost as though he had ceased to care. Mr. Richard O'Sullivan was also present, on behalf of the Prosecution, but, as it turned out, was not called upon to speak.

Mr. Ward began by placing all the trial evidence before their lordships and went on:

"The Defence was that it was not murder, but that there was great provocation and the prisoner had killed his wife without intending to murder her. In other words, that he was guilty of manslaughter but not of murder."

The prisoner, Mr. Ward continued, was interviewed by the police on the night of February 22, when he made two statements. The first was a complete denial of everything; but later, realizing how much the police already knew, he said: "I wish to tell you the truth", and went on to make a second statement.

"This second statement," said Mr.Ward, "is important because the grounds for appeal are based largely upon it."

The grounds for appeal, Mr.Ward went on to say, were that the learned judge in his summing-up had mis-directed the jury as follows:

1. He had told them that both statements could not be true and it was for them to decide what was the truth. If they found that the second statement was true, it did not amount to sufficient provocation for a verdict of manslaughter.

2. He had told the jury that this statement had been so enlarged upon by the prisoner in his evidence in the witness-box as to make two different stories; whereas he had failed to direct them as to the prisoner's mental condition when he had made the second statement to the police; that he was under stress and could not be expected to remember at short notice all the details of something which had happened three months previously. When he gave evidence in court the prisoner had spent two months in a cell during which there had been ample time to recollect all the details. There were not two stories; they were the same except that the first story had been added to.

At this point the Lord Chief Justice interrupted to observe: "The jury might well have had to ask themselves if there were not two stories."

After some argument, Mr.Ward went on to place the remaining grounds for appeal:

3. The judge had severely criticized the prisoner's conduct in not sending for help, but had failed to draw the jury's attention to the prisoner's evidence on oath that he had believed his wife to be dead. Dr.Keith Simpson had stated in evidence that the prisoner might well have thought her dead at the time, but the judge had not directed the jury on this.

4. The judge had been severely critical, in his summing-up, of the prisoner's attempts to conceal the crime, but again had not reminded the jury of the prisoner's sworn evidence, that he had done so for the sake of his four children.

5. The judge had failed to direct the jury properly in law as to the degree of provocation necessary to reduce the offence from murder to one of manslaughter.

6. The judge had failed to direct the jury properly as to the burden of proof which must be discharged by the Prosecution.

Mr. Ward had spoken for forty-five minutes with occasional interruptions from their lordships. He now added in conclusion:

"It is an interesting fact that the jury were out for more than two hours, which means there was indecision. In my submission, if they had been properly directed they might well have returned a verdict of manslaughter."

This brought an audible sigh from the Lord Chief Justice who remarked: "It is sometimes put to us as grounds for appeal that the jury were only out for five minutes!"

It was no use. In giving the judgement of the Court in what he described as "this distressing case", Lord Caldecote said they were unanimous in the opinion that the judge's comment about two stories was a proper observation to make to the jury. Altogether, the criticism of the judge's summing-up appeared to their lordships to be ill-founded. It appeared to them that the whole matter had been adequately and accurately put to the jury. The appeal must therefore fail.

Manton was taken back to Bedford Gaol, this time to occupy the condemned cell.

‡

Was Manton, then, convicted of murder instead of manslaughter largely because he had chosen to be co-operative and to help the police by giving them as many details as he could recall at the time?

Supposing he had refused to make that second statement, as he had every right to do? Or supposing he had confined himself to the first few words of it--"I killed her, but only because I lost my temper. I never intended to kill her"--and not said another word until he entered the witness-box at his trial? There could not then have been "two stories", nor would the judge have been in a position, on that count, to implant doubt in the minds of the jury as to the reliability of the prisoner's evidence. True, Manton had received the usual caution before making the second statement-- *"I must warn you that anything you say...."*. Yet, on the face of things it would seem that Chief Inspector Chapman might well have added: *"I must also warn you that if you alter one jot or tittle of the statement or enlarge upon it in any way at your trial, things will go badly against you."*

‡

The failure of the appeal came as a bitter blow to the relatives and friends. Only one remote possibility now stood between Manton and the gallows--a reprieve; and as soon as it was known that all else had failed, a petition was drafted, which the local Member of Parliament, Mr. E.L.Burgin, undertook to hand in person to the Home Secretary. The grounds set out in the petition, and it's wording were as follows:

> *For many years he has resided in Luton, where he is well known to be of good character, of sober and peaceful habits and a law abiding citizen. He was proud of his humble home and deeply devoted to his children.*
>
> *He was a hard and conscientious worker, always striving in the interests of his home and his children, and during the past four years has devoted himself to the service of the National Fire Service.*
>
> *During his married life, and particularly for the past two years, he has suffered grave provocation and abuse from his wife, her conduct having led to estrangement and separa-*

tion. That but for the unprovoked and unjustified assault by the deceased on November 18th., when she threw a cup of tea into his face, he would not have been driven to commit this dreadful crime.

That the crime was not pre-meditated.

That his attempts at concealment of the crime were actuated only by his great love for his four children and his desire to remain with and care for them.

That having regard to all the circumstances, it is proper that clemency should be shown to him.

There followed a full scale campaign to obtain as many signatures as possible to this petition, and barely a fortnight was left in which to do so. Manton's two boys applied for their annual holidays and devoted the time to securing organizers and in canvassing for signatures themselves. Two hundred volunteers came forward to man signature stands on the streets, in local cinema's, the Town Hall and the Corn Exchange. Colleagues in the N.F.S. waded in and spent their off-duty hours lending a helping hand. Seldom can there have been a more widespread drive to save a condemned prisoner's life.

The execution was fixed for July 2, and by the evening of the last day of June almost 30,000 people had signed the petition. For a town with a pre-war population of barely 70,000 which included children and babies, these figures give a fair indication as to the trend of public opinion at the time. Mr.Leslie Burgin had an appointment with the Home Secretary to present the petition the following day.

He never kept that appointment.

Shortly before 10 a.m. on the morning of July 1, there came a bolt straight out of the blue when the Home Secretary, Mr. Herbert Morrison, himself telephoned Mr.Burgin to say that His Majesty the King had ordered a reprieve and there was, therefore, no need to present the petition that morning.

Somewhere in high places, at last, someone had reviewed the whole case and seen fit to advocate mercy.

Manton was at once removed from the condemned cell, to begin a term of life imprisonment; nominally twenty years.

6

If Manton had really intended to kill his wife, Rene, he could hardly have chosen a worse time, place or method. His desperate attempts to conceal the whole ugly business from the children alone vouch for this. Furthermore, if it were *not* a terrible accident resulting, as he maintained, from a complete loss of control, how had he hoped to prolong the deception of those first three months? Besides Mrs. Bavister, there were any number of Rene's friends and relatives who would not have been hoodwinked indefinitely. It was pure chance, in fact, that the truth remained hidden as long as it did.

Barely thirty years have passed since then; too early for recriminations or criticism. Suffice it to say that, quite apart from the abolition of the death penalty, with the increasing number of crimes of pre-meditated violence that are dealt with so leniently in the Courts today, it is highly unlikely that a crime such as Manton's would be met now, as it was then, with the uttermost severity of the law.

Twenty years. With full remission for good conduct he would not be too old, upon release, to start a new life. But did he want this? How could he face the children now that they knew he had killed their mother? Clearly, they understood and had long ago forgiven him; but for Manton the curtain of remorse and shame would always hang there between them. Things could never be the same again....

At the time of his arrest Manton was in the prime of his life and apparently in good health. Yet it was not long before he was undergoing medical treatment in prison. In all cases of sickness or disease, the chances of recovery depend largely upon the individual's will to survive. Manton did not seem to have this will. Although everything possible was done for him, his condition deteriorated rapidly. He was in fact a broken man.

After serving less than four years of his sentence, "Bertie" Horace William Manton died in the prison hospital.

ACKNOWLEDGEMENTS.

"Luton News" November 1943 - July 1944.

"Beds and Herts Saturday Telegraph" November 1943 - July 1944.

"Pictorial" (Luton) June 1944.

"Cherrill of the Yard", by ex-Superintendent Cherrill, of the Fingerprint Department, Scotland Yard.

Dr.Keith Simpson Article on the *"Luton Sack Murder"*, appearing in the "Police Journal" 1945.

Editors Notes:

1. The Freedom of Information process shows that Public (Prison) Records, Ref: PCOM 9/1028, held by The National Archives, are closed for 75 years or more from the date of conviction (May 17th. 1944) and in this case will not be able to be viewed until 1st. January 2023.

2. Apparently, Internet information since 'Bertie' Manton's sentencing, shows that he was imprisoned at "Parkhurst" Prison on the Isle of Wight and died there in 1947.

3. This crime was publicly known as *"The Luton Sack Murder"*

CPSIA information can be obtained
at www.ICGtesting.com
Printed in the USA
LVOW08*0125290917
550311LV00004B/4/P

9 781460 298831